HUGH JOHNSON
IN THE GARDEN

HUGH JOHNSON
IN THE GARDEN

THE BEST GARDEN DIARY
OF OUR TIME

MITCHELL BEAZLEY

HUGH JOHNSON IN THE GARDEN
by Hugh Johnson

First published in Great Britain in 2009 by Mitchell Beazley,
an imprint of Octopus Publishing Group Ltd
2–4 Heron Quays, London E14 4JP
An Hachette UK Company
www.hachettelivre.co.uk

Distributed in the US and Canada by Octopus Books USA:
c/o Hachette Book Group USA
237 Park Avenue
New York NY 10017
www.octopusbooksusa.com

Design and layout copyright © Octopus Publishing Group Ltd 2009
Text copyright © SALINGHALLPRESS 2009
Photographs copyright © Hugh Johnson except first page, sixth
 page and eleventh page of inset section, copyright © Harpur
 Garden Images

ISBN 978 1 84533 485 7

A CIP record of this book is available from the British Library.

Set in Bembo

Colour repro by Dexter Graphics in the United Kingdom
Printed and bound by C&C Offset Printing Co., Ltd. in China

Commissioning editor: Helen Griffin
Senior art editor: Juliette Norsworthy
Designer: Lizzie Ballantyne
Copy editor: Diane Pengelly
Project editor: Georgina Atsiaris
Production manager: Peter Hunt
Proofreader: Sarah Higgens
Indexer: Sue Farr

CONTENTS

INTRODUCTION

My first anthology of Trad's Diary sucked the pith out of my first 18 years of horticultural musings. The column started in 1975, when I was asked to remodel the 100-year-old Journal of the Royal Horticultural Society and we renamed it *The Garden*. I made much of the fact that it was Volume 100 (rather mysteriously, since Volume I appeared in 1866).

The Garden seemed an auspicious title. The last magazine to bear it was founded by William Robinson. In 1875, exactly a century before, Gertrude Jekyll had called on Mr Robinson in his Covent Garden office: a meeting momentous in gardening history. As for Tradescant, I borrowed what seemed to be an abandoned name (I could find no claimant) from King James I's celebrated gardener, the first to introduce foreign plants to a newly curious England.

History, as we all know, has done nothing but speed up since then. Events, discoveries, fashions – the grist (along with the weather) to a diarist's mill – flash by faster and faster. Memorable changes were documented in my first anthology. Conservation and garden history both appeared for the first time as important factors in horticulture. We grew richer, employed more gardeners (in the 1970s professional gardeners were a threatened species), bought more plants and more gadgets, conservatories came back into vogue, we travelled more to visit gardens and started to use computers. One of their first fruits was *The Plant Finder*, which hugely expanded our choice of plants.

By the 1990s the Internet was becoming a familiar concept. Then 12 years ago the World Wide Web opened a universe of information and exchange that has left nothing untouched: certainly not magazines and their contributors. What you need to know is two clicks away, and discussion with fellow-addicts in any subject, gardening included, wonderfully available.

What does a habitual diarist do? He finds more and more to write about, has more matter at his disposal, hears more rebuttals from his readers – generally, in other words, has to stir his stumps. The natural move to make, in fact, in the teeth of the cybergale, is to go online, which is what Trad did in 2008. Satisfying as it was, month by month, to see one's jottings coming back from the printer handsomely bound, it is even more exciting to launch them on the ether with immediate effect. Better still is the luxury of pruning them later to be handsomely reprinted, as this diary now is in *Hortus* magazine.

Recollection in tranquillity allows one to see trends emerging. Political correctness, ever more throttling to free expression, makes me glad this is only a gardening diary. While more and more money is poured into gardening it seems to generate few really new ideas: grasses and topiary are the icons of the age. The philosophers of horticulture allege there is nothing new to say: does it have to be new, though, to be beautiful?

The 1990s saw Trad's own gardening world expand into central France. The stimulating differences between soils, climates, traditions and conventions became an important theme. A few years later it was North Wales and the opportunities offered by high rainfall and acid soil. Central to it all for 34 years has been my own Essex garden, my daily preoccupation, now beyond maturity and demanding decisions.

Global warming is the elephant in the garden. We have not had a destructively cold winter in Essex for 27 years. We cheerfully plant or leave out things only recently classed as tender, secretly hoping, perhaps, that normality will return and kill them off. It would be doubly perverse, though, not to experiment and enjoy growing things our predecessors couldn't. Carpe diem should be the gardener's motto.

Gardening is all about pleasure, and Trad has been extraordinarily lucky to be able to share his pleasures in growing and weeding and propagating, in talking to gardeners and visiting gardens worldwide for so many years. Extremely lucky too in the tolerance of three editors of *The Garden*: Elspeth Napier, Susanne Mitchell and Ian Hodgson. For many years I also enjoyed the friendly carping (it is their job) of an ideal sub-editor, Jeremy Kirk. Diane Pengelly, who has made editing this volume another pleasure, has been a loyal friend over the years. To them all, and to all my readers, I offer a gardener's blessing: may your ground elder evaporate and roses perfume your life.

Hugh Johnson

1993

KEY OF THE DOOR

Trad reaches years of discretion this month, a curious and not at all unpleasant feeling for a greying gardener. Years of discretion? A likely story. Comes of age, anyway.

Eighteen years, 216 columns and nearly 200,000 words since Trad began, some sort of milestone seems appropriate. I shall mark it by recalling to younger readers how that distant June saw the metamorphosis of the stately old *Journal of the RHS* (then in its 100th volume) into the bright-plumaged thing you have in your hand.

In the process it was felt (the old *Journal* habitually used the passive voice) that a more personal touch would appeal at least to the more frivolous element among the then Fellows. Trad was press-ganged to write a diary-cum-gossip column ... and you know the rest.

'Why Tradescant?' was one of the first readers' questions of the new regime. The answer is simple. I was looking for a pen name that was unmistakable, a sort of Atticus or Peterborough, but that spelt gardening – at least to the initiated. There was no Tradescant Trust in 1975, few knew the name of the most illustrious of royal gardeners – and nobody still bears it, as I was at pains to find out. Very few even knew how to pronounce it (the accent is on the second syllable – a funny place to put it, I still think).

LOST FOR WORDS

Gardens Without Borders was the title of a winter Channel 4 series about some of the loveliest (not necessarily the grandest) gardens of France.

It was a bright idea: to take a party of keen amateurs from Yorkshire on a guided tour and let them make the inevitable comparisons. The itinerary was excellently planned: a circular trajectory starting and ending in Normandy. Some of the gardens (Kerdalo in Brittany, for example) are already celebrated; others certainly deserve to be.

So what was the snag? It was the usual television problem: the self-conscious appeal to the lowest common denominator that emerges as wilful banality. Searching our language for comments on the beauty around them, 'interesting' was the fattest plum anyone found.

It is the long-established custom among English gardeners to wear the ugliest imaginable clothes – especially anoraks in primary colours. Going abroad for some reason brings out the worst in everyone's wardrobe, as a glance round a cross-Channel ferry or an airport lounge too painfully testifies. Just by being in these exquisite places, therefore, our party spoiled the beauty they had come to see.

❧ July ❧

ELBOW ROOM

I wonder what I'm doing wrong. The magic of wallflowers (apart from their wonderful smell, on the winey side of violets) was that they grew on walls. You didn't – at least I didn't – plant them there, but an old wall beside where wallflowers grew acquired plants that became almost shrubby and lasted for years, hanging on like a dinghy sailor in a squall but giving their adopted home that wonderful seal of approval that only self-sown plants can give.

Or plants that layer themselves. A bough of a shrub, or better a tree, that has felt so comfortable with its elbow resting on the ground that it has taken root always looks like the mark of a mature – even a serene – garden. The oriental plane at The National Trust's Blickling Hall in Norfolk, which now covers perhaps half an acre with its boa-constrictor branches, is one of the best examples I know.

Now I'm happy to report that the walnut tree by the back drive here has declared itself satisfied by shooting up vigorously from where a branch has drooped down to the daffodils. Perhaps the wallflowers will indicate their assent too.

❧ August ❦

THE PLANTSMAN

So great and all-pervading an influence has Chris Brickell been on the RHS since he became Director of Wisley in 1969 that it is tempting to call this month, since he retired as Director General on 31 July, the first of the PB (post-Brickell) era.

Relatively few of us can remember the AB years, or imagine the Society without his special blend of courtesy, modesty and authority. In botanical or taxonomic matters it is wise in any case to defer to Chris. But it is also wise in matters relating to human relations, ecology, conservation, travel, publishing – in fact just about anything to do, however peripherally, with horticulture. If confirmation were needed, the length and volume of the ovation he received at the pre-Chelsea press lunch, with the Prime Minister John Major as guest of honour, was a vivid testimonial.

It is absolutely in character for Chris to be embarrassed by the phrases that are doled out as a matter of (very proper) form to an important administrator (and much more than that) retiring from office.

SOURCE OF LIGHT

Truly wise and helpful generalisations about gardening are few. It takes a Russell Page, a Humphry Repton or a Leonardo da Vinci to crystallise observations into axioms. The one I have in mind was Leonardo's 'The trees that are between you and the sun are far more beautiful than those which have you between the sun and themselves', echoed and put rather more plainly by Repton: 'All natural objects look best with the sun behind them; all artificial objects with the sun on them.'

Of course they were thinking on the grand scale: of trees and buildings, if not of whole landscapes. What reminded me of the principle was the fine spring evenings when the low-angled sun caught and fired up the young growth of plants on a pergola, spires in the border – and indeed of trees in new and still-translucent leaf.

I would take issue with Repton, though, on the word 'behind'. The most beautiful effects come not when you are squinting directly into the sun through a plant, but when the light is angled at 30 or 40 degrees. Then the profile of the plant, the colour of its leaves and the detail of its design are brought into the sharpest relief.

What practical use can be made of this observation? Bear it in mind when planting to the south and west of your viewpoint, whether patio or kitchen window (the one over the sink is the most important in the house).

From the chives and pansies in the foreground to the maple and white foxgloves in the middle and the birch in the background (plus of course the vine on the pergola) each leaf and flower is etched on my mind.

The reverse view is flat. Although, as Repton says, the house looks okay from there.

THE MONTH OF MAY

The moment in May when the hawthorns add their mass of flowers to the already splendid candles on the horse chestnuts is the climax of the spring. This year it seemed more so than ever. The weight of white tugged at the hawthorn branches, bowing down the trees in cascades that gave a glittering frame to every other object. The all-important white on a painter's palette can be used for eye-catching highlights, or to give the whole picture a sense of life and freshness. May blossom refreshes the very soul.

❧ September ❧

ROOTS

It is nearly 30 years since the Garden History Society came into being, and almost impossible to believe now that it began life as a tiny clique working in an almost totally neglected corner of scholarship.

Archaeology and research in archives, aerial surveys and detective work on the ground are now integral to the treatment and planning of any site where a garden has stood for a considerable time. Restoration is almost automatically preferred to re-design. Our garden consciousness now has an extra dimension: it is not just this season we see, but a whole history of society and taste expressed in horticulture.

Authenticity, the faithful following of what research digs up about the past, can occasionally be carried too far. We have far more and better plants than, for example, 17th-century gardeners had. Would they, we might ask ourselves, have denied themselves the lovely plants of China and Japan had they been available to them? Should we not follow the spirit rather than the letter and add better plants we know they would have enjoyed?

On the other hand, craftsmanship was available then that nobody can afford today. Even a good garden wall, let alone elaborate stonework, is so expensive that we go without – or make do with more or less trite reproductions.

The past, it seems to me, should stimulate our imaginations – but not limit them. The first step is to know and understand it – and this the Garden History Society above all has equipped us to do.

PS: www.gardenhistorysociety.org

CLARY

Salvia sclarea var. *turkestanica* has been given various rude names. 'Hot housemaid' is one that comes down the ages, full of evocations of a very different era. True, it pongs, but what a wonder its presence is, looming suddenly enormous, self-sown in dusty corners, catching and holding the light in its unpindownable pale blend of violet and white and pink and grey, spiky with bracts (these are the smelly bits) but solid with its broad rough basal leaves. It volunteers here besides catmint and *Rosa* 'Ballerina' and pale-pink mallows, shoots up under *Rosa* 'Albertine' ... in fact it has an unfailing colour sense.

✺ October ✺

DELVING DEEP

Who has really pondered landscape design for almost the whole of the 20th century and produced a string of masterworks to prove it?

There is more than one answer to this question. Roberto Burle Marx, the Brazilian genius who designed Copacabana beach, whose landscapes are massive abstracts in exotic colours and textures, and who was the first person to be exercised about the Amazon jungle, is certainly one.

But the philosopher-designer I have in mind is Sir Geoffrey Jellicoe, because the first of four volumes of his collected writings came out in June from the Garden Art Press. Volume 1 starts with 'Soundings', a new introductory essay that dives in at the deep end. Jellicoe explores the elusive relationship between creative practical design and the subconscious.

In his own design he has drawn on many of the great artists of this century for inspiration. He sees powerful design as springing from the subconscious and being controlled by it. Over 70 years he has developed ideas and formed techniques for creating landscapes that appeal and satisfy on both the conscious and subconscious levels.

I am not good at following the jargon of art criticism, but when Jellicoe expounds the work of Picasso or Paul Nash in terms of landscape design, I am hooked.

LONG SERVICE

We're already into late summer and the 'winter-flowering' pansies are still at it outside the kitchen window. They were installed by Mrs Trad in late November as edging between her new kitchen-herb garden and a much-used curving stone path.

Over nine months in flower they have seen innumerable other flowers come and go, but they have yet to find a mismatch for their gentle, rather washed-out, slightly stripy/blotchy shade of lilac – or is it lavender?

They have been the fetching ribbon to the blue of scillas, the fresh green and purple of chives, the yellow of Welsh poppies, the clear pink of *Rosa* 'Anemone', the hot orange of lilies, the flaring white of *Spiraea thunbergii* (not all of these in the herb bed!), the strong growing-green of grass – and we're still not tired of them. I'm sure they like the shade, because the herb garden faces north-east against a corner of the house. Happily so do the herbs.

BARK AS THERAPY

If there is one plum unjob in the garden, a reward to keep for moments of well-earned tranquillity after the tedious and sweaty bits, it is surely peeling birches.

It is a summer job, ideal for early mornings or late evenings in July and August when the tree has grown enough to need to shed its snake-like skin. You stand in the birch's shade and gently, deliberately, unbandage it. A few strips unwind with satisfying ease, uncovering a fresh layer of bark as tenderly tinted as a nude. Little snags make it interesting. You prise very gently with your fingernail at a recalcitrant corner to start another uncovering; the dusty, lichenous paper crackling quietly as it comes away.

Any birch will do. Native silver birches are as satisfying as any. But *Betula utilis* var. *jacquemontii* has rich creamy layers to explore, *B. papyrifera* powdery goal-post white, and *B. albosinensis* blushing flesh tones. One day, somewhere, I will find an American river birch to undress. The river birch wears black.

DRESS SENSE

Trad ventured on to the evidently touchy subject of clothes in gardens recently, in relation to a certain television series. It was a good mailbag-filler, and a surprising number of readers called for more.

At the risk of sounding like Jeeves to the Berties whose instinct is to pep the place up with a spot of purple (the socks in question, you recall, were eventually given to the lift boy) I have an incident to report that illustrates the problem nicely.

Graham Stuart Thomas had a party of visitors in his garden not long ago that included one orange jumper, one scarlet ditto, and a dress in bold zigzag. His garden is exquisite, delicate, the daily delight of the practical master of modern gardening. Of course he was too polite to say anything. His visitors had come a long way ....

But colour is colour – and can destroy colour. If it is eye-catching it is bound to be a distraction to others. We cannot all make ourselves elegant, but we can think about what we put on when we go garden-gazing. It needn't be mud-coloured either, just quiet, and in colours as far removed from fluorescent as we can find.

Green is a good start. So is medium grey, blue, white or light-pink in summer. Since we have to share the loveliest gardens with so many visitors these days, a modest dress code like this seems to Trad to be merely common courtesy.

❦ November ❦

MOPHEADS

What is it about hydrangeas that makes them such potent creators of a certain garden mood? I mean, of course, the common or mophead hydrangeas, hortensias to the Victorians (and the French), which form great dowdy pinkish mounds in seaside gardens where the secateurs sanded up years ago.

Well tended, well pruned, they are formal things: the proper tub-plants to flank a stately doorway. Caught by a shaft of light in sandy woodland they can be a more startling icy-blue than any other flower. Ranged along the bottom of a wall they stamp it with seniority as few plants can. What gives them this power?

They breathe an air of artificiality that refuses to blend with other plants. Unlike their more graceful cousins the great gangling *Hydrangea aspera* subsp. *sargentiana*, the soft *H. aspera* Villosa Group or the floppy *arborescens* or *quercifolia*, their destiny is to dominate, like a centrepiece in a salon. They finish the summer and bring in the autumn of spiders' webs, slow dawns and chilly gusts;

their mops turning to parchment skeletons, their powerful presence still intact.

Why hortensias? It was one of the prodigious de Jussieus from Lyon, a family that dominated French botany for three 18th-century generations, who gave them the name. Hortensia means 'of gardens'. The genus (as it was) *Hortensia* was thus by definition the *most* garden plant: almost unimaginable in the wild.

BOOK CROP

Perhaps because the dazzling annual choice of new gardening books so cruelly feeds our feelings of inadequacy, I suspect we all keep at our elbow some of the original books we turned to for help when we first started to garden with intent.

It would be interesting to have a poll of which books are most generally kept within arm's length. The book that gave me my first inklings, much comfort and even the first glimmering of confidence was *The Modern Flower Garden* by Brigadier C E Lucas Phillips, the sequel to his famous *The Small Garden* (and more famous *Cockleshell Heroes*).

I don't know how many other military men have beaten their swords into the potent pair of spade and nib, but soldiering seems to be ideal training for recruiting and instructing novice gardeners. Lucas Phillips starts with first-class organisation of ideas, then writes with a kindly bluffness that eminently becomes a soldier. He is no waster of words. Here is *Euphorbia characias*: 'Similar [to *E. Wulfenii*] but has a maroon eye. Hideous.' Had I been one of his men I'm sure I would have followed him anywhere – and not only out of curiosity.

The new books of this season are mounding up in gleaming piles in the bookshops now. Choose, if you can, between Rosemary Verey on *Garden Plans*, Christopher Lloyd's *Flower Garden*, Anthony Archer-Wills on *The Water Gardener*, David Austin on roses, Jane Taylor on shady gardens and dry gardens, *Some Flowers* by Vita Sackville-West, not seen since 1937, and even *Highgrove* by Himself.

JE SOURIS, TU SOURIS

The grey grass of August on a gritty ridge in the centre of France is a miniature rush hour on the Circle line as field mice and voles in tens of thousands scurry along their corridors, sometimes on the surface, sometimes in tunnels.

The breakfast, lunch and dinner area (for human inhabitants) at Trad's hide-out is in a sunken arbour with vines overhead and the ground at sitting eye-level, a herb bed for foreground. As you sit popping cherry tomatoes in your mouth, an agreeable little furry fellow pops out of a hole a yard away and fells a basil stalk with a bite. You say 'tut' and he leaves it for you to savour with the tomatoes.

What beats me is that the buzzards, constantly wheeling overhead making their oddly feeble (but nonetheless haunting) mewing cry, never seem to spot the most blatant mouse manoeuvres. There are scores of the serene broad-winged birds of prey, but I have never seen one stooping, nor carrying a catch. Their rest-stops are stag-headed oaks and walnuts in the fields where they sit looking wise and watchful (but are probably fast asleep). What they clearly need is some tactical instruction, a pep talk, or possibly contact lenses.

Meanwhile I can only assume that the *Crocus tommasinianus* and *Narcissus pseudonarcissus* that I buried so confidently last year have plumped up the tunnellers into tastier morsels than ever.

❧ December ❧

AGONY AUNT

It is a lucky member of the Society who has never had cause to consult its Agony Aunt, Audrey. I'm not sure she will like being described in such unscientific terms, because Audrey Brooks, who retires at the end of this month as Senior Scientist at Wisley, has always kept the low profile that befits a diligent researcher.

On the other hand her sympathetic letters have gone out in their thousands to gardeners worried over sickly specimens, frantic over pests or distraught over dendrogenous deaths.

They have brought the comfort of scientific certainty, even if the alarming message was that you, too, have honey fungus. Or if uncertain, as must happen from time to time, Audrey would often unleash one of her famous little pamphlets (*Faulty Root Action* is my favourite) which have the great merit of making you take a long close look at the ailing plant and try to figure out for yourself what was going on down there.

Audrey hails from Kent, graduated from the University of Aberystwyth, and after apprenticeship at Wisley with Donald Green succeeded him as chief scientist. If this sounds as though the lab is the only part of Wisley she frequents, nothing could be further from the truth.

As Examinations Officer she has been consulted by hundreds of young people heading for a horticultural career, work she loves and which has made her much loved and respected. She is deeply involved with village and church life at Wisley too, as Parish Clerk and Churchwarden: a familiar figure with headscarf and trug bringing flowers from the garden to beautify the church. These duties, I understand, she will not relinquish as she retires.

NONPAREIL

What flower of the autumn ideally combines elegance with endurance? What holds its perfect rings of petals, like dishes of light, in random flights 3 feet above showers of leaves as handsome as a vine? The Japanese anemone, of course.

It is hard to think of a garden picture that would not gain as it were a ray of light from a covey of these flowers. The first encounter with them I remember was in an abandoned flower bed on the Kent Downs where they survived to raise a pale-pink cloud above the tangled grasses as the summer drew to an end. I have vivid memories of them in great cooling white drifts under the sun-baked wall of a château in Périgord, filing like a row of little lamps across the gloom of a rain-soaked garden in Argyll .... Now they manoeuvre like butterflies in a breeze outside my study window.

1994

❧ January ❧

ANOTHER CREED

Autumn is perhaps an odd season to choose for spring-cleaning, but once you become aware how overgrown and blurred a corner of the garden has become, there is no putting off the pleasure of rolling up your sleeves and setting to.

It was our 'Japanese' pond that had drifted out of focus over the years, and if any kind of garden demands to be kept crisp it is the kind that emulates, however inadequately, the Japanese style. We knew when we built our little waterfall, planted our maple and pine, installed our stone lantern and stepping stones, that we were laying ourselves open to the remark reputedly made by a Japanese diplomat in such a setting: 'We have nothing like this in Japan.' But an infidel can still find pleasure in the decor of another creed, however half-understood.

What really lets us down is not lack of formal correctness, but a dearth of small sandalled figures bending with brush and bamboo bucket to retrieve or adjust each fallen leaf. Once a petal is out of place, you can no longer pretend you have even a pastiche of a Japanese garden.

It was a most satisfying job anyway. First I uncovered the rocks, screened by water irises and swamped by hostas, that pretend to be a naturally outcropping ridge that disappears into the pond to re-emerge the other side. Next I realised that the pine I have kept bushy all these years by pinching out its growing tips was also hiding the rocks. I waded in with saw and secateurs and reduced its foliage by half. Now you see through it, which seems to make it more, not less, important.

There was plenty more tidying and simplifying to do before I thought I saw a glimmer of Kyoto. But at last I have dared to do something I've always wanted to: introduce the bamboo note in stout poles propping the branches of trees. Why there should be something appealing in a thick bamboo sticking out of the water and tied to a pine branch I'm not sure. But I've looked at it (and its sharp-focused reflection) from all angles, and it speaks to me. In Japanese, of course.

SOIL AND SOCIETY

Television gardening has advanced by light-years in quality and interest – or so it seemed on the Friday in October when the BBC's enthralling *Englishwoman's Garden* series was followed on Channel 4 by an essay on soil that was quite beautiful to watch.

The two programmes were nicely complementary. In the first Rosemary Verey, brilliantly vague in close-up, was intercut with Penelope Hobhouse, equally tight-shot, laying bare her innermost thoughts. Then Mrs Verey was giving her young gardeners their morning trot round Barnsley House while Mrs Hobhouse was at her publishers, briefing the sales-force about her latest book. They were together at Chelsea, where Mrs Hobhouse gave her outspoken view of the judges who had failed to give Mrs Verey's garden a gold medal.

The programme combined 'lifestyle' with a touch of Anthony Clare: had almost everything in it, in fact, except raw horticulture.

The soil-science programme rivalled *Life on Earth* in picture-quality. The photography was so lovely, whether wandering over the Burren or a ploughed field, that I became a mite impatient with the lecture parts, with students dutifully fingering sand and clay to feel the difference. It scrambled to a dutifully horticultural conclusion, advising against planting azaleas on chalk and vice versa. But all this felt like a (quite unnecessary) justification for what one remembers: the pictures.

Of course there is still a place, and a need, for bean-planting programmes. But may we please have more of the science and the social side of gardening? And come to that, of its literature and its art? We have the cameramen to keep us all distracted with its beauty.

GROUNDSWELL

The idea of County Gardens Trusts is a fairly recent one, but so productive of useful initiatives that the founding of a National Association (in October, at the

Museum of Garden History) had an air of inevitability. A body of volunteers in 18 counties (with another dozen in the wings) has important potential.

The county trusts each originated in a group of enthusiasts who wanted gardening to have an independent voice in local affairs. Some were inspired by the need or desire to preserve an old garden, others to document their county's principal gardens, others to create new gardens. Underlying these efforts, as Gilly Drummond, Chairman of the extremely active Hampshire Gardens Trust and of the new Association, told me, is the aim to 'secure the base of the pyramid'. The way to secure it, she feels, is by such simple initiatives as giving children gardens at school, by giving volunteers the chance to design as well as to weed and rake, and by coordinating this low-key, self-help approach with relevant statutory and scholarly bodies – the NCCPG (National Council for the Conservation of Plants and Gardens), for example.

PS: www.nccpg.com

❧ February ❧

CHROMATICS

Stationary high pressure has kept the garden in a trance for the last three weeks. Without a breath of wind, a drop of rain or a nip of frost the trees have undressed as quietly as in a bedroom, their leaves falling round them like petticoats to lie in perfect circles at their feet.

This is something I've never seen before: each tree's whole canopy of leaves a distinct disc on the grass. No two discs are exactly the same colour: even of two oaks standing side by side, one's leaves are a darker, rustier brown.

The sorbuses have the widest range not only of colours, but also of leaf textures, from the big round plates of the king of whitebeams, *Sorbus* 'Mitchellii', yellow one side, grey the other, to the crisp fretwork of *S. esserteauana* or *S. scalaris* (both Szechwanese rowans). As for their palette, no colour seems to be missing except blue. There is the pinkish plum colour of *S. vilmorinii*, almost matching its faint-pink berries, fading to white. Next to it, their garments just overlapping on the ground, *S. hupehensis* is the mingled yellow, orange and pink of a ripe peach. Before its leaves dropped the tree seemed to be lit from within: a 300-watt bulb at least. Now it stands raw-boned but festooned with ivory berries.

The berries of *S.* 'Joseph Rock' are bright-yellow; its puddle a Fauve blend of green, plum, brown, splashed with orange and scarlet. The straight trunk of

S. alnifolia rises from a circle of parchment ... and then there are the maples: Norway bright as butter but Caucasian more saturated, less sulphur and more canary. The Japanese maples this year are disappointing, but made up for by the pyrotechnics of *Berberis thunbergii* and the soldier-red of the chokeberry.

When leaves have fallen on bushes below, or landed on yews or cypresses, there is another new effect: a paint-splatter sometimes almost hiding the ground colour. The huge dirty-brown leaves of *Populus lasiocarpa* smothered a cotoneaster like a nasty accident.

No two autumns are alike. This time horse chestnuts are like marmalade, spindles like pallid new Beaujolais – and yet some usually reliable fires have not kindled at all.

A GALLANT GARDENER

The most passionate of collectors and most generous of gardeners died in October. Maurice Mason must have left more friends enriched both mentally and horticulturally than any other gardener of our times. To visit him in his two dendrological extravaganzas in Norfolk, to hear his throaty 'dear boy' greeting and feel the hospitable warmth that he and his wife Margaret generated was as much as one could wish from any gardening friendship. Informality and hospitality masked but never hid the extraordinary scholarship the Masons shared and wanted to share with everybody.

No friend left them without a bosomful of choice and rare plants. No one ever forgets a plant the Masons gave them – or its history.

Maurice was as merry and giving as he was earnest and ambitious. It's no wonder plants grew so well for him.

❧ March ❧

HYDROPHONICS

I hope I have readers who have reached the necessary state of mind for the proper appreciation of the many sounds of water. None of our major universities yet has a Chair of Hydrophony, as far as I know, but I can think of many less useful (and more stressful) studies.

Water makes noises by hitting things; most often, itself. The volume of sound depends on the amount of water involved, also on the acoustics of the environment where the concussion occurs. (Jargon already: this must be serious stuff.) The pitch of the sound also depends on the quantity of water, but more on such variables as the speed and shape of the flow (eg, a small-bore pipe or a large one) and the height from which the water falls.

When water is falling into water (volumes being equal) a lower fall produces a lower note than a higher one. The so-called 'drum' falls at The National Trust's Studley Royal in North Yorkshire, for example, are broad but low enough to produce an imaginary drumbeat. A single drip from a tap is in the soprano range. To the listener, a single fairly steady noise, whether high or low, soon becomes 'white noise': not heard without conscious attention. Two or more sounds, on the other hand, create a harmony (or discord) that emphasises slight changes in pitch in either or both. The listener remains aware.

Is this piffle? Trad has been messing about with taps and pumps to find out. More messing (in a warmer season) is required before he can issue a proper bulletin. But so far this much seems true: two (unequal) falls make a more interesting sound than one. A fountain provides a range of notes, but (unless it is a great gusher) all in a high range. A fountain and a fall together need the bravura of the Villa Lante to make them look right, but they make a lovely noise.

DULCE DOMUM

So many of the great gardens of the land are so well publicised that it is possible for a privately-owned garden, even one of the most historic and perfect of its kind, to be overlooked and undervisited. This seems to be the case with Rousham House, a text-book landscape if ever there was one, the starting-point for an appreciation of William Kent's genius and still in the Dormer family that commissioned him in the 1730s.

If you pore over books of classical English landscapes you know Rousham already: its seven-arched arcade of Praeneste above the River Cherwell, its Venus 'surprised' among the cascades and grottoes, its bathing pool fed by the most seductively sinuous rill under the trees. Volumes have been written about the symbolism, literary, social and moral, of its statues, and of its surprising design in the woods along the riverbank, almost excluding the mansion.

I am happy to leave interpretation to scholars, and see it as the work of a great designer and an intelligent patron amusing themselves on what you might almost call a domestic scale, at least compared with the vast parks of grander families.

The Dormers of today remain modest and welcoming. Their little guide says it all: 'Rousham is uncommercial and unspoilt. Bring a picnic, wear comfortable shoes and it is yours for the day.' Compare and contrast with gardens where even the exit is barred by a souvenir shop.

BARK BITES BACK

My hedonistic thoughts about birch bark in October provoked a sharp rebuke from the person best qualified to speak of birches: their eminent collector Tony Schilling. He thought my words might encourage readers to seek out birches not their own to peel. Heaven forbid. A writer who advises 'take cuttings now' is not suggesting you take your secateurs to Kew. But I admit it could have been taken in that sense.

More profoundly, though, he disapproves of peeling birch bark at all. He likes it in its natural state, hanging in shreds and tatters round the trunk and branches, scuffling in the wind, here creamy and there grey-green with lichen. You can tell who is the gardener and who the explorer.

❧ April ❧

WATER TABLE

Any mention of flooding by anyone who was no more than wellington-deep last winter risks upsetting those who had to take to dinghies. When you live on a gravelly eminence, though, and the water table still manages to make itself conspicuously visible, it is not something you can leave out of your diary.

January's 55 mm of rain was not a particularly high figure, until you added it to the 72 of December, the 42 of November, and especially the 60 and 80-odd of October and September. The last four months of 1993 gave this dry corner of England 254 mm, or 10 inches, or over half our annual average.

This was what gave us ponds where ponds have never been before. They came quickly, but seem to be going down extraordinarily slowly – to the great satisfaction of the ducks, now reinforced each morning by a squadron of Canada geese who appear to pop in for breakfast on their way to duties elsewhere. Ducks and geese are naturally drawn to the flood-pond in preference to the permanent ponds nearby: its bottom is lovely grassy wormy soil – or was grassy before they turned its edges into dejected dark-brown mire. Presumably this is what all of it will be when the waters finally recede. Meanwhile its rippling surface dances with morning light, mocking my tidy-mindedness.

NO SHOW

Contributors to the *Orchid Review* please skip this item. Trad is all aglow at having a cymbidium bristling with six flower-spikes all half the regulation (or Show) size. The plant – it goes without saying – will win no prizes, but has won the heart of one not passionately attached to the waxy magnificence of properly nurtured cymbidiums. The poor softy is bowled over by the modest beauty of a feebly coloured, almost apologetic apparent wildling.

A little neglect and lack of feeding is all it takes. The plant has spent the last two winters indoors, and summers in the greenhouse under the staging, watered when remembered. I'm sure we don't deserve to be so lucky, but a healthier-looking plant is hard to imagine: it looks set to flower for months on end, twinkling with the little drops it squeezes from the base of each flower.

༈ May ༈

CRASH COURSE

Although of course his journey was wholly and necessarily in the cause of his horticultural education, Trad just happened to find himself in the West Indies in March at the same time as the England Cricket Team. His sensitive readers will not wish to be reminded of what happened at Arnos Vale, the Oval of St Vincent. But next day, in another part of the island, Trad was introduced to two gardens of surpassing beauty and interest, one new and one astonishingly old.

The botanical gardens of Kingstown are contemporary with those of Kew, with a foundation date of 1763. They fill a perfectly situated narrow valley above the harbour, leading up to the white-gabled Governor's Mansion. The view beyond stretches far up into the craggy rain-wreathed *mornes*, the jungled mountains, to the island's centre.

It is not the West Indian way to label plants, even in botanical gardens, but instead a guide attaches himself to each visitor and performs – it is the only word – the entire botany, history, economic uses, pharmacology and folklore of every plant in view at assault-rifle speed. Torn between the stately mango, the glossy breadfruit tree with its bright-green fig leaves, the massive teak, the elegant mahogany, the sexually ambiguous nutmeg, the jolly coffee tree with its bright-red berries, the tortured screw pine and the voluptuous blossoms of the frangipani and the cannonball tree, Trad forgot almost everything he was told – including the name of the most important tree in the garden, positively the one and only survivor of its race, rescued from the last violent eruption of Mont Souffrière but now apparently impossible to reproduce by any means. There were vigorous new shoots in the crown that looked as though they would take root on any suitable volcano. Not so, it seems; or if they do, they soon wither.

The new garden was no less interesting, and even more beautiful – at least to an English eye at home in pergola'd walks and grassy glades. It is the recent creation of Joan du Boulay Devaux, of the family that was first granted the land at Souffrière in 1713 by Louis XIV. (Their neighbour's plantation, Malmaison, gave its name to the palace west of Paris where the Empress Josephine collected roses. As a girl she had played with her Devaux cousins at Souffrière.)

Mrs Devaux's garden, under a shading over-storey of coconut palms, Norfolk Island pines and mahogany, lines the little Diamond river below where its cool falls resound through the forest. Even with his instant education in Kingstown, Trad could not hope to name a fraction of the plants, from blushing lilies to towering hibiscus, that throng the winding stream and threaten the clearings.

Scarlet anthuriums form stiff clumps among cascading white begonias. Hummingbirds seem particularly attracted to heliconias, with their lurid red and yellow lobster-claw flowers. The vanilla vine wraps itself round the cocoa tree. Fast bowling, bumpers and crash helmets seem to belong to another place and time altogether.

WHAT'S IN, WHAT'S OUT

Trendspotters at Chelsea this month, doing their rounds of the newspaper and magazine gardens where surely the derniers cris are to be found, will have no trouble identifying the continuing obsession with history that gives us William III's Hampton Court garden (*The Sunday Times*), the parson's pleasure from Barchester (*The Daily Telegraph*) and the approximation of a French 18th-century garden (*Harper's & Queen*).

There is another fashion evident, though: one most neatly captured by Mary Keen and the photographer Marijke Heuff in their new book *Decorate Your Garden*. It is the trick of introducing 'found' objects, of evoking vaguely picturesque notions with a ladder here, an old boat there – a hardy perennial, the old boat trick. The *Evening Standard* 'finds' old glass panes and bottles in its courtyard garden. The *Sunday Express* an old railway ticket office. Next year, perhaps an old airport terminal?

⁑ June ⁑

FORESTS OF THE MIND

No one could ask for a better planting season than this spring, either in Essex or in Trad's obscure corner of France – which is just as well since it saw frantic activity in the forestry department, filling former barren fields with sweet chestnut, sessile oak, and pines black, Scots and maritime (how will they do without a sea view?). Shower followed shower on already well-soaked land.

It is the common practice to wait two years before transplanting oak seedlings – long enough to have a plant about a foot high to deal with. As it happens, there was very little seed in central France two years ago, so we were planting one-year seedlings we could hardly see. My pious hope is that the deer are as short-sighted as I am. There is already evidence, though, that the hares are not.

Why is there such satisfaction in settling a tiny tree in the ground which (we hope) it will cover with its soaring crown in a century-and-a-half or so? Already in my mind's eye these open slopes are tree-shadowed, shot with slanting light, filled with birds and sheltering wood sorrel and anemones – not to mention, of course, deer.

It certainly helps that we are filling in between woods that have already stood who knows how long. The feeling of continuity is strong. But there is also the excitement of planning the rides, the access and vantage points of the future – and even sneaking in trial exotics. They may be the first sugar maples, cryptomerias or nothofagus ever to taste the gritty Allier soil.

Meanwhile the potager, my sister's inspiration and laboratory, yields more immediate returns, fortifying the hungry task force (thirsty, too) that sets out daily to teach brambles the lesson they are so reluctant to learn.

THAT YE BE NOT JUDGED

Paintings give critics enough trouble, heaven knows. But when it comes to judging gardens we are in still deeper water. The simplest way – simplistic, indeed – is to judge the gardening rather than the garden. The technical competence route is the Village Hall way – and often the Horticultural Halls way, too. Beyond it, what else is easy and objective? Rarity is relatively hard to argue about. But once you get into the realm of taste, aesthetics, call it what you will, subjectivity takes over: the judge is as much in the dock as the garden.

So how do you want your garden (supposing you are so competitive) to be judged? I have a simple answer: on the mood it creates in the majority of the people who see it. Are they all affected in (approximately) the same way? Are they calmed, stimulated, even inspired? Some will always poke around looking for labels, while others will sit quietly with their thoughts. But in the end the garden should satisfy them by giving them a strong simple memory to take home.

⚜ July ⚜

OUT OF THE STRONG ...

Magnolia flowers scorched by frost are a sad sight, but such a common one that a sigh is as much reaction as they usually provoke. The sigh becomes a deep groan when a vineyard is blasted by late frosts. It can mean a whole year's income lost. Together with hail it is one of the worst hazards of wine-growing.

What I never expected to see was a whole oak forest scorched and brown at the end of April, the sight that met me when I arrived in the Allier to take advantage of a month of heavy showers for some last-minute planting. There had been a week of torrid weather at the end of March. The great oaks of the Forêt de Tronçais had started to spread their heart-stopping canopy of brilliant olive-green – then one night the thermometer went down to -4°C.

It was enough, in that moment of tenderest young tissue, to brown and crisp every leaf and flower-bud like a grill. Four weeks later a second set of leaves was emerging – but at the loss of a great deal of growth, and presumably a year's acorns.

Needless to say the local wisterias, even lilacs, were equally disconcerted. Trees earlier in leaf – birches, cherries, horse chestnut – were not affected at all; nor were the limes, still in bud. But ashes, walnuts, planes and even sweet chestnuts were shrivelled brown.

Yet oddly it is this tendency of the climate of the centre of France to cut back early growth that is credited with the famous quality of its timber. It is the slowest oaks (so long as they are straight) that eventually make the best furniture. Wine barrels, too. A lesson in patience indeed.

CHANGING KEY

There is much more to be said about the various sounds of water (touched on in March) – not to mention its other qualities. I made the simplest of discoveries the other day playing around with a copper spout – a tap really – that feeds a stone tank with a steady gentle arc of water from a height of about 4 feet.

Left as an uninterrupted stream the water made a rather low-pitched note, loud enough to inhibit conversation near at hand, and steady enough to be boring. But by obstructing the U-shaped spout with a small vertical obstruction in the middle of the flow, the sound was transformed. My brother-in-law tried it first with a plastic plant-label. The instant result was to change the pitch from baritone to soprano, as the interrupted water splashed down sparkling with much less concerted weight. We soldered on a half-inch square of copper sheet in the centre of the U, across the flow, in place of the label – and now the spout sings an infinitely prettier tune.

TOO EASY BY HALF

A reader has asked me whether I know of any sterile form of *Alchemilla mollis*. She is tired of digging up its seedlings all over the garden. I suppose as lady's mantle it has always been popular in gardens, but it does seem to have begun something of a reign of terror since it became so fashionable 20 or so years ago.

I can see the same thing beginning to happen with *Smyrnium perfoliatum*, that wonderfully quick and easy bright-lime-green umbellifer which appeared from obscurity in the Chelsea Physic Garden in the mid '80s, was given an award at Chelsea (the Show) and its seed eagerly scattered.

Lush waves of it now throng Trad's borders. In May it rivals euphorbias in sheer lovely freshness. Unlike lady's mantle it soon shuts up shop, but I am told that in Battersea Park, at least, it is (or was) getting out of hand. How tempting it is to scatter some new exciting seed; how little one can tell of the possible results.

❧ August ❧

SPIRIT OF THE AGE

It is no earthly good trying to predict the particular pleasures of any Chelsea (and not much, I admit, rehearsing them again three months after). But this year's show made such an impact that it is worth reflecting on whether it was talent, timing, emergence from recession, or some other stimulus that gave us such powerful images as the abbey garden with its old mulberry tree and a fair bit of Salisbury Cathedral, the wonderfully aromatic patch of Queensland, the 'French' formal garden, frozen in time and perfection, and indeed Mr Maidment's collapsing greenhouse, dandelions and all.

Can anyone detect a trend in such diverse images? Nostalgia, perhaps – but only to the extent that gardeners are rarely revolutionaries; we build naturally on recollections, whether of natural scenery or the artifice of others. Besides, Chelsea was full of new ideas too.

For what it is worth, Trad's conclusion is that we are seeing a real renaissance of the gardener's art. All over Europe the turnstiles are spinning, the tills are ringing, and money in huge amounts is drawing more and more talent into every branch of the gardening industry. Hampton Court is solid enough evidence. Paris had a new garden show this spring, too, at St Cloud, to add to the brilliant success of the Journées des Plantes at Courson.

The flow of ideas, plants and skills around Europe is unstoppable. Is this something to be surprised at? Only if you can remember how morose the gardening world was 15 or 20 years ago. That was when the Professional Gardeners' Guild was formed in a spirit of last-ditch defence of values most people thought were doomed.

PS: www.domaine-de-courson.fr

JERMYNS

Trad paid an overdue visit to the Sir Harold Hillier Arboretum at Ampfield, Hampshire in May to see the relatively new area across the road called Brentry Woodland in all its springtime glory. The sight and scent of the massed rhododendrons on one of spring's few sunny days was almost overwhelming.

They have the most magnificent setting possible for such a collection: scores of mature Scots pines, their grizzled heads soaring on glowing orange trunks 90 or 100 feet above the floor. The enormous task of converting this high wood, then full of straggling *Rhododendron ponticum*, into such a paradise had quietly been going on for nearly 20 years before it was opened to the public by the county council in 1990.

In the arboretum proper, and especially in the gardens around Jermyns House, Sir Harold's great work continues triumphantly. It struck me again what a tranquil and lovely house Jermyns is, asymmetrically gabled, pale cream with a dark slate roof, backed with huge trees and facing a prospect of ravishing specimens of every sort.

Ceanothus 'Puget Blue' (very dark) and *Olearia* x *scilloniensis* (dazzling white) were perhaps the star performers of this particular day. But my heart went out to the crazily-leaning snow gum, *Eucalyptus pauciflora* subsp. *niphophila*, whose cream-and-grey trunk must be the most beautiful in England.

❧ September ❧

NYMPH IN THY ORISONS ...

It is over 15 years now since I first visited Ninfa, but the vision of this dreaming garden-ruin, deep in the Campagna south of Rome, has never left me. It stuck in my mind as a place so beautiful and extraordinary that even the potent word garden could hardly stretch to encompass it. When I went back in May this year, my highest expectations were more than fulfilled. Surely this is the loveliest spot on earth.

Ninfa was a city of the plain. From 800 AD to almost 1400 it lived, traded, worshipped (even crowned a pope) within its towered walls and churches. Far above it, dizzily far, perched on a 1,300-foot cliff, hangs the ancient town of Norma. From a lake at the base of the cliff the River Ninfa (the name means nymph) flings itself, as clear as crystal, wide as a street and fast as a trotting horse, under the walls, past the barbican and the old Palazzo Communale, under bridges and through jumbles of ruins, to slide glittering under a final embattled bridge and gigantic poplar into the light and stillness of the countryside.

After the city was sacked in 1382 its inhabitants never returned. Mosquitoes from the Pontine marshes made it a place of fever into this century, its streets and houses a medieval Pompeii.

Then in 1920 Prince Gelasio Caetani began to uncover the buried stones, strip the ivy from roofless churches, and plan the garden that has now reached such spectacular but serene maturity.

The Caetani family had owned Ninfa since 1297. They became gardeners by degrees as three generations married English or American wives. Prince Gelasio, half English, planted the cypresses, evergreen oaks and planes that dominate the ruins today: at 75 years old they are in resplendent maturity. His brother Roffredo, Duke of Sermoneta, and Marguerita, his American Duchess, embroidered this Italian canvas with fruit trees and roses, magnolias and wisterias, irises and lilies and with a romantic abandon that is completely English in spirit. Roses climb high in cypresses, tender plants find shelter in the still-frescoed apses of the four remaining churches. The pair also played games with springs and rivulets to fill the garden with the many voices of water, from tinkling treble to booming baritone.

Their daughter Lelia, married to Hubert Howard, was the last Caetani of Ninfa. When the Howards died they entrusted stewardship of the indefinable magic they had helped to create to their young curator,

Lauro Marchetti. Happily the future of Ninfa is ensured by endowment as well as spiritual succession. And what remained a secret for so long is now beginning to emerge.

BALEFUL TALE

How far from those pellucid waters to the turbid subject of blanket weed.

It is not usually Trad's way to spoil the fun by submitting a good story to too much scientific investigation. But a rumour going about that the bane of blanket weed in a pond could be conquered by a bale of barley straw seemed too far-fetched to pass on unchecked. The bale has been in the pond, therefore, for six weeks now, and the following has been the order of play:

- Step one. Despair at the endless camouflage-green filaments choking the surface and glued firmly to the sides.
- Step two. Locate a barley field with friendly farmer attached. Negotiate a sackful of straw.
- Step three. Wade in, rake, roll and scrape as much weed as possible from the water. The long rolls drying on the bank now turn a lustrous silky green that almost makes you repent.
- Step four. Weight the sack with stones and drop it in. For extra conviction Trad used a sack at each end of the pond. They look like baby hippos. The water browns encouragingly round them. Remaining scraps of weed turn brown too.
- Step five. Visit daily for six weeks. Observe the daily increase in delicate green strands of blanket weed growing back apparently undiscouraged.

A further report will follow.

❦ October ❦

SENSITIVITY

There is nothing so stimulating as a forthright, well-argued alternative view – and, in horticulture, few things rarer.

I have not yet read a new American book called *Why We Garden: Cultivating a Sense of Place*. But the title beckons, and so does an article by the author, Jim Nollman, in the avowedly alternative *Interspecies Newsletter*.

This paragraph, partly borrowed from the (not normally inspiring) philosopher Schopenhauer, is a fair sample: 'Bad gardens copy, good gardens create, great gardens transcend. What all great gardens have in common is their ability to pull the sensitive viewer out of him or herself and into the garden, so completely that the separate self-sense disappears entirely, and at least for a brief moment one is ushered into a … timeless awareness. A great garden, in other words, is always mystical no matter what its actual content.'

The crux of the paragraph is that word 'sensitive'. We have all heard visitors to gardens walking around seeing nothing while they discuss their slug problem back home. But Nollman goes further. 'Neither the language nor the forthright pragmatism of horticulture', he says, 'is able to plumb the depth of what I consider to be an … intuitive relationship with the garden.'

Not everyone will follow him into his questioning whether man is the only sentient being in the garden, and whether or not the plants, and indeed the pests, have feelings too. But I have great sympathy with his view that more things happen in a garden than mere horticultural routine – and on planes we know little or nothing about. The better a garden, the more of 'a sense of place' it has. I shall be reading Nollman's book.

MEDIATION

This sounds to me like an idea whose time has come: The Mediterranean Garden Society.

Exiles from these shores to what they fondly imagine will be the softer conditions of the Mediterranean are almost invariably amazed by the extreme conditions they encounter. The notion that anywhere where 'tender' plants flourish is by definition kindlier is based on a deep misapprehension.

Here, in Britain, is where gardening is easy, the climate equable, the possibilities almost infinite. There, under pitiless sun, often on terrible soil, in the sporadic rainfall and sometimes literally maddening winds, far from competent nurseries and with very few relevant reference books, the bougainvillea can seem a small reward for all the plants you can't grow.

OVEREXPOSURE

After five weeks of subtropical weather this summer it is very noticeable that leaves without their full ration of chlorophyll are like sunbathers without Ambre Solaire – except that they go black, not red.

It is common for the fresh yellow leaves of the 'golden' philadelphus to burn in bright spring sunshine. Now every plant with even a touch of cholorisis, indicated by a certain pallor in its foliage, is quite seriously scorched. Here *Acer rubrum* has been blow-lamped; so has *Acer pseudoplatanus* 'Brilliantissimum'. *Magnolia salicifolia* is crisp at the edges, little *Berberis thunbergii* 'Aurea' (not chlorotic, just yellow) has lost most of its leaves.

Even the white-variegated *Aralia*, whose spreading leaves usually provide the coolest-looking dappled shade, has started to shrivel and turn brown.

❧ November ❧

MARSH LANE

Monet's garden we all know. But how many other gardens can you think of created by painters, sculptors, architects or designers for their own delight that survive for us to enjoy?

I can think of only one: the garden made by Sir Frederick Gibberd at Marsh Lane, Harlow. Gibberd, who died in 1984, was both an architect and a landscape designer with a masterful eye and a powerful sense of place. He was also a passionate art collector and highly competent plantsman. Going back to Marsh Lane the other day I realised that his garden must certainly be one of the most 'important' – to use the collector's term – in Britain in the history of the mid-20th century. It is certainly one of the most beguiling.

When Gibberd planned Harlow New Town he very sensibly found himself a promising site nearby. Marsh Lane is a sheltered plot sloping gently down to the little Pincey Brook that runs into the River Stort. He built a simple, airy house with lofty rooms to display the collections (largely of works by his friends, from Edward Bawden to Henry Moore) that so inspired his own vision of landscape. The 9 acres around, bordered on the east by the brook, he planned not just as a garden, but also as a setting of rooms, glades, groves and alleys for sculpture and architectural trophies.

He planted bold masses of trees and shrubs, as many as 15 Lombardy poplars, for example, to encircle one statue, and a ring of Norway maples as a setting for another. He channelled springs into quiet ferny runnels to the river. He made pools and falls in the little river itself, using massive boulders from a Welsh reservoir. He built summer houses to command vistas; used piles of stones, logs of wood or outcrops of clipped yew or box to direct the eyes or feet; and as a centrepiece used a short but monumental avenue of limes, preposterously tight-planted and humblingly tall, leading to a stone swan opening her wings for flight.

In so busy a space, so subdivided and full of incident, it needed inspired judgement to create a flow of alternate concealment and revelation; to pace the changes of mood. Gibberd had that skill. He also called for a high level of expert upkeep, but the effect was, and is, unique. Since his death Lady Gibberd (whose own credentials in the art world are formidable) has maintained his vision impeccably, for Gibberd was not one to let his works perish with him. Happily he left Marsh Lane in trust for the benefit of Harlow, its people and its visitors, perpetually.

OMNIA GALLIA

It came to me in the interval of *Arcadia*, Tom Stoppard's puzzle play at the Haymarket theatre (whose characters include Lord Byron, off-stage, and a caricature of Humphry Repton in the style of Thomas Love Peacock, called Mr Noakes) that any idea about the English landscape as we know it being an invention of the 18th century is absurd.

If the essence of Englishness is curves and of Frenchness straight lines, these dominant shapes were drawn ineradicably on our respective countries not centuries but millennia ago by our forebears who made our roads. If the rolling English drunkard made the rolling English road, he surely also set in train the forms of landscape that we recognise as native, and indeed the sensibility that approved of them as natural and right.

Nor was it Le Nôtre, of course, who gave France its arrow-like avenues, but Julius Caesar – with a bit of help from Napoleon.

❦ December ❦

GARTENHAUS

I'm not sure how many perfect rococo gardens still exist to be visited and wondered at, but certainly few as complete as the worldly pleasure-ground of the prince-bishops of Würzburg at Veitshöchheim in northern Bavaria. Trad was invited there the other day after a glorious concert of appropriate music in the prince-bishop's town house, the Residenz in Würzburg, where Tiepolo painted his most outrageously gorgeous ceilings.

Though still a little unclear about exactly what rococo means, at least in garden design, Trad was captivated by what really amounts to a maze liberally sprinkled with hints and clues. It is an odd, lopsided garden, an enclosure of some 30 acres neither directly (certainly not axially) related to its house, nor depending on the surrounding landscape in any way. The house, in any case, is only a modest schloss, stressing the fact that the garden is the main feature.

Hornbeam and lime hedges make the criss-crossing allées, leading here to a grass theatre, there to a fountain-packed pond, there again to a gazebo, a 'Roman' ruin or a grotto-pavilion covered with snails, shells and grotesque animals. Some 'rooms' between allées are entirely shaded with limes pleached to form a ceiling. Everywhere there are statues, mainly of the pastoral kind, with the same shepherdess popping up again and again, oddly piggy-featured and wildly décolletée. (Trad loved her.)

Next stop was Weimar, near Leipzig, to see a *Gartenhaus* of a very different kind: the deeply tranquil cottage where Goethe used to retire to write. It lies in a valley so romantic that Trad was reminded of Fountains Abbey. Any shepherdess here, though, would surely come thoroughly colletée, and with working sheep.

PLANTERBOUTS

I had been lured into thinking that 'planters' on pavements were the nadir of misbegotten effects in horticulture. But now comes a more ingenious method of installing a garden where no garden should be: the sponsored roundabout. The new development is to allow some local business to sponsor cute little flower beds in exchange for an advertisement – a distracting hoarding just where drivers should be looking to their right.

French provincial mayors are notoriously unable to distinguish between a shopping street and a public garden, with catastrophic results for the integrity of France's urban landscape. Now our councils are achieving the same visual discord along country roads. Radial slices of cheery, multi-coloured bedding cutting into the green sobriety of the countryside are yet another form of visual pollution.

1995

❧ January ❧

DÎNER SUR L'HERBE

Gardeners who went to the magnificent reborn Glyndebourne opera this summer were a bit bemused by some of the planting on the slopes that connect the higher level of the new opera house with the old garden below. I suspected that a last-minute panic accounted for such eccentricities as ornamental cabbages – and were they courgettes or melons? – trying to fill the bare ground. Next year I'm sure the true plot will emerge and be as splendid as the rest.

In the old garden I went to check on a feature that has always caught my eye: to the right of the main vista over the ha-ha there is a clump of *Macleaya microcarpa*, that aristocratic cousin of the poppy with creamy plumes above massive glaucous lobed leaves, translucent enough to show the orange sap that flows in their veins. *Macleaya* in a border is a runner. At Glyndebourne it is given a place of honour on its own, a huge patch in the grass where the mower can keep it in bounds. This year I found it somewhat diminished – but my real interest in it is as a potential plant for wild gardening in France.

Establishing tough perennials in grass, rather than in beds and borders, was an idea propagated by William Robinson in the 1870s (and no doubt others before and since). It seems to me particularly suited to the sort of garden that flows without boundaries into copses and meadows. What I have in mind is random but substantial blocks of, apart from *Macleaya*, such plants as *Phlomis russeliana*, *Persicaria mollis* (*Polygonum molle*), *Acanthus spinosus*, perhaps such geraniums as 'Johnson's Blue', certainly Japanese anemones, maybe doronicums for early spring. The trick will be to give them a good start in a well-dug patch, well manured and (for a year or so) well weeded. Then simply hope they will thrive, survive the rabbits and form clumps as redoubtable as bamboos.

ENTR'ACTE

Even if I were of the school that likes to put the garden to bed in November, this extraordinary month would have stayed my hand. With the temperature in the last week still steadily in the mid-50s, dipping at night to the mid-40s, the borders are still packed with (admittedly slightly dishevelled) perennials and (slightly soggy) annuals flowering fit to bust. Roses are still unfurling quiet little half-strength blooms, while the winter brigades of mahonias and jasmine are already up to full power. My most confused plant is a prized *Daphne tangutica* (now Retusa Group), its pink scented flowers almost covering its smart dome of British Racing Green as though it were April.

This suits my winter philosophy nicely. Far better to have fading memories of the season past than the sterile theatre-without-players that is a garden tidied away for winter. For us the autumn jobs are in those places where long-established plants no longer bear close inspection: climbing roses half-full of dead wood, ivy choking shrubs – and worst of all the combination of the two. If we have learned one thing this month, it has been never to let ivy, even pretty variegated ivy, climb the same wall as a powerful rose. The eventual tangle of dead rose branches and live ivy is a fiendish foe.

❦ February ❦

THE ACID TEST

Hands up anyone who hasn't got a Leyland cypress either on the premises or the skyline. Not many hands. And yet we all know, don't we, that this vegetable monster will grow inexorably to 100 feet plus; a tower of dull green that will be extremely expensive and awkward to remove when the time comes.

So far the ones I planted (as windbreak, space-fillers and to help nurse better trees) have been culled by felling. One or two I have topped at 30 feet or so, which checks their progress – for a while. Now I hear that this arboreal Hydra will sprout back into life however hard you cut it – in other words like yew, rather than the closely related Lawson's cypress. Once a Lawson's cypress is cut, browned by shading or otherwise discouraged from growing, it never (in my experience) puts out new growth.

To put Leyland to the test this winter we have removed every branch from a vigorous young tree about 20 feet high, leaving it as a bare spar which could almost be described as avant-garde sculpture. I shall report later on whether it fuzzes green again, and whether it contrives to grow new branches. It would be an interesting development. Imagine the rows of narrow columns that you could create. Such vertical hedging, as it were, has many possibilities.

PS It didn't sprout, but became an ivy-covered pillar surviving (so far) 13 years.

MARSH LANE (CONTINUED)

I wrote confidently about the future of Marsh Lane in the November issue, knowing that Sir Freddie's will left it in trust to Harlow. But wills can be contested, and its future is now not so certain. In view of this a public meeting in Old Harlow recently founded the Friends of the Gibberd Garden Trust to try to ensure the future (and future accessibility) of this very special place. More than a hundred people came to the meeting, which followed a lecture on the garden by Jane Brown, whose *Gardens of a Golden Afternoon* established her as the leading authority on Gertrude Jekyll and Edwin Lutyens.

Both the local and county councils are among those discussing what can be done to save the garden and to give it the role that Sir Freddie intended. Trad will be happy to help readers who would like to contribute to this worthy and urgent cause by putting them in touch with The Friends.

PS All's well. The National Lottery helped the Gibberd Garden Trust to secure it. See www.thegibberdgarden.co.uk

FINGERS CROSSED

I look out of my study window at the green bole of a copper beech tree about 30 yards away, the ground beneath it covered with the brown leaves and husks of mast which the worms have not yet tugged industriously down into the soil.

This is where I try to grow winter aconites. 'Try', because out of the 20 I planted some years ago, only five survived. They are slowly, very slowly, building up strength. A couple of very frail-looking seedlings have appeared. But do I have the confidence to do the necessary: dig them up as they finish flowering, as though they were snowdrops, divide them and replant them to cover more ground?

The situation should be ideal: the grass has almost given up the ghost in the dense shade, so there is no competition. But then I've seen them take over lawns in gardens they really approve of. Perhaps – another thought –

the greedy beech roots are starving them?

Why is there a special pleasure in growing such wayward, elfin plants – plants whose instructions always include the words 'with luck'?

PS Progress is still slow, but dividing and replanting is succeeding.

✤ March ✤

PLUS ÇA CHANGE

It is teatime. The sun that gleamed on wet birch trunks this afternoon, and picked out willow catkins like pearls against the sombre sky, is setting in a cold rim of bilious light between the chasing clouds and the black horizon. The fire crackles red in the hearth. I sit surrounded by books and magazines, catalogues and plans in that most luxurious horticultural moment: anticipation of the year ahead.

I have the tired parts of the garden firmly in my mind: parts of the borders where Michaelmas daisies are wandering off in search of better soil, *Veronicastrum virginicum* gets shorter every year and monarda has evaporated almost entirely, or where my indulgence of handsome, self-sufficient volunteers – a spotted hellebore or a white foxglove, clary or Miss Willmott's Ghost – have brought about an unfocused muddle.

This will be the year I dig up a miserable chlorotic magnolia; replace a woody ceanothus waving high above the wall; steel myself to prune a *Rosa moyesii* whose 20 barbed trunks soar 15 feet in inextricable entanglement. But not now – and that list is already written.

Yet the greatest winter indulgence is not turning pages of sickeningly beautiful picture books, still less of clamouring catalogues fatuously touting 'novelties'. It is joining fellow gardeners of the past whose company, in the pages of their books and magazines, is as vivid as that of any contemporary.

I have just looked up the March issue of *The Gardener's Magazine* of 1835 to see what occupied horticultural minds in this season 160 years ago. It was the month when the melancholy intelligence reached England of the death of David Douglas, in the Sandwich Islands, on the horns of a wild bull. 'No man', writes John Claudius Loudon, the magazine's 'conductor', 'ever introduced so many beautiful hardy plants into Britain.' Douglas was 36.

The issue contains enthusiastic reports of the new colonies of South Australia and the Swan river in the west, and discusses the progress of the first hardiness trials of acacia and eucalyptus in Monmouthshire, Edinburgh,

Dublin, Dundee and in the Horticultural Society's gardens. It carries reports of orchids collected on the Spanish Main and Demerara ('justly has Demerara been called the land of mud'), of the virtues of the new *Garrya elliptica* (introduced by Douglas in 1828), and an ingenious idea for covering wall fruit-trees with ivy to protect their fruit.

It debates the relative merits of green and white asparagus (the green, it reports, being eaten by the French chopped up to resemble a dish of peas), and declares that pines can be propagated by cuttings of young wood in sand 'like ericas'. Would that it were so.

It also prints a sour reflection on farmers as gardeners. Cottagers, it says, are on the whole pretty good about their gardens. But 'there is hardly any class of the ... community to be found more utterly ignorant and destitute of taste, in respect to gardening, than the great majority of our farmers.'

Time for another log on the fire. How little life changes in the countryside.

ON THE DOWNS

In January, Trad sadly reported the death of Dick Norman, the saviour of the Hanbury Gardens at La Mortola. Alas in December he was followed to the grave by his elder brother Mark, who, in his time as Treasurer of The National Trust, was described as managing its affairs 'with flair approaching genius'. Mark Norman gardened at his old family home, where he lived for most of his life, Moor Place at Much Hadham in Hertfordshire.

As boys, though, both were deeply affected by the gardening of their uncle, Sir Mark Collet, one of many relations and forebears who, since the 18th century, had been directors of the Bank of England. The Collets lived at St Clere, near Kemsing on the Kentish North Downs.

A great swell of chalk downland rises above the 17th-century mansion of St Clere. With its hanging beech woods and clumps, it is the sort of scene that Tristram Hillier and Stanley Badmin so often painted with their special sort of infatuated realism. (Nobody was more infatuated with these fields and trees than the young Trad, who lived at the edge of the park as a lad.)

The great surprise of St Clere, though, comes at the top of the Down, where a wayward outcrop of greensand allowed Sir Mark to plant an exotic pinetum richly decorated with rhododendrons; an improbable sight in a landscape formed almost entirely of chalk. The pinetum is still there, now in its maturity with some interesting new planting, in the middle of one of Kent's most perfect bluebell woods – in spring heavy with the Chelsea smell of azaleas.

HORSE MANURE

I learn from a local land agent's newsletter that horse manure is henceforward to be classified as Industrial Waste, which means it can be tipped only on a site with a licence to accept such noxious materials. I am, of course, taking steps to have my borders classified as such sites.

To what end this pointless and apparently endless classifying of everything? Except, of course, to justify the employment of persons who have nothing whatever to do but make a nuisance of themselves.

⚘ April ⚘

BOTANY BAY

Trad is an avid explorer of botanical gardens at all times, but avider than ever when they are in that most delectable weather-belt, Australia, in our coldest months.

The three cities of the south-east, Sydney, Melbourne and Adelaide, each put forward strong contenders for the prize of most historic/ beautiful/ interesting garden. Sydney must be allowed to win on historical grounds, because the slopes of Farm Cove, where the garden lies, was the first land cultivated by the colonists of Australia in 1788.

Miraculously they remain entirely green; the one promontory of all the ins and outs of Sydney harbour not built upon, yet with all the water-traffic swirling round it on its way to Circular Quay and the Opera House. The garden has lovely corners, especially a bravura display of annuals, excellent roses, and some mighty trees. If it has something of the feel of a public park, though, it is because of its wide open lawns, and of course its matchless situation.

Melbourne's botanical garden overlooks the little River Yarra, with its navy of sculls and eights, from the slope opposite the city centre. In a city full of space and trees it is the dominant green hill, laid out much as John Claudius Loudon might have advised in his 'gardenesque' mood, its weird rockeries now softened by time and the shade of its colossal trees, but still with every mark of botanical intent, including a fern gully which almost amounts to an artificial rainforest through the relentless use of sprinklers. Melbourners resort to this garden in their thousands for concerts and dalliance without changing its character of a great collection full of venerable specimens.

In this judgement of Paris it is Adelaide's garden, though, that wins Trad's heart – both for beauty and botanical interest. The aptly named Colonel Light, who laid out this city of enlightenment, surrounded its serene central grid-pattern of streets with a broad green belt of unbuilt-on land. The garden (founded in 1855) lies in this belt, the inner core of a 'botanical park' whose huge old trees dapple little picnic parties with the sort of light Tissot loved. Within the stately iron gates of the garden the pace of horticulture revs up – culminating in a spectacular new rainforest glasshouse, 100 yards long and 100 feet high.

It is one of the great experiences of the garden world to walk through the dry 'Australian forest', where kauri pine, stringybarks and blue gums, 'mountain ash' and river red gums raise their silvery canopies far overhead, stirring like eddying pools in the slightest breeze; and through the doors of the vast fan-shaped conservatory, into the still, steamy world of palms and tree ferns and epiphytes. Silvery light filters down from the gleaming spars of the roof, through a perpetual mist from a hundred fine sprays. The building seems to dissolve among the dark plant forms wrapped in cloud.

The garden is rich in more conventional horticulture, too: rose and herb gardens, broad brick paths under shady pergolas (very necessary where the temperature frequently reaches 40°C) and massive specimens of exotic trees from the northern hemisphere.

But Adelaide has other strings to its bow: five botanical gardens in all. The biggest, and newest, was opened in 1977, 500 metres up on Mount Lofty where sea winds from the Great Australian Bight deposit a west-country quantity of rain. The native red gums and stringybarks form the setting for a rich collection of flowering trees and shrubs, and especially of splendid conifers, from round the world, sheltered in a mountain cleft where springs converge to form a broad lake.

As the old-established private gardens of the Adelaide hills testify, this is one of the most privileged climates on earth: the Mediterranean without its winter.

POT LUCK

The blue shimmer of flax, hanging like a mysterious lake between the hedges, is a lovely addition to the landscape. Oilskin-coloured fields of oilseed rape daubed on the early summer countryside are met with mixed emotions.

This summer you may see something less familiar suddenly shooting up at an alarming rate into a 9-foot green forest. Hemp is back. It is 24 years since the Misuse of Drugs Act banned *Cannabis sativa* from our fields. Not only a valuable crop, but also the industry that processed it, was lost. Hemp produces excellent paper, rope, strong cloth (the word canvas comes from cannabis), oil, and the best horse litter. Pot-smoking stopped it all.

But French and Dutch breeders have now produced a strain of cannabis to frustrate pot-smokers. They have bred out the tetrahydrocannabinol that gives it its entertainment value.

❦ May ❦

BOOKWORM

What does this column think about the Lindley Library debate? Should it have a new home purpose-built for it in Westminster? Should it be regrouped in splendour in a new centre of horticultural learning in a much-augmented Wisley? So many readers have asked that I feel obliged to reveal my posture. Unfortunately sitting on the fence is not the most graceful posture to reveal.

But there are many questions to be answered before the best solution comes to light. A fundamental one to start with: is a library a collection of books (and periodicals and manuscripts and paintings), or is it a place? For years the Lindley Library has been housed mainly in its inadequate quarters in the Old Hall, partly in even more inadequate quarters at Wisley.

Would it make a radical difference if the balance tipped in favour of Wisley? Do the 3,000-odd annual library visitors need instant access to the whole collection? In a few years' time, when researchers will turn to computer screens as a matter of course to consult libraries all over the world, how much will the location matter?

But scholars need to *feel* books – and of course to see the originals of paintings. We (I include myself) feel a nervous anticipation as we close upon our quarry on the shelves, then let our eyes run along the spines of neighbouring volumes, greedy to read them all for every reference, every hint about our subject. Serendipity is the unlooked-for clue in the next book along.

Living in the country, I go to London (and Cambridge) as a matter of course to spend a day shelf-crawling. It isn't something you can hurry; its very essence is the unexpected.

TRAVEL SUPPLEMENT

The Abbey of Fontevraud is the great shrine of the Plantagenets in France. King Henry II is buried there with his queen, Eleanor of Aquitaine, and their son, Richard Coeur de Lion. It is the greatest 'religious city' left in Europe, covering

34 acres with its abbey church, cloisters and courts, refectory, chapter house, dormitories, hospital and its famous Romanesque kitchen with 20 chimneys.

Fontevraud is a few miles from Saumur and its bridge over the Loire, very near the road taken by scores of thousands of us every year on the way south. Yet until four or five years ago it remained an unvisited secret. Napoleon closed this magnificent institution, which in its time had been ruled by 36 abbesses, 16 of royal blood, and turned it into a common gaol. A gaol it remained until 20 years ago, when restoration began to transform it into the Cultural Centre for Western France. Three floors of cells had to be removed from the very church itself ....

Why do I mention it here? Because among the restorations are those of a medieval herb garden, and several unique (as far as I know) trellis enclosures with examples of all the crops, fruits and flowers grown by the order of monks in the Middle Ages. The former Prieuré St-Lazare, the leper hospital, has been transformed into a comfortable but suitably simple hotel (its restaurant is arranged around a cloister) approached through a well-labelled herb garden. There are concerts at the abbey throughout the summer. The Château de Villandry with its spectacular vegetable parterres is not far away. Gardeners going south will find it a singularly rewarding stopping place.

For those not going so far, the verdant little poplar-lined valley of the River Authie, 80 kilometres south of the Channel Tunnel, has another abbey garden, this one a nursery and garden centre as well. A few years ago I mentioned the unusually enterprising nursery of M Cousin near Calais. He is now installed with a wide collection of plants, particularly shrubs and fruit trees, in the precincts of the handsome baroque abbey of Valloires. The hamlet of Argoules nearby caters rather well for the inner person, too – but let me not venture down that road.

PS: www.jardins-de-valloires.com

❧ June ❧

BACK TROUBLE

The newsletter of the Professional Gardeners' Guild has surely reached the point (at its 67th issue) where it could, if it wanted, describe itself as a magazine. It reminds me, indeed, more and more of the old *Gardener's Magazine* in which John Claudius Loudon brought together the news and views of (mainly) professional gardeners between 1826 and 1845. It unites practical tips with moments of nostalgia, reports of plant-hunting journeys with brisk exchanges of opinion, offers with suggestions, experiments with experience.

One article in the April issue especially caught my eye. In *Back Trouble*, Robert Milne discusses the best design of spade, and finds that longer handles on spades, forks and hoes afford him considerable relief from long-term back pain.

When I began gardening in France I wondered at the quaint design of the local tools. The British D-shaped handle on a short shaft is unknown in the Bourbonnais and, I believe, in France generally. Tools just have a long pole, chin-high, to hold them by.

Four years later I have completely abandoned my imported British spade. In fact I can't remember what the D is for, except for hanging from a hook. The change of grip to a straight shaft comes completely naturally, and the extra leverage in digging is astonishing. With a long-handled hoe, as Robert Milne explains, you scarcely find yourself bending at all.

Fifteen years ago I asked the spade-manufacturers of Britain why they no longer made straight spades like the old Essex model for cutting clay. Their reply was that the standard kind with an angled blade is 'ergonomically' perfect. I expect they will give the long straight handle the same blank stare.

LE MOMENT CRITIQUE

Watching the mid-April frosts gnawing away at the young growth on everything from box to walnut to ash to oak, not to mention the flowers on magnolias and the bright young shoots and flowers on *Pieris*, it becomes apparent that there is a critical moment when the slightest frost will destroy young tissue.

Deep in the oak woods of Sussex where we spent the weekend, one could see how trees in frost-pockets had sometimes suffered, but sometimes not: if their new leaves had been hardening even for as much as a few days they could resist slight frost.

Well-sheltered trees in relatively warm spots were just as frost-tender if they were unlucky with their timing. The earlier and more beautiful the spring, of course, the greater the chance of retribution. On the other hand some wildly precocious plant may just get away with its daring by leafing in a window of warm weather, even in February, long enough to harden its leaves before the cold comes back.

We have a poplar from Korea whose pale tender-green leaves are an invitation to destruction every winter. This year it got away scot-free. By April it thought it was summer. Just as well poplars don't usually put on Lammas shoots.

❧ July ❧

FAITES SIMPLE

Early May was the rather riskily late moment for a planting session at Château Trad in central France – possible only because the rain had been almost constant there all spring. For once there was no frost to check the superabundant growth of all last year's planting; on all sides the growing green was almost bright enough to hurt your eyes.

So what did we plant? With a few exceptions the answer is: more of the same. In my thinking if one 'Gloire de Dijon' or 'Alister Stella Gray' (just to mention roses we planted last year) looks good and does well, three or four (or six or eight) will look better. Oaks are the main theme of the farm, supported by pine, wild cherry, birch, and the wild service tree which laces the hedgerows here. The odd flourish of a walnut or a tulip tree, or any purposeful row (eg of willows or poplars) just serves to domesticate the landscape. But repetition is the true source of strength in design, and what goes for the macrocosm of landscape goes for the minimicrocosm of our garden, too.

It is after all the basic French gardening formula: symmetry by definition implies two of everything but, as Le Nôtre knew, 200 is a good round figure. The difficulty, of course, comes with the decision: which of all our favourite plants shall we plant again, and again, and again?

QUIET AUTHORITY

It is one thing to be the great authority, editing and directing a formidable reference book – and a very different thing to be an author alone, with his judgements, his sensibilities, his tastes and memories. For many years now Chris Brickell has been the ubiquitous arbiter of horticulture (as well, of course, as the first Director General of the RHS). *The RHS A–Z Encyclopedia of Plants and Flowers* could be the magisterial work it is (and the commercial success) only under his baton.

But now we have a personal book of a kind he has had to deny himself, and us, for too long: *Christopher Brickell's Garden Plants*, published by Pavilion Books.

CDB is as notable for his modesty as for his learning, not to mention his persuasive powers. Modesty gives his writing a gentle, slightly old-fashioned flavour that recalls the great gardening writers before our era of novelties and certainties.

He will start a passage on a splendid and essential plant with 'I would venture to suggest ...', but then go on to give a more considered, rounded picture and estimate of it than anyone else ever has. This is thoughtful and experienced, but also vivid and positive writing by a plantsman who truly loves his subject. How good to think that we can look forward to Brickell expounding on his loves for years to come.

GOSLING-SCROTCH

As goosegrass years go, this is proving a relatively light one. Goosegrass (you can call it cleavers, cleggers, hayriff, burweed or even [in East Anglia] gosling-scrotch – I doubt whether anyone likes it enough to call it *Galium aparine*) is one of the weeds I class as more irritating than infuriating. Its speed and spread can be astonishing, especially as the whole sprawl of nature's Velcro arises from one stem no thicker than 15-amp fuse wire. It can overtop shrubs before you notice it has started. It regularly clogs hedge-bottoms, and insinuates itself into beds and borders just enough to blur the focus without really drawing attention to itself.

But even a hefty infestation is not heavy work to remove. In spring before it flowers you can usually roll most of it up into an inconsiderable ball, which you can hide (I get scolded for this) in any out-of-the-way corner. Teasing it out of plants is rather soothing work, I find.

It is a different matter when it reaches the seeding stage, covering everything it touches with little green pellet-like burrs. It is particularly fond of socks, and soon gets into your shoes as maddeningly as gravel.

SUMMER BEDDING

What last year could have been called Conservatory Row at Chelsea, the road north of the marquee, really needs a new name after this year's show. There was scarcely a living plant to be seen inside any of the ever-more-elaborate structures. Most were living or dining rooms of some sort. One was even a rather comfortable-looking bedroom. But are these conservatories? 'Home Extension Row' doesn't have quite the same ring, does it? But then one wonders whether some of the exhibitors have turned up at the right exhibition.

❧ August ❧

LIKE AS THE HART

Why did I ever think a fountain was a simple thing to grow? I should have known better: nothing to do with water in the garden is straightforward and reliable. It not only has a life of its own; it also contains or supports myriad forms of life, from fish to geese (more on these later) and dragonflies to duckweed.

Last year I installed a very simple submersible pump in the shallow water of a small concrete-lined pond. Up shot the glistening jet; for several days it gave me great joy to visit it – until I became aware that it was shrinking. All was not well.

When I waded in to retrieve it I found the pump's filter was blocked with debris, from dead and rotten leaves to water snails. The filter was not hard to clean, but a few days later it not only needed cleaning again, but I also found the jets of the nozzle were equally clogged – and not so easy to clean.

I will not bore you with the various dodges I tried to screen the pump from detritus. None worked; the pump stopped, and an electrician pronounced it dead from stress. He suggested a more important pump above water level, humming away in a little house of its own on the bank. I was not keen to start a housing estate on the bank – in any case, I pointed out, whatever filter I put on the suction pipe in the water would quickly clog up too.

My right-hand man, Eric Kirby, has a more penetrating intellect. In the bottom of the pond are several deepish holes designed for water lilies, formed by sinking old beer barrels when the pond was built. (A sudden oath from the water garden usually means that someone has found one of them by stepping in up to the thigh.) Eric's scheme was to put a pump at the bottom of one of these holes and put a sort of filter bed of larger and smaller shingle on top. The filter bed is suspended in a metal box that sits in the opening of the hole.

One refinement has already been necessary. The tiny filaments that detach themselves from duckweed get through and eventually block the fine apertures in the fountain nozzle. Answer: larger apertures (but of course a lower jet).

For the moment the plashing is perfect. But in the meantime, on another pond, a family of Canada geese is growing apace, making the grass around an extremely unsavoury sight.

I think I'm learning why the Japanese so often have imaginary water in their gardens ....

DRAMATIC EFFECT

I'm afraid Trad trod on a tender spot in January when reporting on the plantings around the hugely successful new opera house at Glyndebourne. He mentioned the cabbages and courgettes beside the steps up to the entrance as apparent evidence of haste to get something growing in time for the first season.

Not at all, says this year's programme. Expect to see more unconventional planting. And we did: the giant hogweed standing proudly where less imaginative gardeners might have installed a plant with – shall we say? – more breeding.

✤ September ✤

DOG DAYS

You can safely send your mower off for servicing in July these days in our part of the world. No grass has grown for a month, the lawns are mottled green (the shady or clovery parts) on a delicate fawn ground. One aims for the overall wholemeal effect, but a degree of greenness seems unavoidable.

No grass grows, but no mowing means everything else charges ahead. Deep-rooted weeds rashly advertise their presence: a touch of Roundup sees to them. More problematical are the root suckers from trees. Poplars are worst. They delight in demonstrating the almost incredible amount of ground they occupy, at least as wide a radius as their height. The aspen is the most absurd show-off of the lot, but the white and grey poplars, and even the Lombardy, have the same exhibitionist instinct.

I will spare you a description of the un-grass around the duck pond. Since a pair of Canada geese arrived last spring, wearing smarter livery than any airline, the area has been comprehensively wrecked. I failed to take a friend's advice to prick their eggs, so now a team of five is making the surroundings of the pond extremely unsanitary, to put it politely.

Is there a good Canadian recipe for goose, I wonder?

IN A BIND

Another all-too-evident result of so little rain (only 2 inches since March) has been to give such deep-rooters as bindweed pole position on the starting grid.

As a rule we don't water our borders, except locally when planting. Their relatively slow growth this year has given bindweed the chance of a lifetime to scramble up and smother everything – well perhaps not everything.

The problem is always how to apply a powerful systemic weedkiller without killing the plant being used as a climbing frame. The tactic we are trying this summer is to push in fresh-cut bamboo canes, like slim green antennae, wherever bindweed is emerging, from phlox, geraniums or even clipped box.

The bindweed seems to be falling for the ruse, taking hold of the canes and whizzing to the top. At this point it is to be drenched in a substance it will transfer to its roots with fatal effect, without harming other plants. That at least is the theory.

What would we do without weeds? Half the entertainment, and all the bile, in gardening come from the perennial combat with plants in the wrong place.

ROAD AND RIVER

Normally I avoid the Hayward Gallery on the South Bank as one of the worst of London's concrete blunders. But this summer's exhibition redeemed even this awful building. The seven rooms glowed with the genius of French landscape painting, contrasting the Impressionists with their more conservative contemporaries whose paintings were hung in the Paris Salon, and who earned relatively large sums from state patronage.

There are obviously extremes of both manners, but they meet in the middle, and some of the paintings would be hard to categorise as Impressionist or its opposite without knowing more about the artist. Even Van Gogh might well have taken inspiration from Paul Guigou, a painter of Provence considered decidedly square.

But why has Trad turned art critic? Because I was so struck by an element of design that seems almost too obvious to mention. At least 90 per cent of the landscapes (of both schools) took either a road, a river or a path as their main theme and perspective. Virtually every artist used the device to bring the viewer into his picture. The lesson for garden design does not need spelling out.

EVENSONG

There have been truly golden evenings, and on the most golden of all we were at Garsington Manor, looking out over Oxfordshire from one of the most evocative of all gardens.

By some almost occult means, Leonard Ingrams has succeeded in concealing a very substantial opera tent (I can think of no other term) beside the gabled grey manor without obliterating, or even detracting from, the formal gardens the Morells made in the 1920s.

Our opera was Haydn at his fluffiest. The singers come rushing on to the terrace through the box-edged flower beds and Irish yews. The very garden statuary comes to life: the chorus of naked lead wrestlers break their classical poses to cause havoc on stage. Haydn's plot, if it can be called that, made a weekend at Blandings Castle seem a straightforward and sober affair.

On this most Blandings-like evening the view over the Thames Valley was lowland England at its most sublime. Below in the foreground, wobbly old yew hedges, sheltering venerable statues, surround the broad rectangular pool. Beyond, a patchwork of ripe cornfields and dark woods gently lead the eye to the softly contoured downland that culminates in the old trees of Wittenham Clumps.

A sudden scale from a tenor tuning up bursts from the open windows of the house, and a soprano balances on a vertiginous note. Gnats swarm over the water in still air. Such evenings hover between reality and a golden dream – and they have been everywhere this summer.

RIP

My experiment (reported in February) in cutting back a Leyland cypress to see if it would sprout from the trunk has produced what many will consider a desirable result: a dead Leyland.

❦ October ❦

THE TREE PROPHET

Few things have made me so sad as the news of the death of the dendrologist Alan Mitchell. I have been lucky enough to have had three great teachers and sources of inspiration in my life: at Cambridge my supervisor, Dadie Rylands, who taught me to love words; the late André Simon, who taught me to love wine; and Alan Mitchell, who showed me trees and ensured that I looked at them properly.

Alan could truly be described as the tree prophet. Striding through a wood or standing with the wind in his white hair sizing up a giant specimen, he was like a figure of classical mythology. Poussin might have painted him.

Even in the woods he kept something of the sailor (his first calling) about him: forthright, disciplined, commonsensical. Yet you could almost feel the trees repaying his ardent feeling for them – for or against; he was no indiscriminate tree-worshipper. His pithy descriptions still ring in my ears when I see trees we discussed together. When he called the hybrid wing nut, *Pterocarya* x *rehderiana*, 'the fastest thing on roots' it must have heard him. It certainly responded.

There is a practical way of honouring Alan Mitchell's memory. The recently formed Tree Register of the British Isles (TROBI) carries on from his unique record of notable trees (part of which he inherited, in turn, from the Hon Maynard Greville).

TROBI is a charity that organises the efforts of those who record trees. Its register covers well over 100,000 notable specimens and makes its information freely available. A donation to the Tree Register would be put to good use to continue the great Mitchell tradition.

SHORT FRONT AND SIDES

By the end of August, rain or no rain, the banksia rose on the tallest, broadest wall of the house is seriously outstepping its bounds. Eight-foot shoots of green growth are waving above the gutters and gesticulating like a triffid across the path.

I take heart from a pithy note in *The Gardener's Magazine* of August 1835 (a source I frequently turn to for solace, some are unkind enough to say like Lord Emsworth to his 'Whiffle' on *The Care of the Pig*). 'The Rose Banksiae', writes a correspondent in Caernarvonshire, 'throws out, when much clipped (even with common shears), an increased quantity of blossom.'

OLEANDISSIMA

The pride of Saling this summer has been the hottest plant on the place: an oleander in the conservatory, pressed against the glass – and indeed offering grateful shade to other plants with less thick skins.

It is a single pale-pink variety – I don't know its name – which grows boldly upright, unlike a double white we have which droops despondently under its burden of flowers. In three years it has grown to 8 feet and now fills a 14-inch pot.

The pot is the reason I mention it. Oleanders have me baffled. They thrive in the most arid places imaginable: on Mediterranean airport perimeters and the centre strip of the Naples ring road. But put them in a pot and they demand water twice a day and food twice a week. They reward their feeder handsomely. But in nature they must surely have an astonishing root system that no pot could accommodate.

ZEALOUSY

I shifted nervously in my chair just now as I wrote about a 14-inch pot. What have the Whitehall Thought Police got in store for us gardeners? If they can threaten a fine of £5,000 for offering a pound of apples for sale, what might the penalty be for measuring pots in inches?

It would be pure farce if it were not so sad – and sinister. The citizens of Holland blithely buy and sell in pounds when half a kilo is what they mean. In French markets they talk of *livres* just as they did before the dreaded Corsican and his decimals. The idea of prosecuting anyone who persists in speaking the language of his or her childhood is zeal so misplaced that it could, alas, only originate in the Looking Glass Land of Whitehall.

Of course we should ignore such fascist decrees but (as we read every Sunday in Christopher Booker's *Telegraph* articles) thousands have already been bullied into submission by 'directives' far more damaging than these, applied with sadistic rigour.

The man Europe most needs at this perilous hour is the great trimmer Talleyrand. '*Surtout, Messieurs, point de zèle*' should be at the head of every 'directive' of the European Community. Not easy to translate, but perhaps 'Whatever you do, Gentlemen, don't overdo it' gives the idea. Not that anyone in Whitehall would understand it.

FAXACEAE

I have just received my first plant by fax. It came out slowly, with much stuttering, but in good order and crisp detail. It won't grow, I fear, being a mere piece of paper, but sending even the likeness of a plant down a telephone line seems rather wonderful to me.

I think it was Jim Russell who originated the photocopy herbarium. His vast records in box files are certainly an early example of turning simple office technology to the service of horticulture. (*The Plant Finder* is a magnificent extension of the principle.) What more simple, then, than to fax the photocopy? It shows every little hair and wrinkle. On the other hand there is always the post.

❧ November ❧

WEST OF EDEN

It occurred to me, on two matching (also matchless) visits this autumn, that the advice 'Go west, young man' was probably aimed at a gardener. It is the world's west coasts that (to easterners at least) make gardening seem too easy to be true.

The first visit was to Portmeirion in Snowdonia. How could I have let myself reach my middle years without visiting this fantasy-land? Everyone has seen pictures of the glittering little 'Italianate village' by the sea. 'Italianate' (an ugly, slightly sneering word at best) does not begin to describe the achievement of Clough Williams-Ellis in blending elements of Welsh, English (and to be sure Italian) architecture into a seamlessly elegant, constantly witty opera set. What nobody had told me was that it all began with the garden – or at least the planting possibilities of this sea-girt headland on his estate.

In the village the gardening is unashamedly flowery, taking advantage of the chance to let hydrangeas or fuchsias grow on unchecked to massive proportions, yet fine in detail and clearly under discreet and discriminating control. In the woods along the seashore and the rocky heights above, the distinction between native and exotic has been happily forgotten.

This is the idiom of architecture interpreted in woods and glades. The guidebook warns you that you may well get lost. We did, immediately. I'm sure it is another Williams-Ellis joke to have a fragmentary (also ambiguous) signpost system. The happy result, until it comes on to rain, is the sense that you are discovering an untrodden Eden – although I wouldn't vouch for summer weekends.

Within two weeks of this visit I found myself exploring a coast so similar that it was like half-waking from a dream. Puget Sound, the intricate pattern of bays and islands sheltered from the Pacific by Vancouver Island and the Olympic Peninsula, has the same made-for-gardening climate. A seashore walk on one of the (uninhabited) San Juan Islands was Portmeirion with the madrone, the tall red-trunked *Arbutus menziesii*, as the dominant note.

Logging the giant coastal firs, spruces and 'cedars' of the Northwest rapidly gave Seattle a millionaire class. As fitting accommodation for this new gentry, the Olmsted brothers (whose father designed New York's Central Park and instigated the first National Parks) laid out a seriously senior housing estate on the Highlands, densely wooded bluffs overlooking the Puget Sound from northern Seattle.

There are Olmsted mannerisms here: sunken roadways crossed by stone bridges, stone pergolas, stone-edged pools and cascades. Everywhere there are thujas and firs of prodigious height sheltering long-established dogwoods and maples, and rather more rhododendrons than I would have planted.

The difference between Washington and Wales is more marked than it seems, though. Washington's gardeners are never allowed to forget that north of them lies an ice-bound continent, and that just occasionally, without warning, it sends down a blast of air at practically no degrees Fahrenheit at all.

DO IT NOW

The nursery trade has been urging us to plant in autumn for years – and beginning, I fear, to despair as the instant gratification of containerised plants fits the mood of spring so much better. 'Let it die in the nursery rather than in my garden' is the prevailing sentiment.

But this year has taught many of us that autumn planting is far from foolish. Trees and shrubs planted in October, while they are still making roots, are far better able to face a dry spring and summer than our Easter plantings that need constant watering to establish at all.

Given our usual kind of open winter these days, in fact, it may be a better bet to give plants as Christmas presents than to wait for the spring.

SAUCE FOR THE GANDER

Following September's appeal, kind readers have sent me a number of recipes for Canada goose. For example:

Take one plump Canada goose and prepare for cooking.

Place in a large boiling pan and fill pan with water.

Add three large river-smoothed stones, say 6 inches in diameter, a large onion and herbs to taste.

Bring to boil and then simmer for 24 hours.

Throw away the goose and dine.

❧ December ❧

SCORED FOR WIND

The orchestration of this autumn has been quite different. Usually there is a sudden flare-up in the brass section: all the strident colours appear at once, while the drums roll for winter as the wind whips away the leaves.

But this October summer was still in an infinitely gradual diminuendo, with assorted *da capi* from here and there in the orchestra. Delphiniums and daphnes have both seen their openings for a short, sweet passage.

The crescendo of autumn is even more gradual. Fruit is first: the arching stems of *Cotoneaster sternianus* with their little scarlet fruit; *Crataegus orientalis* with its round orange hips against its fretted grey leaves. Under the grey-leaved *Pyrus nivalis* the green-russet little pears are dropping in profusion. The tiny berries on the Washington thorn, *Crataegus phaenopyrum*, gleam like redcurrants. But only the amelanchiers have so far given a brief show of orange and scarlet leaves. The Japanese maples brood on in ever-duskier, bronzier green.

At this moment the conservatory is the most vibrant spot at Saling. It is all Bee's doing. Bee is our perfectly named new gardener, who arrived last winter from an establishment which, I gather, was slightly stilted in its approach. Trad Hall is not like that at all, but Bee has nonetheless been oxygen, nitrogen, and come to that phostrogen to us and our plants all year. And just now where it shows most is in the conservatory.

Lists of plants are tedious, but try to picture a bank of purple streptocarpus nestling among pink and white pelargoniums, the whole embowered in jasmine, passion flowers and *Mandevilla*, flanked by little orange and myrtle trees full of fruit and framed with dark *Salvia guaranitica* and pale *S. haematodes*, while the oleanders flower on and the white trumpets of daturas scent the air.

Wattles are already blooming, and so is *Mahonia lomariifolia* (which seems to be able to bloom in either autumn or spring – or indeed both). By the conservatory door *Choisya ternata* is in full late bloom beside the honey-scented *Buddleja auriculata*, blooming early. Pink nerines are sparkling right on cue.

Mrs Trad has decorated the hall with a mixture of the blood-red dahlia 'Bishop of Llandaff' and richly berried holly, with flower buds of loquat and glistening berries of *Viburnum opulus*. And a bowl of apples perfumes the passage. No mists so far, just mellow fruitfulness.

Perhaps I am too easily satisfied. There is so much richness all around that my critical faculties (such as they are) are registering nothing but plusses. *Serious* gardeners are not like this. They know a better form of nerine; a bigger passion flower.

Perhaps we divide naturally into the contemplative and the competitive. If all your plants must have Awards of Garden Merit, all your maples burn in autumn like the tail-lights of a winter rush hour on the M25, you are a competitor. If you are happy that God made any nerines at all, and enjoy the slow decay of trees, tail-lights or not, I will call you contemplative – whatever your friends may say.

DEER FODDER

As visitors are not slow to point out, the effect of my planting in the heart of France has so far been more like one of Christo's set-piece wrapping-ups (Reichstag, Pont-Neuf and so on) than a fledgling arboretum. Not that I have bubble-wrapped the barn. But every tree is jacketed in a black netting sleeve 1·7m high – the browsing reach, they tell me, of a red deer tempted by something out of the ordinary. Black rectangles march up hill and down dale with such authority and panache that I wish I had thought of applying for a Brussels grant for a significant work of art – or at least looked for a sponsor.

I have been reassuring myself that the invisible trees are happy in their wrapping, presumably yes (or alternatively no), because two years after planting a good number have popped out above their casings. My cryptomerias (the redwoods of Japan) are showing their dark-green nose-cones and the tops of red maples are already correctly colour-coded.

How will we know when to release the trees from their unnatural confinement? Perhaps the sleeves will slowly disintegrate so the deer won't notice. Perhaps I should plant thickets of willow for them to plunder – it seems to be their favourite salad.

For the moment, though, I am much more worried about my tiny seedling oaks, unprotected in the open fields. Caviar to the roe deer, they seem to be.

OUT IN THE COLD

Our olive tree has to take its chance this winter. It has outgrown its old place in a pot in the conservatory and been planted outside against the snuggest wall we have – if walls can be snug.

England is not entirely an olive-free zone. The Chelsea Physic Garden boasts an impressive full-size one – but then London, especially near the Thames, has a practically Mediterranean climate. More to the point, the late John Codrington, officer, painter, and highly original gardener, grew a fair-sized tree on the wall by his front door at Hambledon on Rutland Water. I wonder if it's still there?

As with many nearly-hardy plants, the best hope lies in really well-ripened wood at the onset of winter. 1995 should be as good a start as they could hope for. But even in Tuscany whole olive-groves can be destroyed by extreme winters. We shall keep a fleecy shawl handy.

1996

❦ January ❦

NATURE'S RICHEST CLOAK

Musing upon the colours that made last autumn so exceptional, and the reasons why so many leaves turned to tints I have certainly never seen before, it seems to me that the single most unusual factor was the incredible stillness of the air for week after week.

The high-pressure zone that parked itself over the Channel prevented even the gentlest zephyrs, while it also kept the thermometer uncannily steady. Without frosts and without physical damage leaves simmered on and on, finding new combinations of creams and greys, bronzes and oranges, pinks and tawnies, the colours of cigars, pewter, parchment; even black. Then, still windless, they fell vertically to form a neat pool under each plant.

Some of the loveliest effects were where leaves lodged in the lower branches of a neighbour: a red maple in a dark spruce, a pale-cream and grey one in the glowing copper of a beech. (Why, by the way, do we call dark-red beeches 'copper' when they are nothing of the kind?)

One of the sights of October for me was the great rug of Virginia creeper, planted presumably by William Robinson, that covers most of Gravetye Manor, his house near East Grinstead and now one of England's best hotels. It seems strange to cover such splendid Tudor stones with an all-smothering creeper – and it must be an almighty labour keeping it from blocking the windows, gutters and every architectural orifice. But what a spectacle it was, glowing, flaring, smouldering; here green, there buttery where the flames had not yet reached. I'd love to have a Virginia creeper, but I think I shall compromise and grow mine up a tree, as nature intended.

A GREAT PATRON

The name of Maecenas has come down through the ages as that of the liberal patron of Virgil and Horace. If horticulture, and especially its dendrological branch, has had a Maecenas in the last 30 or 40 years it was surely the Belgian plantsman and diamond-merchant Robert de Belder, who died in October.

The benevolent patronage, creative flair and intense involvement of Robert and his wife Jelena made their two homes, Kalmthout near Antwerp, and later Hemelrijk near the Dutch border, into something approaching a private college for the study of plants and the formation of young gardeners.

The de Belder family was famously warm-hearted, welcoming plant-lovers from round the world. There were always students around them; whether from Holland, England or Japan made no difference. They were active collectors, particularly in Korea and Japan, with vast knowledge and unstinting generosity. The de Belder collections of *Rhododendron yakushimanum* and their breeding of *Hamamelis* ('Jelena' is a famous orange cultivar) are perhaps their two best-known achievements.

Robert had not been well for some years, but he spent the last summer of his life, one of the most glorious, in twice-daily drives round the quiet acres of Hemelrijk, where placid ponds reflect a wonderful variety of the plants he loved.

❧ February ❧

BOOKWORM

The fog has closed in on the frozen garden, the rimy branches and the iron ground. It is reading time again; reading and looking up in the special dot-and-carry rhythm that garden books induce. I find I never read gardening books one at a time. The first book I pick up leads me to look up what someone else has to say on a plant or a place, to turn to *The RHS Dictionary of Gardening*, to thumb through a couple of other books and consult *The RHS Plant Finder*. Which leads me to think about another part of my garden and get sidetracked once again. After an hour I have seven books open all round me, a sheet of notes and only a dim memory of the number I first thought of.

Nigella Lawson wrote in *The Times* the other day that gardeners and cooks respond to books in quite different ways. Cookbooks, she said, are an end in themselves; gardening books a spur to action. Is this the right way round?

I always assumed people bought Delia Smith to cook with, not to dream about, while on the contrary they buy Penelope Hobhouse or Rosemary Verey's latest gorgeous production for a trip into dreamland … or at least into the sort of half-focused reverie I was just describing. I dare say planning menus and borders comes to the same thing really: a mixture of emulation and dissatisfaction leading to stern but short-lived resolutions.

MENU SUGGESTION

Gardeners who have to contend with deer are ready to go to almost any length to protect their plants. There is a whole folklore catalogue of deer-repellents, ranging from lion dung to the sweepings of the hairdresser's floor. None seems to work, at least for long. The Society publishes a list of plants that deer reputedly leave alone, or perhaps eat last, but the deer population goes on rising. Europe-wide, it seems, it is at an unprecedented level. What can be done?

One practical suggestion that has come my way is to ask your butcher for venison. Venison is the most naturally-reared meat you can buy. In Germany it features on almost every menu. Yet we seem culturally disinclined towards it. If we were to make venison even a small part of our diet you can be sure that the deer population could soon be under control. With our present disinclination to eat beef this seems a good time to start.

I hadn't intended this to be a cookery supplement, but I was rash enough in November to give a recipe for Canada goose and have been taken to task for my flippancy by a reader who knows better.

Canada geese, she assures me, make very good eating if you remember that they are game birds, devoid of fat, and cook them accordingly. First, choose a young bird. Young birds have narrow, pointed feathers; as they get older the feathers grow blunter and rounder. Even a young bird needs hanging for up to seven days in a cold place. Then it needs a long slow roast with plenty of butter or dripping, stuffing with apples, onions or prunes, or sage and onion. Or a casserole.

The bonus, not provided by pheasant, is the down. The feathers should be plucked first, then the exquisitely soft down. How many geese you have to eat before you can fill a duvet she does not say.

LES NEIGES D'ANTAN

Colour schemes are for later, when the garden is fully clothed. As spring begins, colour of any kind seems to be an end in itself. We not only tolerate, we actually enthuse about juxtapositions of colour that we would describe as swearing in the summer months.

We accept (we have to – they're everywhere) daffodils of searing yellow in splodges under cherry trees of lurid pink. We even welcome the muddy magenta of bergenias and the alarming magenta of honesty in the same picture as the crude chrome of forsythia. For years the bullfinches helpfully de-budded the forsythia for us. When they went we had no option but to dig it out.

Am I a wimp to prefer white to yellow? A white forsythia would be a marvel. The white-flowered honesty – especially the form with white-flecked leaves – already is one.

❧ March ❧

GORMENGHAST

When the leaves are on the apple trees they are the most wholesome sight in the garden. There is a particular spot I pass daily where the mossy fork of an old tree is framed by a dip in a yew hedge: a symphony (no, more of a ballad, really) in greens and greys. Those stout, rounded, deep-green leaves cast shade of a special quality. Lunches under them are dappled like a Tissot.

Wholesome does not describe them in winter, though. The gnarled twistings of the bare branches are a gothic fantasy. The problem is years of neglected woolly aphis. It is astonishing how this tiny wretch with his sticky white overcoat can penetrate the new bark and scar it for life. As he digs deeper in, the twig appears more and more cankerous, with grotesque swellings and contortions. Eventually the whole crown is – well, gothic with knobs and writhings. Luckily I am a Goth. From a distance, at least, the gnarled crown has an almost sea-coral effect. I love it.

But this month is treatment time, starting with the slow and intricate operation of pruning almost half the crowded, criss-crossing old branchlets out of the crown, opening the rest to the light and air. In early spring we will open fire on the aphids with Tumblebug or something similar, and keep at them until they disappear. I'm already looking forward to sitting under a cleaned and rejuvenated tree. Cleaned, that is, except for the moss. All that will be missing, despite all our efforts, is mistletoe.

FIGURES IN LANDSCAPE

Where did I read the other day the opinion, finely expressed, that statues have no place in modern gardens? If the author was referring to plaster Venuses of the sort that have regrettably been sighted at Chelsea recently I would wholeheartedly agree. But his comment was more general: that statues are 'static' (I'd spotted that, too) while modern horticulture was 'dynamic'.

Would this not then make them an apt contrast and complement? No, I think he was saying: gardens are becoming more and more 'natural'. Apparently random swathes of ecologically compatible 'plant material' are the coming thing. A stone figure in a pseudo-natural scene is out of place.

What rot. I immediately thought of the pulling-power of the sculptures (figures among them) that make Sir Freddie Gibberd's garden at Harlow the electrifying landscape that it is. Or indeed the graphics, busts and fragments that are almost the whole point of Ian Hamilton Finlay's Little Sparta.

Japanese gardeners, whose faithfulness to nature can teeter on the edge of parody, seem to make no distinction between nature (in the form of rocks), art (lanterns and water-troughs) and architecture (temples, gateways, fences and the rest) in composing their pictures.

Nor should we. The only sin is to borrow some sentimental irrelevancy from another time and place – in other words, a plaster Venus. Any object made or found that leads the eye into the garden space and beguiles it among the plants, or even instead of plants, can be valid garden sculpture.

❧ April ❧

THE SUSSEX KEW

I have to admit with shame that until recently I had not visited Wakehurst Place since the aftermath of the great storms, to see how the Royal Botanic Gardens have recovered from the devastation, and the loss of something like 15,000 trees. The answer, of course, is ingeniously, laboriously and astonishingly.

The Wakehurst of today is a more complete botanic garden than ever it was, more artfully and horticulturally designed, more botanically organised, more full of 'visitor interest'. What it has inevitably lost for a century or two is the mystery of exotic plants in the comfortable shelter of native woodland: the illusion that Westwood Valley was actually in the foothills of the Himalayas.

Unavoidably, new planting on such a scale will look raw for a generation.

But the site is so exceptional, plunging from the sophisticated horticulture around the mansion by stages of plantations and glades, water and rocks to the lake at the bottom – and across the lake the untamed wildwood – that one is soon carried away by the excitement of potential steadily being realised.

One corner I had never visited before is the willow beds in wetland flooded by the lake, a self-contained landscape hemmed in by steep slopes and woods and crossed by a wholly oriental-looking wooden causeway. Without the slightest self-consciousness it is a perfect evocation of China. This, and the dream-like view along a sinuous valley with the Ardingly reservoir gleaming in the bottom, from the high ground where a whole wood was blown down, are landscapes to memorise for inspiration.

UNDER GLASS

There has been plenty of time in the last wintry March weeks to concentrate on the plants in the conservatory. It has never looked better. We have an eight o'clock rendezvous every morning with Bee for a critical look before she gets started on the preening of the plants: feeding, adjusting, leaf-polishing. The effect is what I have always dreamed of – a bright space bursting with buoyant growth, the walls densely clothed with vines and climbers, the floor an obstacle course of plants in flower, bud or just refulgent healthy leaf – and all this with a miserly approach to heating aimed only at excluding frost.

The crowding pink buds of jasmine are still only on their marks in their infinitely slow and tantalising build-up to flower. Even the tender noisette rose 'Maréchal Niel' is making buds that look ready to challenge them. Anticipation is daily more exciting.

At one end tall plants of creamy mimosa and white-flowered *Sparrmannia africana* emerge from a young jungle of azaleas, bamboo and ferns. In the centre white cyclamen and hyacinths crowd the staging, above a miniature orange tree in fruit and a far-from-miniature clivia. A primly upright *Veltheimia* stands on a table with an unnamed orchid spraying scores of pink-and-white flowers, jostling a 4-foot *Fuchsia paniculata* which has not paused in its tiny, upright, mauve-pink flowering for 12 months. Then come the crystal-pink camellias 'Donation', 'Brigadoon' and a red-and-white striped one called 'Mikenjaku' I am less certain about. Its bud-scales open with such reluctance that rather than fan out, the flowers appear to be extruded.

Jerry Harpur came one sunny day to photograph it all. I didn't know whether to be chuffed or miffed when he asked if we had bought in plants specially for the occasion.

❧ June ❧

COLD CREAM

To a cold Cornwall in the last week of March for a garden-visiting weekend advertised in these pages by Heritage Tours. Our spirits sank on the road west to see not the slightest sign of spring in the woods and hedges. Devon was still winter-brown, Cornwall too at first sight. Which made what we saw in its gardens seem all the more miraculous.

First to the 'Lost' garden of Heligan, which should by now have altered its sign to the 'Found' garden. The coaches in the car park were ample evidence of the power of a suggestive name. What has been found is intriguing: the mechanics of an ambitious Victorian garden on the grand scale almost intact – especially the frame yard, bothy, toolsheds and a pineapple pit which is apparently unique (and even full of pineapples).

There are some good plants, too, but heady claims that a rockery walk evokes the Himalayas were bound to lead to disappointment. A brave effort, but it should not distract anybody from the qualities of gardens that haven't been mislaid.

Trewithen, for example, is a house with no dramatic natural advantages; no streams, lakes or sea-views. This is pure inspired horticulture – starting with an excellent small nursery. The entrance to the walled garden is by Alice in Wonderland out of Japan: through a cottage so low-eaved that you emerge bent double – on to a long lawn that frames the facade with a consummate sense of proportion.

That day the *Magnolia campbellii* by the house, towering twice as high as the Georgian parapet, was a whole cloud formation of glistening pink in the pale-blue sky. We were absorbed for hours in the wandering woodland paths beyond, discovering beauty after beauty, never out of sight of a tall magnolia or without the petal-fall of camellias carpeting the ground at our feet.

Arriving at Glendurgan, now in the care of The National Trust, we felt an odd sense of familiarity. The lie of the land is uncannily similar to Wakehurst Place, specifically Westwood Valley with its stream down to the lakes – or in this case, the Helford estuary. The essence of the garden is cross-valley views, including one of a bizarre waist-high boxwood maze looking for all the world like a fanciful tea-plantation, and another of what is surely the country's biggest tulip tree – its vast knobbly bole, low-branched, on a dinosaur scale.

There is an agreeable scent of money in the air in National Trust gardens; such no-holds-barred infrastructure; such attention to every detail of stake and label, path and drain, step and handrail.

By this time our acquisitive instincts had taken us to Burncoose Nurseries, where the forbidden fruit – as far as eastern gardens are concerned – is potted and (rather reasonably) priced. The back of the car was nearly full when we arrived at the garden that really took away my heart: the Magic Jungle – while we are coining phrases – of Chyverton.

Nigel Holman gardens Chyverton, all 20-something acres of it, alone. It is not for lawn-edging fanatics, but for those whose heart almost stops when, crossing a stream full of the yellow spathes of *Lysichiton* by a mossy stone bridge, they find themselves under 50-foot rhododendrons in flower round grassy glades where priceless plants have been – as it were – put out to grass. Why does it make me so happy to see exquisite (and some very rare) little trees seemingly fending for themselves in a wood rather than dotted in beds on a close-mown lawn? Because I'm certain the trees prefer it that way. Because they have an air of belonging, as though they have seeded themselves – as I'm sure many have.

There is a very clear affinity of style, as well as landscape, between the great Sussex gardens and Cornish gardens planted or replanted in the early years of this century. Buttoned up against the March wind it was not obvious that Cornwall has a great advantage of climate. But the evidence was all around us in the plants. Heritage Tours are right to drag us there in March ... and there are a dozen more great gardens to see next year.

JAMES RUSSELL

I have just heard with great sadness of the death of Jim Russell, which I am sure will be recorded more adequately on other pages. A whole generation of great plantsmen is passing, and none, I think, greater than he.

His great memorial is at Castle Howard, where he created a 50-acre arboretum in one winter of heroic work. In December his friend George Howard (then Chairman of the BBC) found a nice little chunk of budget (not the BBC's) that had to go before the end of the year. When Jim heard of it he called Harold Hillier and gave him an order that virtually amounted, or so I'm told, to three of everything. When the trees came, though, the ground was ice-bound – and stayed that way for weeks. When at last it thawed it was a tree-planting to remember – and 18 years later its memorial (now more than 100 acres) is very leafy and very real.

❧ July ❧

PAINTING THE LILY

Would you have second thoughts about planting exotic species in a landscape where no one has ever done it before? I certainly did, and third and fourth ones too, before finally standing on my spade in a little hidden combe at Château Trad in deepest France.

Two springs rise in this unexpected cleft in the hillside under tall oaks and wild cherries. Last year the springs, and most of the trees, were densely over- and undergrown with brambles, sallows and elder. The lie of the land was revealed only by a great deal of hard work.

It is beautiful already, in its quiet way, with ferns, spurge and foxgloves scattered in thin grass and dappled shade. But I couldn't help seeing it as a chance to apply some of the brighter colours of the spring and autumn – and some of the lovely scents, too. In April I made up my mind, surveyed the soil (here dust-dry, there saturated, and everywhere full of roots) and dug holes in the likeliest places. My plan was to limit my palette to a few plants that (I hope) will look as though they just might occur there naturally.

I have planted the yellow pontic azalea, now called *Rhododendron luteum*, both for its May flowers and its autumn colour; *Clethra alnifolia* for its intensely sweet-smelling white flower-spikes in August; *Gunnera manicata* for authority; *Euphorbia palustris* and bluebells.

Clethras love damp soil, and so does the euphorbia (although at Saling it seems equally brilliant in the dry). Graham Thomas describes its flower-colour as gamboge – a wonderful word, derived, believe it or not, from Cambodia. Clethra leaves turn yellow in autumn, the euphorbia – and of course the azalea – fiery orange. In the streams I have put shuttlecock ferns and on their banks the yellow candelabra *Primula florindae*. Now all I have to do is stop the brambles from coming back.

Am I right or wrong in seeing these additions to the local flora as such a major step – almost amounting to a moral dilemma? If it was obviously related to a house it would be labelled a garden and the issue wouldn't arise. It's the ambivalence of an exotic planting in what amounts to virgin woodland that raises the question. Native plants are there by right: each niche has been hard fought-for. But scatter foreign seed and something by definition will lose, or at least be challenged for, its slot.

So long as it's the brambles I think I will be forgiven.

OLIVE BRANCHES

The green woodpecker has taken a peculiar fancy to a tree I also happen to like very much, and we are pitting our wits against each other.

The tree is a *Phillyrea*. I don't know an English name for it, although it has been grown in England at least since the 17th century. To John Evelyn its 'verdure' was 'incomparable'. It is, and looks like, a relation of the olive tree, only with very dark-green leaves. I have encouraged it to grow with seven strong stems to make it as like an olive tree as possible.

Perhaps the woodpecker has a Greek soul: he certainly loves to spend his time among the tree's branches. But he is methodically ringing them with neat little drills that could have killed them if I had not seen what was happening.

I'm not sure what to do. I have rigged a cat's cradle of black string between the stems and bandaged the wounded ones. But now he has started work on the base of the tree. As if the deer were not enough ....

BAMBI TROUBLE

Wherever I go I hear yet more stories of deer demoralising gardeners. Some of their assaults seem almost ferocious: all the bark eaten on old apple trees in a vicarage garden bordering on the woods here, for example. But I also hear of incessant incursions into suburban gardens as far away as Marin County, north of San Francisco. The population explosion seems to be universal. In France, in Germany and Holland correspondents are hunting for remedies. But each time someone suggests a new trick, someone else tells me it has been tried and doesn't work.

The latest suggestion is intriguing because it takes a different tack. Deer will come, or so I'm told, to a certain sort of whistle on a bamboo pipe. Eureka. So now we have a stag summoned to order, what next? I'm not sure that reasoning with him will solve anything.

✹ August ✹

PARVA SED APTA

More evidence of the sudden conversion of fashionable France to gardening: Jean Tiberi, the mayor of Paris, gave the sort of reception usually described as 'glittering' on a golden evening in June to launch an exhibition of garden history at the Bagatelle.

As it fell in the same month as the 25th birthday party of our own Garden History Society, the two parties provided an interesting comparison. The Society was celebrating a quarter century of distinguished existence, research, conviviality, tours and publications that have shed more light on the origins of our gardens than anything that has gone before – the rock on which (among other things) a thriving network of County Gardens Trusts is founded. It was a family sort of affair, with the President Mavis Batey as materfamilias.

The bash at the Bagatelle was something else. This pavilion deep in the Bois de Boulogne is one of Paris's best-hidden treasures. Parisians know it for its lovely rose garden (and the fact that it was built in 63 days by the brother of Louis XVI at the age of 17. Marie Antoinette bet him he couldn't). On this summer evening *tout Paris* was treated to champagne, canapés, and an excellent and comprehensive survey of fashions in gardening from ancient to modern times in paintings, photographs, models, books, tools, captions, statues, tapestries and furniture. Those who remember the excellent garden exhibition at the V&A in 1979 will get the idea.

The motto on the pediment of the mini-château of La Bagatelle is one that could be borrowed by much humbler toilers than the young Comte d'Artois: *Parva sed apta*. Small but just right.

... AND IN THE GREY CORNER

Of the numerous joys and surprises I experienced on a visit to Northumberland this spring (a vast new arboretum at Howick Hall; the lovely quarry garden at Blagdon; and the extraordinary ungardened quarry, the very essence of picturesque landscape, at Belsay Castle among them) the most intriguing was the presence of red squirrels – and the absence of grey.

My hosts had a food-hopper outside their dining-room window to enjoy the antics of the little red charmers. I had forgotten just how beautiful they are. When I asked the Forestry Authority for the latest on efforts to suppress the dominant invading grey and reinstate our native red squirrel, though, I was surprised by what I was told. The grey squirrel, they told me, is not just stronger than the red, weighing nearly twice as much, he is more adaptable and proficient at exploiting differing sources of food.

What is odd is that grey squirrels are better than the reds at using the food supplies provided by broadleaved woodlands. Grey squirrels compete with red in conifer forests on more or less equal terms, but then use oaks, beeches, chestnuts and other sources of fat fruits to build up their families to go back into the pines and spruces to oust the reds. Paradoxically, we need more non-native woods of pure conifers to maintain our native squirrel population. Needless to say the destruction of broadleaved trees in favour of conifers is a programme with few supporters. So the only practical way to redress the balance is to wage war on the intruder.

Two new weapons have been developed for this fight. One is a hopper for poisoned bait which differentiates between the species on the basis of their size, weight and, seemingly, curiosity. The other is a contraceptive, also in bait, to help the greys in their family planning.

PS See *www.europeansquirrelinitiative.org for the latest in this one-sided war.*

Q&A

Every year at mid-summer, the Garden Festival at Hatfield House attracts more and more people. This year (its 14th) the combination of a cold May and a warm June had filled the gardens with spring and summer flowers together: iris, peonies and roses basking in gentle sunshine made an unforgettable picture.

The informal gardeners' question-and-answer time is one of Hatfield's annual delights – largely due to Jock Davidson, formerly of Rochford's great house-plant nursery. I don't know where Jock gets his gags but I loved this question and answer: 'Which is the most dangerous plant to sit under in the garden?' – A water lily.

September

ON THE OTHER HAND ...

In September last year I tried to get all scientific about blanket weed in the pond and messed about with bales of barley straw. I must have learned some philosophy since. Yesterday I went in in shorts to enjoy the stuff, and found that reeling it in is as good as a day by the sea. It comes up very like a fishing net and smells not unlike seaweed.

The skeins of it gleamed on the bank like iridescent fabric piled in a *souk* until I carted them off to mulch suffering shrubs. Blanket weed, in fact, has become one of the mini-pleasures of summer (I hope it hears this).

❦ October ❧

WORDS AND PICTURES

You don't need me to remind you how gardening literature has changed in the past few years. Without question the biggest physical change is the quality of colour reproduction in books and magazines. You only have to look at your back numbers of *The Garden* of, say, 1990 to see how relatively dull and muddied colour-printing was even then. Going back to 1980, you wonder how we ever accepted such approximate images.

I have just rewritten my book of 1979, *The Principles of Gardening*, to be re-issued this month with a new format and title [*Hugh Johnson's Gardening Companion*], and I find the vitality and crispness of the pages quite thrilling. There are more new garden books than one can possibly keep up with, beautifully executed and illustrated by a dozen excellent specialist photographers who would scarcely have made a living ten years ago. There are also good-value reprints of almost every classic of the past … the choice is dazzling.

But I am heartened too, that with so much glamorous material claiming our attention there is still room for a more reflective, modest style – a fact proved by the tenth birthday this summer of *Hortus*, whose creamy cartridge paper, black and cream photos and woodcuts perfectly accompany gentle, leisurely, scholarly writing.

With such riches in print, what contribution can the frenzied world of cyberspace offer the gardener? According to Chris Philip, who put communications technology to spectacularly good use when he created *The Plant Finder* (now *The RHS Plant Finder*) with Tony Lord, the answer is a great deal.

This has not been my experience so far, in the odd hour I have spent doodling at my computer. The 'gardening forum' I popped into, like many other 'forums' (wine was one), seemed to consist largely of frustrated penfriends killing time with any old trivia. The 'library' was the most useful feature – although nothing like so agreeable as a few shelves of good books.

I admit I have not delved yet into the World Wide Web, which is reputedly brimful of good stuff if you know how (and have time) to find it. But then I confess that sitting at a keyboard is very far from being my favourite way of gleaning information.

PS Has any aspect of gardening (or life) changed more than this? Mine was by no means a Luddite view in 1996. Now I blog away myself. Hortus – *paper, woodcuts and all – is the only unchanging medium.*

POTAGER, POTAGEST

Every year it's the same quandary: the August close-down coinciding with the season of surplus in the kitchen garden. For various reasons we always seem to be away from home for the great surge of veg that needs daily picking to prevent beans from becoming gross, courgettes bolsters and tomatoes from rotting.

What's more when we are just on the point of picking up our buckets and spades, the kitchen garden is suddenly the jolliest part of the whole place. Runner beans are a wall of green and red; sweet peas a pyramid of red, white and blue; artichokes classically handsome in grey; purple cabbages rotund as abbots; leeks silvery and alert; roses promiscuous; and down the centre path the marigolds and nasturtiums that reseed themselves every year are fighting colour duels with a sort of avenue of purple orache over head-height – which in autumn will perform all sorts of chromatic U-turns. Marigolds climbing into a tall blue-grey fuzz of borage is the nearest approach to visual good taste in this harlequin assembly.

Friends can be encouraged to come and help themselves to the August bounty – if they are not at the seaside too. But the chances are they have a glut of exactly the same things as we do – a good reason to grow only the most obscure veg.

❧ November ❧

THE SCARCE RESOURCE

Yes, this is repetitious – but so has the weather been. A total of 8 inches of rain in the first nine months of the year, following a total of 16 inches in 1995, means 24 inches in 21 months. The extraordinary thing is that, grass and new plantings apart, most of the garden is surviving. Just starting, indeed, to put on a passable show of early autumn colour. They say summer rain just evaporates and does no good, but 1½ inches in August must have given hope, if not life, to plants that had had nothing since May.

Meanwhile a visit to northern California has given me much clearer ideas about irrigation. Rain there is a winter phenomenon, jealously stored. Nothing (at least nothing that isn't native) grows without irrigation – even, these days, the grapevines. Hidden in every bed, shrub, pot and vase, and in the ground around every garden tree, is a black hose dribbling life on a time-clock.

And what gardens it gives life to. My guide in the Napa Valley was Molly Chappellet, whose own garden is one of America's most marvellous.

It lies high on a hill facing range upon range of purple mountains, with a glittering lake far below. Her single-storey raw wood ranch-house has almost disappeared behind the trees and vines that smother it. In a sense you have to look for the garden, too; so skilfully is it blended into the surroundings. Behind the house are olives and cypresses, beyond it oranges and lemons, but around it you pick your way through flowers and vegetables mustered by attributes that only Molly ever thought of.

At vintage time when others have chopped down the towering brown stems of artichokes and fennel, she chops off their leaves instead, leaving their skeletons standing as sculpture. She sows a late patch of maize to tower with its golden beards next to giant tobacco ... and for mulch she uses the grape pomace from the Chappellet family winery. Within a year the skins rot away, leaving the dark pips gleaming like a bed of caviar.

Through this machismo parade of giants you creep to find a quiet collection of flowers and vegetables in soft shades of purple, ending in a cascade of orange pumpkins and strange sea-green gourds as big as turkeys.

We visited designer gardens where the theme was grey, clipped and orderly; soft painterly gardens where waving grasses and the butterflies on sedums make the picture; an astonishing Italian garden enclosing a Tuscan villa either five or 500 years old, and finally the unique Anglo-Chinese garden of Peter Newton and his wife Sue-Hua on Spring Mountain.

Spring Mountain is one of the steepest parts of the Napa Valley, deeply scoured with ravines. Its vineyards are like the Douro Valley port country: perched in opportunistic scraps on terrace and ledge, in scallops and wedges of green. Among these and crowning a long ridge, the Newtons have concealed with infinite art a large winery and a courtyard house of strong Chinese inspiration surrounding a Chinese stone garden, all within a profusion of gardens such as only the English make – when they have mastered the art of irrigation.

❧ December ❧

RETROSPECTIVE

I love the uncorseted look of October borders: the jostling for space of plants with a whole summer of growth behind them, sprawling on the lawn, leaning heavily on box hedges, flushing as their leaves turn, dissipated and beyond caring. Annuals now overgrown and flowering fit to burst,

Michaelmas daisies, chrysanthemums (if I can still call them that), sedums and the last Japanese anemones, euphorbias and salvias are mobbing the autumn roses, which seem almost wan in comparison with their summer vibrancy, and certainly with the rowdiness of their companions.

If there is a gap in the border in October, there is a good reason to choose something to fill it. I have just spent a profitable morning in a nursery that grows its own plants to memorable effect (Glen Chantry, at Wickham Bishops in the willow-growing heart of Essex). Most of my haul, admittedly, was more Michaelmas daisies – ones I had never seen before. There is a distinct danger of favouring the autumn at the expense of the spring if you garden in this undisciplined fashion.

This seems to have been the year of the white cosmos. I don't know why, but almost every garden I have visited has had the same idea and given this wonderful annual a star role. We, certainly, have grown other colours and found them dowdy, but the white is quite dazzling. Perhaps others have done the same. Certain white flowers reflect light with the brilliance of a crystalline surface: cosmos is one, the annual white mallow another. Petunias or tobacco, in comparison, are merely whitewashed.

The cosmos we planted in France at Château Trad in April was looking a bit neglected and sleepy after the summer. A good dead-heading and a drink in October and it moved back into top gear.

Another flower I have seen more of this year than ever is the kindergarten-level nasturtium. Perhaps the new idea is to pamper it and give it triffid energy. But how wonderful it looks, scaling hedges and walls, ignoring every traffic sign to surge through borders well over the speed limit. It looks particularly well in combination with the pumpkins and the fancy gourds that have had such a year in the limelight. I fancy it was Caroline Boisset's eye-opening display at Vincent Square last autumn that gave the cucurbits their break. This kind of instant entertainment gardening can go too far – but so can more solemnly tasteful kinds.

1997

❧ January ❧

BRIMMING OVER

Last autumn produced an almost overwhelming harvest of fruit. The apples were endless, the pear trees breaking, wild plums were as red as tomatoes, the loquat stooping with fruit, and a medlar tree a marvellous sight as the red leaves falling revealed hundreds of russet hips, sepals flaring.

Two crops gave us special pleasure: the 'Vranja' quince, whose huge knobbly yellow fruit Mrs Trad promptly converted into fragrant dark-amber slabs of quince paste – perhaps better known by its Portuguese name of *membrillo*. (*Marmelo*, the quince in Portuguese, is the origin of the word marmalade.)

Elizabeth David once described the quince as being to fruit what truffles are to fungi. Put one quince in a basket of apples (or a single truffle in a basket of eggs) and its 'unearthly savour' permeates everything. As *membrillo* it is certainly one of the most positive and penetrating of all fruit flavours. Among wines it matches (mimics, maybe) the inimitable flavour of Hungarian Tokay to perfection: one of the winter's perfect combinations.

Trad meanwhile seized the chance of an astonishing crop of grapes on a single vine of Pinot Noir to throw down the gauntlet to Burgundy. The vine itself has a history. It started life 20 years ago as a cutting from a champagne plot owned by Bollinger which, mysteriously, has never suffered from the fatal vine-louse *Phylloxera*. Its sap is the pure blood of old ungrafted champagne vines.

A pergola is not the approved way of growing wine grapes, but by early November it was such a noble sight, hundreds of dark bunches contrasting with the yellow leaves, that it would have been absurd not to make the vintage. The best bunches gave 25 kg of fruit, which while I write is fermenting as 15 litres of fine-smelling wine.

BRINKMANSHIP

The carp is a fish that can apparently live longer than a man. My recent observations suggest that it is also endowed with an elephantine memory. At least this is my conclusion from the fact that several carp we were given by a neighbour for our little spring-fed hill-top pond in France are ceaselessly trying to enlarge it.

They were reared in a lake, and they simply don't believe their watery horizons can have shrunk, and spend most of their time gnawing away at the muddy brink to enlarge them. Not entirely without success.

What brought me to this conclusion was watching a fine old torpedo of a mirror carp, 20 years at Saling, which I gave to a farmer friend for his new reservoir. Since he launched it into its spacious new quarters it has hung about the shore as though the thought of unlimited depths and breadths is too much for it to take in.

❧ February ❧

AFTER MANY A SUMMER

I'm sure there must be a Chinese expression that means 'May your bamboos flower'. It was after all the Chinese who coined the curse 'May you live in interesting times'.

We are living in interesting times now, at least those of us who grow a common but very beautiful bamboo. Suddenly its graceful fountaining clumps are putting on a new sort of beauty, something never seen here before. All over the soft green and fawn of its stems, purple bracts are opening to reveal purple and green grass-flowers.

Its drawing against the sky, of leaves like little blades or brush-strokes, is darkened and thickened. As the flowers open (at every node on some culms, as though purple blood were spurting out) the weight arches the stems outward and downward. I have just spent an hour watching a plant against the summer-house wall. (It thrives here because the gutter brings it all the rain from the roof.) It is the loveliest thing in the garden on this bright December day, silhouetted against the opal sky, the light-yellow of remaining larch needles and the squirrel-brown of swamp cypress.

All this is made poignant by the probability that the plant will die – or at best be reduced to a long convalescence. If I can't tear myself away it is because the swan's singing betokens the end.

David McClintock tells me (and what he doesn't know about bamboo is not worth knowing) that this species first flowered in Europe 20 years ago, in Denmark, and started flowering in Britain about five years ago. It normally sets quantities of seed, which should be sown with dispatch in the hope of notable new specimens. (In China its flowering and seeding have given rise to plagues of rats that have devastated farms.)

You may have noticed that I am being coy about its name. I bought it as *Arundinaria murielae*. Wrong, says *The New RHS Dictionary of Gardening*: it should be *Thamnocalamus*. Wrong again, says David McClintock: the latest name is *Fargesia murielae*. One thing is sure, though; it is Muriel's bamboo. Muriel was Mrs E H Wilson, whose husband brought the first plant from China. Let us settle for *murielae*, then – and leave botanists to their sport.

JACK SPRAT

Graham Stuart Thomas, whose writings I regard as holy writ, makes an interesting observation on hollies in an article in the tenth-anniversary edition of *Hortus*. He says that in general male plants are more open, irregular and rangy: female ones neater in shape.

What surprised me was that I have noticed exactly the opposite tendency. At Château Trad in the Bourbonnais one hill is so covered with mature hollies that we call it Hollywood. But here the shapely, compact and darkly gleaming trees are the males; the females are generally spindly, with longer more horizontal branches and much less foliage. What they lack in leaves, though, they more than make up for in sumptuous masses of berries.

Could the shape of a holly depend not just on its gender, but on its nationality as well?

IN A BIND

I suspect that the great majority of gardeners, given a simple choice between a 'green' or organic way to solve a problem and a 'brown' or chemical solution, would choose the former. If only they knew one.

But there are garden menaces whose destruction by green means is either impossible or just too laborious to contemplate. I am looking at a serious infestation of bindweed through a vineyard.

Covering the ground with black plastic for a couple of years might possibly do the trick without offending green sensibilities – though it would present plenty of other problems. Any sort of cultivation would obviously only make matters worse by spreading bits of root everywhere.

Or have I missed a solution that I should have spotted?

❧ March ❧

UNDER WRAPS

Two days in Oslo in January was a reminder of snow at its best, in a place where they do winter in style. Norwegian snow, even in the busy main square of the capital, is immaculate, iridescent under the spangling hoarfrost on birches taller than we know how to grow. Our East Anglian snow seemed half-baked in comparison. In reality of course it is only half-frozen.

The day the snow melts is a good time to try that most difficult thing – looking at your own garden with fresh eyes. Especially when the transition from white to green is instantaneous and complete: no grubby grey piles by the hedges.

The arrival of snow is a great revealer of shapes and masses you had not been so aware of before. But it is deceiving: its cloak of perfection is a wicked flatterer. Perhaps you can learn from its added emphasis, but snow and leaves are not the same, and its blue shadows cannot be reproduced in another season.

I looked hard and long, therefore, when I drew the curtains this morning to see what had been under wraps for two weeks. How full the garden looked, how busy with incident. The temporary sense of order and serenity had evaporated. Even at this low point in the year the colours and textures are infinitely complex – perhaps more so than in summer.

After snow even the moss on trees and paths becomes dramatic; its intimate detail emphatic. The familiar forms of iris and hellebore take on new life, the grey leaves of pinks, the purple of heucheras and every commonplace of the resting border is promoted to new value. And in some ways all this complexity is oppressive.

Is there anything to be learned from the simplicity of snow? Only, I think, that simplicity of design and strength of impact go hand in hand.

ILLUSTRIOUS PRECEDENTS

Last autumn Essex joined the list of counties with their own gardens trust (there are now about 30). Already the Steering Group has become a Council of Management, with responsibilities ranging from surveying to archival research; the whole operation swinging into action with the precision and elan of a military campaign.

Listening to the developing plans for every aspect of the county's historic gardens, new gardens, gardens for schoolchildren and gardens for wildlife, I realised that never before in history has the past been so lovingly tended, or the horticultural future so eagerly nurtured.

It is hard to believe, with so much conservation activity all around us, that 20 years ago there was practically none. A very few were aware of the need in the early 1970s when Graham Stuart Thomas, in *The Gardeners' Chronicle*, first proposed the setting up of National Plant Collections. Nothing happened, though, until in May 1977 we devoted a whole issue of this journal to conservation issues. It sent out such ripples that the following year the RHS held its first conservation conference – from which flowed the National Council for the Conservation of Plants and Gardens, and perhaps indirectly the County Gardens Trust movement.

The trusts have enormous potential for harnessing energy and goodwill to eminently useful ends. Nobody thought of Essex as being particularly endowed with gardens or gardeners until the trust focused our minds. Now we realise that, for example, the Petre family (the present Lord Petre is Trust President) had one of England's first great collections of American plants at Thorndon Hall, that Humphry Repton lived at Romford, Tradescant the Elder gardened in Chelmsford at New Hall, that Ellen Willmott employed 100 gardeners at Warley Place where John Evelyn had gardened two centuries before, the Reverend Joseph Pemberton bred the hybrid musk roses at Havering-atte-Bower, Samuel Curtis of *The Botanical Magazine* lived at Glazenwood near Braintree … and all this without mentioning the great gardens of today, from Beth Chatto's to Audley End to the RHS on its hilltop at Hyde Hall.

Inspired by all these illustrious precedents we see the present and the future in a new light. We have been used to apologising for the past – or at least any part of it that involved imperial adventures. I like to think that we have come to terms with all that, and are ready to be proud of our county – and indeed our country – again.

❦ April ❦

VITAL JUICES

There is nothing like pruning a grapevine for training yourself to think like a plant. When you are cutting away everything but a very small precise number of buds, it matters acutely what those buds are going to do. They are the blueprint for the luxuriant growth of summer. If a bud points upwards, that is the way the shoot will grow; it will be easy to tie to a wire at whatever height you want. If it points sideways out of line, it will be nothing but a nuisance.

In early February the buds are like brown pinheads, scarcely visible and spaced so close that your secateurs hover for half a minute while you decide where to cut. By chance we started pruning on the day before the new moon, a clear still day that grew hot by lunchtime. There was no sap running in the vines; the cuts were dry.

To my amazement next morning when we went to work again the tide was already on the flood. Whether it was the single hot day or the new moon or both I have no idea, but the sap had risen, to start pouring from every cut. Happily they start to callous over and staunch the flow in a few days. But it is painful to see the vital juice welling from an apparently dormant plant: juice that has only to pass through a grape to become wine.

MULCH WARNING

Stop me if you've heard this before, but there is a serious drought looming – indeed here already. It is now two years since the pattern of frequent, if irregular, anticyclones, bringing rain from the west, faded away. In its place we (at least in the east) have had almost continuous high pressure, still air and virtually no rain at all. Last year Beth Chatto at Colchester measured less than 15 inches. Far from the winter filling the dykes (it is two years since the farm ditch ran) January gave us just over a quarter of an inch; the first half of February managed only the same again.

I am laying in a serious quantity of mulch. The only question is when to spread it. Probably it is best to keep hoping for soaking rain until April, then pile it on. To let any of the precious drops evaporate would be a crime.

IN PATAGONIA

The last thing I expected to see in Patagonia was gentle English gardening. But the 'lake district', where the crest of the Andes simmers down to modest peaks on a Scottish or Welsh scale, with only an occasional snowcap in the distance, offers a mild climate, bountiful rain and fertile soil. The landscape of mountain and forest, water and islands is hard to beat anywhere for unsullied purity.

At the northern end of Lake Nahuel Huapi (600,000 hectares, if I heard it right) 60 or so summer 'cottages' cluster round the Cumulen country club, above the golf course that rolls down among huge redwoods and Douglas firs to the brilliant water.

As we wandered from one garden of honeysuckle and roses to another it was just as though we were out on a Yellow Book afternoon, asking names, assimilating ideas, taking notes. But then, as our (Argentine) host reminded us, the settlers of the River Plate were famously described as 'Italians who speak Spanish, dress like the French and wish they were English.' The proof is in their gardens.

The Douglas firs are a serious mistake, though. This is the land of the southern beech, *Nothofagus*, whose most splendid evergreen species, *N. dombeyi*, forms some of the world's most perfect temperate high forest. In drier places it mingles with *Austrocedrus chilensis*, the southern-hemisphere equivalent of the incense cedar; down at the water's edge with the sinuous rosy and tawny trunks of ancient myrtles. For undergrowth it has the curious clambering bamboo, *Chusquea culeou*.

North American conifers were introduced here early in this century. In these benign conditions they grow at frightening speed and sow themselves prodigiously. Douglas fir comes up like cress and goes on up to 30 metres, and much more, blanketing out the native species with precipices of relentless green.

I couldn't help thinking how lucky we are that the Leyland cypress is sterile. What horrors we would face if it suddenly started setting fertile seeds.

❧ May ❧

PUFFING GENTLY

Trying to keep pace with this spring has made me fitter than I've been for a long time. A heat- (alright then, warmth-) wave in March has given us enough dust to ransom all the royal families in Europe. What with doubling round the garden to make sure you haven't missed another opening flower, another shrub inflating its buds, another spear piercing the ground, and attending to bed, border and potting shed duties (as well as airing greenhouses and conservatory, and watering as though it were summer) the hours and days have whizzed by.

This is not a complaint, but a more leisurely unfurling of the season gives one more time to revel in its riches. The annual orgy in the frog-pond, for example, could keep me engrossed all morning, and the whole afternoon would not be too long to gaze up at blue sky through the branches of the red maple, dense with flowers redder than an embothrium. Had we but world enough and time ....

Besides, there are infrastructure jobs that are supposed to be done in winter now looking at me accusingly. The long-overdue revision of what we unimaginatively call the Long Walk has involved shortening an overgrown circle of cypress hedge to let in light, the felling of a thuja that had suddenly (or so it seemed) become a forest tree, radical pruning of ancient shrubs, the installation of a water-pipe and widening and resowing of the grass – all work better done before the spring sprint begins.

And the Red Sea – our pond so named because it originally leaked so badly that chariots could cross it untroubled – has taken to leaking again. It stands empty and forlorn while we argue about alternative ways to patch, plug or line it – or rather while we don't, because we're far too busy elsewhere.

Worse, Bee, whose energy, adaptability and smile have powered the place for the past two-and-a-half years, is moving away to a hive of her own. But change is the essence of gardening. Imagine living on the Equator, with sun-up and sun-down at six o'clock every day of the year, and the seasons marked by nothing more than whether it is raining or not.

GRAVITAS

Beth Chatto's gravel garden should be compulsory viewing for anyone who lives in the rain-starved counties. We went on a winter's day when the sea-fret from Harwich was reaching gloomily inland and sensible citizens were watching the rugger. But even in the glum chill, with not much more than the bergenias in flower, the genius of this most famous former car park was plain to see.

It is completely English. Its sweeping lines, its bays and inlets and islands of planting in the unifying gravel ground hark back subconsciously to 18th-century landscape. But banks and massifs of broom and cistus, rosemary and lavender (and of course rarer and more recondite things I didn't recognise) recall the Mediterranean.

The choice of plants and the deep gravel mulch make it a no-watering garden, an ecological model. Yet striped-lawn fanatics are the only people I can think of who would not find it profoundly satisfying. Even in February.

DICK BANKS

I shall sorely miss Dick Banks, who died in February at the age of 94. I met him when I was 13, when he came to see his son Lawrence (recently Treasurer of the Society) at our mutual house at Rugby. Little did I think that this tall and twinkling person, so kind to small boys, would be my gardening mentor over 40 years later.

I wonder whether anyone has had a better horticultural innings: 67 years of active life in the family's great garden and arboretum at Hergest Croft on the Welsh border. He was, I was so happy to hear, still looking things up in his library (he was a scholar of the best sort, infinitely curious, but without an ounce of pedantry) two days before he passed peacefully to the Elysian Fields.

❦ June ❦

DEEP FRANCE

The electric fence is a wonderful thing: it means we can share the garden with the Charolais mums and their beautiful white calves. It is an odd feeling at first, looking up from weeding to see a vast creamy beast snuffling away at the grass within a few feet. They are so utterly benign, these dairy-monsters, that they cast their massive tranquillity like a spell over the place.

Ten days in April at Château Trad turned out to be a summer holiday. Never have I seen the bocage of central France so radiant. We look down from our hilltop orchard with a bird's-eye view of the oak wood beyond the ravine. Oaks are wildly individual in their sense of time. One tree will be in full piercing-green leaf while its neighbours are just considering opening a tentative bud or two. The colours run from tawny to khaki to russet to olive to electric green across the hill, while here and there a wild cherry proclaims itself with a froth of blossom high in the canopy of the forest.

It is the same with the bocage, the infinitely various monotony of oak-dotted hedges rolling over hill and valley, sketching out the roads, the river and the farms. We are perched high enough to follow the field-boundaries for 5 miles at least, look down into placid farmyards and trace the silhouettes of woods scattered in dark wedges to a distant horizon.

At dawn the valley at our feet is veiled in thin half-revealing mist as the sun touches first the barn and the single tall elm, then the house and finally the garden and the still reflecting pond. At dusk in April the sun set in an almost cloudless sky day after day, in a brief fury of pink, purple and orange, before the strange vision of Hale Bopp's comet appeared, motionless and yet tearing through the heavens dragging its astonishing train.

Who could believe there is no connection between this celestial performance and the month with scarcely a cloud?

❧ July ❧

JACK THE LAD

We have seen plenty of examples recently of the bewildering behaviour of frost. Its ground rules are supposed to be simple: cold air flows like water to the lowest point it can reach and, like water, fills its hollow. Unlike water it can be dispersed by sufficient air movement. Of course, if the wind itself is below a certain temperature, it can aggravate the damage to tender shoots, flowers and leaves.

A wisteria here, for example, is undamaged in the lee of a wall, but totally blasted above it. Contrarily, a 25-foot oak had its fresh leaves crisped brown up to 15 feet (presumably the depth of the frost 'pool') but is perfectly green above that height.

What is even less clear to me, though, is how some new leaves can remain unburnt by frost, others seem to be vulnerable for their first few days only, rapidly hardening off, while others can spend a whole month at their full size, enjoying sun and wind, and still be vulnerable to temperatures below freezing.

An example of the first, in my experience, is the California buckeye, *Aesculus californica* – always one of the first green trees and never frosted. An example of the second is the oak, very variable in its leafing time, but once well in leaf pretty well frost-immune. An example of the third is that most glamorous of willows, *Salix fargesii*, whose buds like lacquered fingernails issue almost magnolia-like leaves, delicately pleated and touched with red. Our plant, the apple of my eye in May, had been in leaf for four weeks in the shelter of a wall when a temperature of only -2°C burnt it like a blowlamp.

In a sense all this is idle speculation because there is precious little we can do about it – and in any case most gardeners feel more aggrieved by the browning of their magnolia-petals or the wisteria than of 'mere' leaves. But damage to flowers is only for that year: damage to growth is a setback to the whole life of the plant – and of course, to a recently installed young plant with its roots scarcely established, may well mean curtains.

A QUIET BROWSE

A deer in the garden early this morning gave me a start. As I made my way through the arboretum, quietly musing, she raised her head from the pond and lolloped off into the trees. She seemed huge, and dark-bronze like the sculpture I wish she had been.

We are used to muntjac, a nuisance but a relatively small one. Unless the deer found me alarmingly huge too we may have to get used to a rather higher browsing level in future.

❧ August ❧

BLESSED RELIEF

Suddenly we were reminded of what it is like to be released from stress. Our very souls have been withering in month after month of drought. Our expectations, even our hopes have been dwindling. We have steeled ourselves to say that a yellow lawn is alright; a 2-inch shoot on a shrub at least a sign that it is alive.

And then came the rain. Two inches in a week (after 3 inches in five months). I never cease to wonder how immediately some plants react, with oaks the most eager of all. Even our 'Concordia', the golden oak which is one of the very slowest-growing trees, put out 9-inch shoots within 24 hours of the first real rain.

Friends tell me I'm a freak to prefer rain to sunshine. But surely the most profound of garden pleasures is to find a sheltered place to watch the heavens deliver what plants need most of all. Branches bending, their leaves heavy and shining, to mingle and block paths, have a grace beyond anything that sun and wind can give them.

Pale soil darkened and gleaming, gutters and downpipes running with a transfusion of new life, open flowers taking the punch of raindrops in the face, the surface of the pool scratched and smeared, jumping in tiny plumes of replenishment: this is horticultural heaven.

No surprise, of course, that weeds are among the first to take advantage. But in the euphoria they seem to drop their guard. A slow steady pull bringing up the whole carrot of a dock may be the greatest satisfaction of all.

HAUTICULTURE

France cannot have seen such a garden-creative period since the belle époque. On each visit (we settled in the centre so that all parts would be equally close for visiting – or equally far away) I discover new works on a humbling scale.

At Château Trad we are content with a potager. Well, almost. But our neighbours, near and far, are spreading themselves with astonishing confidence – astonishing when you learn that their workforce is usually derisory.

In May we headed south across the Auvergne into the Cévennes, stayed the night in the Gorges du Tarn at France's most romantic hotel, the Château de la Caze, a fortress pygmied by the precipices around and even overhanging it, then crossed the rugged Causse Méjean on the way to Provence. This is the season when the weathered limestone of the Causse, at 1,000 metres plus, is a rock garden. For mile upon mile of highlands the principal plants are box and juniper, forming strange shapes like an agitated sea. In May they are illuminated by masses of pink, violet, purple and yellow, blue and white and poppy-red.

Our (eventual) goal was the Château de Bagnols in the southern Beaujolais, a fortress with baroque adornments, restored over five years of inspiration and perspiration by Helen Hamlyn, wife of the publisher Paul. The garden she has made as a setting for what is possibly France's most luxurious château-hotel is a shining example of carrying a bold idea to a totally satisfying conclusion.

An immense grass promenade 200 metres long ties together the château, the old stable block and a bosky lime-shaded terrace. It is like the front row of the stalls to a panorama of wood and vine-clad hills, pastoral foreground to the distant snows of Mont Blanc.

To me the masterstroke is the vast parterre below the promenade. It consists only of four quadrant cherry orchards, outlined with low yew hedges, around a high central fountain. Through each quadrant runs a diagonal path: simply grass mown closer. Outer walls and corner gazebos are frothy with climbing roses. But the stage, as it were, that carries the drama of the view is a masterpiece of restraint – very appetising restraint, it is true, in May when the trees are gleaming red with their harvest.

The French of course are at their most creative when they forget the admonition to *faites simple*. Just up the road from home, a princess with a fairy-tale name is putting the finishing touches to her 'Chartreuse' of four large walled gardens of breathtaking elaboration: every plant from rose to mulberry to lime trained like a soldier or clipped like a poodle.

This is haute-couture horticulture, all the more humiliating to a scruffy English gardener for being the work of one gardener directing 'volunteers' borrowed from the gendarmerie.

❧ September ☙

BRUM SUR MER

Having often marvelled at the soft climate of Dublin (you see almost Trescoid plants in its suburban front gardens) I often wondered why the Welsh coast, further south (Anglesey being the nearest point to Dublin) and apparently more exposed to the beneficence of the Gulf Stream flowing up the Irish Sea, did not obviously exhibit such signs of horticultural privilege.

True the gardens of Portmeirion grow huge fuchsias, but I had always thought this was a coast rather neglected by gardeners. The mountains of Snowdonia provide a magnificent backdrop: the potential is mouth-watering.

Then I discovered the Mawdach estuary, from Dolgellau to Barmouth, transformed by the tide twice a day from a broad tree-reflecting loch to an intricate pattern of shoals and sandbars and gleaming pools. Cader Idris rises to 3,000 feet from the south shore, the bare-headed Rhinog mountains protect the north.

The old Barmouth road, obliged to leave the dangerous estuary and climb the Rhinogs, was one of the earliest places in the British Isles to attract tourists in search of the picturesque. By 1800, Barmouth was becoming a fashionable resort. Then with the building of a shore road the wealth of Birmingham started to move in. In the 1840s there was even a short-lived gold rush: there are still mines in the hills today. Iron-masters built baronial stone houses as their seaside retreats – and surrounded them with lavish gardens – which before long disappeared behind the firs planted to protect them from the sea winds.

Today you can drive along the spectacular Barmouth road almost unaware that you are surrounded by such mansions: that you are, in fact, on the Brummy Riviera.

BUXOMANIA

In July Eric Kirby clips his box bank in the garden here, and each year more and more visitors photograph it. It started 20 years ago when I planted box to cover the impoverished and unstable side of an old gravel-digging.

We made a vaguely Japanese-looking pond with stepping stones at its foot, with a sadly underpowered cascade over rocks fed by a distant hydraulic ram.

The clipped box notion was taken from Kyoto gardens where azaleas are trimmed into buns which flower, to my mind rather facetiously, like a pink rash. Photinias, also popular for their shining red young leaves, are scarcely better. You can't beat the calm authority of box.

Over the years, though, Eric's boxes have acquired a sense of humour of their own. Almost every visitor volunteers a different description: sheep, rocks, a distant mountain range to romantics; buttocks to a young lady painter the other day.

There are 88 of these absurd creatures now, with enough recruits to bring the sum up to 100. Little did I think that while they were growing, box was scaling the social ladder to become one of the most modish plants of all. In case anyone thinks of rustling Eric's, though, I warn them that the gravel they are growing in makes any move a fatal one. I've tried it, and it doesn't work.

TITANIA COUNTRY

It has been the year of the bryony in these parts. Bryony is the spider's web of the weed world: its fantastic streamers with their convoluted tendrils have the spider's ability to leap unlikely distances from plant to plant. I have never caught them at it, but in the morning the aspiring shoot that clasped a branch at waist height last thing at night is waving from the one above your head.

This is white bryony, the athletic one, a member of the cucumber family with a root so large (hence presumably the plant's alarming energy) that it passed for our native mandrake. It was supposed to look like a baby – which with some trimming and a lot of imagination an old one could. Hence associations with fertility.

Black bryony is the shiny-leaved one whose smooth stems surge up unnoticed inside bushes until the shiny leaves, and eventually the lustrous (and poisonous) berries, emerge into the light. It is no relation to the white one in botany, and can't compare in either vigour or elegance.

One of this summer's least expected delights was white bryony cavorting among low pine branches and then draping itself through and among the white papery flowers of a huge old cistus. Its discovery one morning had the impact of utter originality; a fantasy beyond what we call horticulture.

Don't encourage it, though. By the time the greeny-white five-petalled flowers appear it is time to start hauling it out of whatever imaginative lodging it has found itself – or its soft little seedlings will be everywhere next spring.

❧ October ❧

IN ITS PRIME

Distressing as it is to see a plant, pruned or cut at the wrong season, bleeding from the wound, I would never have believed that a vigorous plant could actually bleed to death.

But that's what happened in May when a careless workman, operating a mini-digger right by the house where a shovel was all he needed, chopped through a five-year-old muscat vine. I had just succeeded in training it to cover a large patch of boring wall. I cursed roundly, detached the beautiful green shoots, leaves and tendrils, as dramatically vigorous as only a vine can be, from their pinnings, to carry them off to their funeral pyre – and waited. The sap poured from the 2-inch stump like a spring: a heart-rending sight.

I have seen enough damaged vines recover (after frost, hail, wind or accident) to be sure that, even if the muscat scion was ruined, the rootstock would put up new growth with the characteristic ruddy shine of its American parents. But nothing happened.

The spring flowed for a week, then everything dried up. How can the energy that creates new buds just pour away as water into the ground? Could it be simple shock at being severed when it was growing most lustily?

In a neighbouring meadow the blackened stumps in rows show where a vineyard was abandoned to cattle; seven years ago, I'm told. Yet a third of these vines are still putting up shoots, admittedly only modest ones, having been grazed regularly all that time.

Pondering on this, my eye was caught by Liz Robinson's notes in *Hortus* magazine, where she calls for alum, the principle of the styptic pencil for razor scrapes, to staunch bleeding from plants. There is alum in wood-ash. Had I heaped wood-ash on my vine, could its life have been saved? In winter I am going to dig out the roots to see if I can learn any more – and of course plant another vine.

A BIG DIG

As the water in the well gets lower and lower, I have been investigating the possibility of digging deeper. Which led me to investigate how old wells were dug in the first place.

Ours is very old. The house couldn't be on this site without it, and its origins go back at least as far as the 11th century. It is intriguing to think of the water diviner criss-crossing the ground with his hazel-rod before plumping for the spot – then presumably keeping his fingers crossed all the while the diggers dug.

They started with a sturdy oak frame of the circumference of the proposed shaft laid flat on the ground. A digger stood in the frame and made himself a shallow pit to work in. Then his mates laid three or four courses of bricks, lengthwise, unmortared, on the frame and the digger set about gradually easing the earth out from under this circular wall. He scraped gingerly, because the weight had to lower itself gently and evenly until the top bricks were level with the surface. His mates meanwhile hauled up the spoil in a bucket.

When the top bricks were at ground level, one of the others took over below, starting again with a central hole to work in, while his mates added to the wall above, then eased out the earth to lower the whole increasingly massive cylinder … and so on until – maybe weeks later – the digger's feet began to get wet.

This must have been the trickiest (and most frightening) part of all. To reach a good water supply our hero would have to keep digging around his wet legs and undermining the surrounding brickwork until the fear of drowning combined with claustrophobia made him sing out for a hoist to the top.

No wonder these days we sink boreholes.

PS We dug. Further developments are reported in April 2000, page 136.

❧ November ❧

GREYING SLIGHTLY

We've been reluctantly aware for a couple of years that our conservatory was in need of an overhaul. It has given wonderfully little trouble in its 17 years of life: only two complete repaintings and one new set of blinds.

The blinds are the cedar-lath type, held together with copper rings, that roll up to just under the opening lights at the top. They age to an inimitable silver-grey, the individual laths snaking subtly as they age to look almost as though a living plant is covering the roof. Eventually the laths snap and what looked picturesque takes on a shanty-town air; time for the very considerable expense of a new set of blinds.

This summer we called in the firm that built the conservatory in 1980. The same team, greying slightly, went lovingly over their old handiwork. One problem: we had cunningly disguised the cast-iron ogee guttering as a cornice with only the slightest fall over its 40-foot length. Heavy rain (I can just remember it!) tends to build up and overflow the back of the gutter, eventually rotting the facia. It has all had to be stripped off, the new facia protected with copper sheet and half the lovingly-carved dentil mouldings on the facia replaced. But that's it. A fresh coat of paint and I don't see why it shouldn't do another 20 years with only cosmetic treatment.

When I think of the hours, days, nights, springs and autumns and winters of pleasure it has given us I can think of no greater bargain. Just now the plants it shelters, purple *Streptocarpus*, pink oleander, blue plumbago and white pelargoniums, echo the colours of the Michaelmas daisies, Japanese anemones, caryopteris and marguerites down the borders outside.

DRAMATIS PERSONAE

At last a producer has found something more dramatic to do with a garden than simply saunter round it, with pauses for topical tips. BBC2's *Ground Force* started in September with a wonderfully loony idea. A householder connives with Alan Titchmarsh and friends to hoodwink his wife into going away for just long enough for them to remodel her garden. She comes back home (punctual to the minute) to face a camera recording her delight: 'I can't beleeeeve it!'

This gives Titchmarsh about 25 minutes on screen, representing two days of work for his little band to uproot, fork over, level, plant, unroll turf, rake gravel and describe what they are doing and why. Time is telescoped by fast-forward digging, weeding, trimming ... surely every gardener's dream. The budget for purchases is £700 – most of which seems to go on large plants at garden-centre prices – but also some imaginative non-essentials.

Although some of their reasons have all the daftness of ecological correctness – 'we should have some stinging nettles for the butterflies' – there are enough good ideas, useful tips and pungent asides as Titchmarsh bosses his team along to make good quick-fire television.

The second week had the same storyline. Most of the action, though, was more DIY shed-building than what you or I would call gardening. This brought in the neighbour who was none too sure he wanted a shed in his view. He was easily pacified with a promise of a Russian vine to hide it – and possibly by the camera in his living room.

I shall go on watching this series. I hope they manage to find drama in something more horticultural. The subject of 'nicking' cuttings has plenty of potential. But this is a good start in bringing gardening to life on the box at last. Above all it has the essentials of drama: unity, plot, characters, development, a degree of suspense – and of course a happy tear at the end.

❧ December ❧

FRENCH LESSONS

For years now we have been telling solicitous enquirers that no, actually, the Trad *domaine* in France does not boast a garden. A bit round the house with fruit trees and a little potager where the cows are (not always successfully) excluded, a horse-pond, even a little flower border, a lilac – every farm has one – a vine pergola and some roses on the walls don't add up, in my mind, to a garden: just a smattering of horticultural activity to domesticate the expanse of wood and pasture, hill and steep declivity to the winding, tree-lined river. Nothing at all, in fact, in comparison with the immense, map-like view.

I'm afraid, though, there has been a weakening. Whether it is the urge to conform or the itch to imitate, we have given in. The little skewed quadrangle (if a quadrangle can be open-ended) between the old cowsheds and the red-roofed barn had no sense of place or purpose. Gradually we realised that only a Gallic sense of order, ruthlessly imposed, would bring it to heel.

Out came the tape and spirit level, the pegs and lines. Slowly we convinced ourselves that four quadrilateral beds, two sort of whale-shaped, two closer to square, could be given some sort of unity by crossed paths meeting at a circular stone basin. We excavated the beds, outlined them with old oak barn-timbers, filled them with what passes for soil and the paths with ten-decibel gravel. Then, to our delight, we found a friendly artist-*brocanteur* with a passion for box and enough rooted cuttings to take care of Hampton Court. With his impeccable little hedges installed we were committed. The question was, and still is, what to plant in the four accusing parterres to give them the proper look of inevitability, of being *normale*.

Playing for time, last season we filled them with nasturtiums. I have a passion for this childish plant, so lush, cress-smelling, its orange flowers complementing so perfectly the light-green of its leaves and stems. (Unlike the pink-flowered variety: a prime case of Breeder's Folly.) If only nasturtiums started to sprawl and cover the ground sooner I would settle for them as the annual answer. (This is largely absentee gardening, remember; no fancy bedding.) Their salad freshness enclosed in sober box would make my summer.

Alas, though, their bulk builds only from late July or August onwards. We need something permanent, lowish, weed-proof (and of course *normale*). Lavender? Artemisia? Crushed tiles?

Meanwhile in another part of the wood my rash attempt (notice the first-person singular: no one shares the blame) to garden in an untamed gully goes forward more or less as planned. I have taken on a patch perhaps 30 by 10 metres (or yards if you prefer) along a stream bank in ground full of springs. I planted yellow azaleas, *Euphorbia palustris* and bluebells. Oh yes, and candelabra primulas. All have survived, the primulas have multiplied, and my job now is simply to pull up the brambles that launch their long-jumping shoots from their surrounding encampment. Soon I will have to select from seedlings of oak, hazel, holly and hornbeam that volunteer everywhere.

No one, I should add, is interested in this garden but me. I am simply seeing how much (or how little) you have to do to introduce and maintain a cameo in a wilderness. Its spring moment is marvellous, and its October colours not bad. But the popular feeling, I fear, is: 'Has this poor nutter nothing better to do?'

AUTRE TEMPS ...

Something reminded me just the other day that my parents had a 'sunken' garden, and that as a child I supposed it was something everybody had.

It's not a term you hear any more. In fact I couldn't think where to look it up until I remembered the grand old gold-encrusted half-a-stone volume of Thomas Mawson's *Art and Craft of Garden-Making* (mine is the fifth, 1926 edition) – and even the masterly Mawson hasn't very much to say on the subject.

He makes it plain, though, that the purpose of a sunken garden was to introduce terracing on a flat site where none was called for. You simply excavated a rectangle (it could be an oval or a circle) to a depth of 3 or 4 feet, walled it with brick or stone, and had the fun of walking down steps into a place where the borders were waist-high. It was very much the kind of thing Alan Titchmarsh, with his passion for brick-laying, might spring on you in two days while your back was turned.

There are grander precedents, though. What is the Dutch Garden at Kensington Palace if not a sunken garden? The suburban or Surrey version (the kind my parents had, but in St John's Wood) was just the last dilution of the idea. If Arts and Crafts gardening comes back (and the portents are all around us) we may have to watch our step or be precipitated into a well of nostalgia.

1998

TO THE GREAT WALL

It is a truth universally acknowledged that travel books are more interesting after you have seen the country they describe than they are before you go. You can imagine, then, that if I found Roy Lancaster's 1989 masterpiece, *Travels in China*, absorbing stuff without having got further than Hong Kong, a few days around Beijing has made me devour it more avidly than ever.

November is not the ideal month to go. It was dry and dusty (apparently its usual condition except in midsummer) with the sun making only a wan orange impression on the coal-smog. The flat approaches to the city across the plain reveal only two kinds of tree: poplars (var. *alba*, I suspect; each one is painted white up to 4 or 5 feet from the ground) and unweeping willows, planted with a hypnotic regularity somehow wholly fitting to the outskirts of a great communist capital.

With Lancaster as my guide I had not been prepared for the world's biggest building-site Beijing has recently become. Whole neighbourhoods of traditional low grey-brick houses around courtyards, the *hutongs*, have been bulldozed to make way for shopping centres and vast office blocks with post-modernist pagoda flourishes.

It is the *hutongs*, though, that constitute the past of Beijing, and where you will find its domestic gardening, from a single tree peony growing by a doorway to the considerable walled pleasure-grounds of a senior courtier.

The Chinese passion for rocks bears no relation to that of the Japanese. In Japan all the art is to conceal the art, at least within certain conventional forms. In Beijing there are (at least) two clearly distinct styles. The lucky owner of extraordinary stones, often like great pumice needles, plants them upright in strange aggressive clusters, or incorporates them in steep-stepped grottoes, often disappointingly arid, with no cool alleviating moss.

A flat-stone style, in contrast, simply heaps up sometimes prodigious slabs to form what appear to be the world's worst-built walls. I asked my Chinese companion whether she found satisfaction, even perhaps serenity, in these angular barriers. The answer was yes.

The pretty painted pavilions are the making of these gardens: often either perched on a very artificial-looking hill or central in a little lake. Since there is little maintenance (apart from gardeners displacing the dust with besoms) it is hard to know how many plants are missing from the scheme. I suspect the majority, because in the relatively rare courtyards furnished with bamboos, paulownias, spiraeas or kerrias, or (in November) with newspaper-wrapped peonies, the sense of aridity quickly disappears. One wonderful tree appears time and time again: *Pinus bungeana*, the lace-bark pine, whose often multiple trunk and branches exfoliate, almost plane-like, to shimmer in a jigsaw of silver, white and green.

You see no urbane lace-barks in the country round, north and west towards the Great Wall, two hours' drive out of the city. The poplar-planted plain abruptly ends at the foot of dry brown hills. For miles a dull conical juniper dominates the bare landscape, giving place as you climb to *Pinus tabuliformis*, the standard north-China flat-topped pine. The last orange leaves were hanging on the smoke-bushes (*Cotinus coggygria* is native, it seems, in Asia as it is in Europe), and huge, shaggy, tobacco-brown ones on tall, narrow oaks, *Quercus dentata*. But it took intense bare-twig botanising to identify elms, limes and the *Koelreuteria paniculata* that reach up to the Great Wall.

Chinese mountains are craggier. Perhaps gardeners are not exaggerating, or only slightly, with their stony ziggurats. The Great Wall itself struck me not so much for what it is as where it is: a humdrum military highway with a distinct air of Viollet-le-Duc following the mad gradients of a tortuous ridge apparently forever.

We visited the Wall at Mutianyu, where you can be wafted up in a few minutes by cable car. As we descended the seemingly endless (and beautifully made) stone steps we encountered the spirit that, in China, makes anything possible. A hundred or so workmen were carrying up the iron rods to construct a new cable car – on their shoulders; two to a 20-foot rod. And not just carrying them, but racing, overtaking their workmates, even laughingly trying to upset them over the edge.

MADE IN HEAVEN

There are, I'm told, people who find mahonias spiky and glum bushes to have around the garden. Dear old *Mahonia aquifolium*, the Oregon grape, I admit is a bit of a plodder (though intriguingly varied, from seed, in shape, shininess and general allure). But in November ('No fruit, no flowers ...' – you know the ditty) the jaunty expanding sprays of fragrant yellow fanning out from all the forms of the hybrid *M.* x *media* are the garden's clearest signal that all is not lost. I have always wondered how their parents could have met. *M. lomariifolia* is flowering now, but its supposed spouse, *M. japonica*, waits until February.

❦ February ❦

FRONT ROW OF THE STALLS

How much are you aware of your garden when you are in the house? Unless you spend your time in a conservatory, or a room with French windows in a bay, I suspect the answer is not very much – or only intermittently. In this – admittedly ancient – house the windows are relatively high and small; you have to go and stand at one to more than glimpse the garden. Which window do we stand at most, thus making it the one with the most important view? The one above the kitchen sink, of course.

We have spent more thought on the composition of the washer-up's view than on any other. Now, in midwinter, it is more remarkable for composition than for incident. The only flowers near at hand are those on a miniature *Viburnum farreri* and the purple pansies that we use to carpet the hacked-down herb beds. These are in the foreground, just under the (north-facing) window, framed to the left by a variegated holly and to the right by a brick wall that glows pink in reflection of the teatime sunset. Then there is just lawn but, happily, 30 yards of it to lead the eye to a low curving box hedge which I think of as the stage for seasonal performances. Overhanging the lawn is the protective canopy of a mature walnut, its pale trunk the defining right-hand limit of the view.

Behind the stage the collage of dark masses, arbutus, evergreen viburnums, evergreen nothofagus, yews and more distantly spruce, is interspersed and brightened by the pale verticals of tree trunks, the ivory of birches, and just now the yellow starbursts of *Mahonia* x *media* 'Charity'. On stage, as principal actor in the leafy season, is a 10-foot golden Japanese maple, poised as a prima donna, at whose feet crocuses, then bluebells and tall white tulips play.

And beyond it a grass path leads through the collage to a glimpse of sunlit space, suggesting (at least to me) that something, or someone, is waiting to step into Scene II.

THE LILY, UNPAINTED

In a handful of the houses I visit from time to time I am regularly entranced by exhibits from the world outside. I don't mean flower arrangements, lovely as they can be. It is the sprigs of foliage or flowers brought in for their own sakes, almost as scientific specimens that, for me, have a strange poignancy.

Valerie Finnis famously collected and photographed one each of all the flowers and fruit in her garden week by week, arranged on a little etagere rather in the manner of a school photo. Lady Salisbury at Hatfield House always has a cluster of tiny vases on a side-table as a record or witness to what is in flower on any day of the year. The effect, especially in winter when flowers are small, is a deposit of gems sparkling in the artificial light.

At the opposite extreme are the whole oak, olive or pine branches laid on a table or snaking along a broad mantelpiece, the signature of my favourite Californian gardener – designer Molly Chappellet, in her rambling ranch-house in the hills north of San Francisco. Or, indeed, the long hop bines that Kentish pubs used to hang above the bar.

Why are these exhibits more memorable – at least to me – than stately vases of colour-coordinated flowers and leaves, berries and bark? Perhaps because they are nature unadorned, simply brought to our attention by being put in an unexpected context.

In Japan's grander hotels there is always a seasonal flourish just inside the front door: plum blossom, pine, trained chrysanthemum, bamboo, turning maple … often the whole tree. Usually they are associated with rocks and reflected in water. In the context, I suppose, a simple cut branch would look too crude.

Not at home, though. Drag in a bare birch branch with its catkins and see what it does for your kitchen.

❧ March ❧

HARD HAT

If museums are being forced to get rid of stuffed animals because National Lottery advisers tell them they 'give off the wrong signals' (I read this in the increasingly scary 'PC Watch' column of *The Week*) it must be time for gardeners to start worrying. What potentially offensive 'signals' are emanating from your choice of plants – let alone your ornaments?

Looking round me I can see innumerable causes for offence. There are outrageous 'signals' of sexism, like one female figure typecast as Flora and another shivering in wholly inadequate clothing for the time of year.

I have already hidden the ageist gnome in a pixie house where we may just get away with him as a legitimate resident rather than as an offensive mockery of small people in bright clothes.

Revision of our planting schemes looms. Obviously, the white border will have to go. But we also have a large area without a single Chinese plant, which could easily be signalling wildly about our prejudices. Anyone remotely sensitive to elitist issues must surely have grave misgivings about growing superior forms of anything.

Then comes the perpetual worry of avoiding killing anything, and trying to prevent one creature from killing another. The cats can be confined to barracks, but how do you show disapproval to a ladybird munching aphids?

There is the safety issue, too. Stephen Anderton puts it perfectly in the autumn issue of *Historic Gardens Review*: 'the safety of everything and the excitement of nothing'.

Health and Safety at Work legislation threatens us with red lifebuoys beside every pond. Poisonous plants should go to the back of the border. As for ha-has, perhaps we should forgive our ancestors for such dangerous follies, but then certainly fence them off before the worst happens.

❧ April ❧

BEFORE THE SWALLOW DARES

The lack of extreme weather up to mid-February (and counting) has given the winter-flowering plants a wonderful run. *Prunus* x *subhirtella* 'Autumnalis' has exhausted its supply of flower-buds, but *P.* 'Kursar' is starting: it is a much stronger pink. The winter aconites, after years of patience, seem to have settled for their less-than-ideal billet under the beech tree and are blasting away. The snowdrop seems least moved by a lack of winter cold (does it want snow, perhaps?). It takes its time to perform; perhaps it is one of those cold-blooded plants that are governed by day-length alone.

The winter heliotrope and *Lonicera fragrantissima* already keep their wide territories drenched in scent. Roses and clematis are tempting fate with emerging shoots. I was alarmed to see the south-European ash, *Fraxinus angustifolia*, already in flower in January.

But top prize goes to the plant that has been having its own private party since before Christmas. The hybrid strawberry tree, *Arbutus* x *andrachnoides*, is the plant made famous by the top terrace at Bodnant – and vice versa, come to that. There, its massive smooth red bole glides sideways like a boa constrictor. Our comparative midget (it is only ten years old) has similar serpentine ideas. But just now all eyes are on its canopy of white and yellow heather-bells, in 3-inch sprays from every twig. In still air a faint aura of honey hangs around it. It is the complete winter-performing evergreen. But then all the arbutuses are as desirable as they are amenable.

ALL CHANGE

I don't suppose L Brown or H Repton ever had a sinking feeling when they saw the oceans of churned mud, the stumps and holes at the mid-point of a project. My nerves are more fragile. The scene at the end of the Long Walk, where we are replacing the thuja hedge, is about as dire as can be.

True, if a JCB could ever skip like a fairy (it can't) it would be one driven by my friend Andy Dunn. He could divide snowdrops with his massive bucket. He has just removed the stumps of the circle of assorted 'ferns'. I can't remember who gave this name to all conifers with ferny sprays, whether thuja, Lawson's or Leyland, but it fitted our mixed bag perfectly.

So 40-odd muddy, whiskery stumps are piled up here, a great mound of resiny logs (one touch and you're stuck) there, and he has just picked up the millstone which was the central feature and whisked it to a *rondpoint* in another part of the wood.

We now survey two unusually upright parrotias, flowering as though they were smothered in wild strawberries, a ramrod-stemmed snake-bark maple, a cherry, a huge euonymus and two tall cotoneasters, all of which form part of the circle and now stand as awkwardly as people who haven't been introduced at a party.

The next move is to dig the trenches to plant the yew hedge to form a rectangular room, ending in an apse. There will be four entrances/exits. The axial one from the Long Walk leads to a distant view of a fountain. Two transverse ones are aimed respectively at my favourite oak and a young umbrella pine. And one behind where the altar would be, as it were, leads down another alley to another distant focal point, the temple of Pisces.

The sole piece of furniture for this room is lying to one side, reminding me rather grimly of the poem about Ozymandias. It is a monolith of Welsh granite, a natural block of stone 11 feet long, 2 wide and 1 thick. We are going to erect it (he says confidently) at the meeting point of the two axes, with 8 feet of weathered grey stone, a jigsaw of pale-green, brown and almost white lichens, above ground. The yew hedge then has the challenge of catching up with it.

So far, so theoretically good. I keep forcing my imagination into overdrive to see if I've overlooked anything I won't be able to change in five years' time. I fear it may be one of those garden features that needs a long explanatory notice to stop visitors saying 'What on earth …?' I'm sure no such doubt ever crossed the minds of H Repton or L Brown.

KEEPING DRY

I am sure you have often had the same thought as you issue forth on an errand in a downpour. What did they do before they had Macintoshes – let alone Barbours and Driza-bones – to keep the rain out?

I suppose the oilskin is older – but not that old. Coachmen on Christmas cards are always buried in massive capes and coats of what I imagine is broadcloth.

Mr Macintosh floruit in the 1830s. They tell the charming story in Clermont-Ferrand that his niece was governess to one of the children who grew up to be, as it were, the Michelin man. Her uncle sent her bouncy balls for them to play with – and rubber came to the Auvergne.

Why all this? Because Rosemary Verey put me on to an exhibition at the Pitt Rivers museum in Oxford. It includes a raincoat that could have been the model for the Driza-bone (the Aussie one with a cape protecting the shoulders). It was woven from the fibres of the Chusan palm, the only palm you can grow anywhere in England (should you want to: it grows hideous with age).

The exhibition is called Braving the Elements – conserving plant fibre clothing round the world. Who knows what inspiration mac- and welly-designers may find in it?

❧ May ❧

EL NIÑO

It is hard to imagine, living in our cosseted island climate, what it feels like to be in the teeth of El Niño with no escape. A week in northern California has just enlightened me. The average annual rainfall of the Napa Valley is 24 inches. Since January this year they have had 40.

There was a mixture of sunny days and downpours (they call them showers these days) during our visit. The least drop of rain instantly flooded the saturated soil in low-lying places, but the main effect on gardens was simply that spring is (by California standards) an awful long time coming. It seemed absurd that England was at least as much in bloom as much of California.

We may have mixed feelings about magnolias in mid-March. They make me feel as I would watching troops marching towards an ambush – the frost that is bound to come. But no one can deny the bonus of balmy days when you normally expect a saw-toothed wind. *Daphne odora* is breathing sweetness through my open study window, clashing merrily with scarlet *Chaenomeles*, with daffodils and majestic crown imperials. The garden has scarcely ever looked more enticing.

But back to the mess in California. One of my favourite roads is the narrow, winding Highway One that hugs the coast north of San Francisco, following the San Andreas Fault to, shall we say, a fault. Where it skirts precipitous headlands above breakers from Hawaii exploding on rocks the size of offices, huge landslips that blocked the road for weeks were being cleared. Every 500 yards or so the road had already been remade, while the whole length of it is banked high with the mud and tree-stumps bulldozed daily to keep it open.

At one point the road dives into the calm of Tomales Bay, a long narrow slit in the coast which is actually the fault-line made visible. Trees grow to huge sizes here: groves of eucalyptus, introduced maybe 150 years ago from Australia, are already as tall as any I have seen in their native land. Coast redwoods 200 feet high are just the suckers from sawn stumps bigger than the little cabins that cluster in their dank shade.

Spring was further advanced on the coast than inland. I went to San Francisco's Golden Gate Park to see how much. The beach front was packed with families marvelling at the roaring, glittering surf. Behind the beach is a wall of Monterey cypress couchant, the only tree that, with bushes of *Arctostaphylos*, will sustain and absorb constant salt-laden wind. Within 300 yards of the ocean, Monterey pines and eucalyptus are sheltered enough to be fine straight trees. Within a mile, the Strybing Arboretum luxuriates in one of earth's most favoured gardening climates.

Spring is coloured in northern California by the deep-blue of ceanothus, by vast clumps of arum in ditches, by the congested spikes of tall echium turning purple, and in the woods by tall forget-me-nots, yellow oxalis and little *Dodecatheon*, like cyclamen-pink insects buzzing about. *Clematis montana* soars up big trees faster than old man's beard, decking them with rosy-backed white stars. Oh yes, and by the glow of oranges through the teeming rain.

THE RIGHT TO LIGHT

Why do we have to make such a meal of Leyland hedges? An Englishman's house may be his castle, but does it follow that his garden is his forest? Nobody could be less dirigiste than I am, but the simple French law that a boundary hedge may be 2 metres high and no more, without the neighbour's agreement, seems to me so sensible that if Brussels were to make it a 'directive' no reasonable gardener would kick up a fuss.

And if an obstinate neighbour plants his Leylands a bit back from the boundary? Under the same directive they become a boundary hedge just the same.

HORTUS IN URBE

It is 28 years since we gardened in London, and I admit I had forgotten the snags of city gardening until I was recently helping my daughter and son with their respective patches. Both, I am delighted to say, insist on living where they can see, smell, and even dig the earth.

Snag one, for houses without a side-passage, is of course that everything goes into, and comes out of, the garden through the house. (This was our case when we lived in Islington, and the traffic up five steps and down seven stairs included a fair amount of York stone paving.)

Snag two is no bonfire and no compost bin worth the name. A significant pruning-session – and both our new gardens-in-law needed at least that – produces rather more snaggy, thorny and even heavy wood than the council is ready to accept as household waste. Very decently, it seems to me, most councils seem ready to regard five dustbin bags or so as fair prunings – though reducing rose offcuts to the 3-inch lengths that go into a plastic bag without destroying it is a rather different branch of gardening from the kind we are used to. A real makeover of a city garden – when you finally decide to make the sycamore see reason – requires a financial understanding with the council.

On the plus side, listing and de-listing plants that are really both growable and worth growing in a small, shaded and tired garden is stimulating. Looking at neighbours' gardens (but not too hard at the Chelsea Physic Garden, which seems to have private relations with La Mortola), relatively tender plants are definitely on the list. It could be worth trying an olive, for example, and Irish hedge-type fuchsias are no problem at all.

❧ June ❧

EX CATHEDRA

Now I know what it's like to garden – or rather fail to garden – in a wheelchair. I fell and broke my Achilles tendon, in circumstances I won't bother you with, and shall have two more months to become familiar with what many people are stuck with for life. It certainly makes me realise what grit and resourcefulness a long-term wheelchair-user must have. Sticks give me more possibilities, but hardly enough to get excited about – and certainly not in this season of blessed rain and beanstalk growth, when they sink in (as does the wheelchair) at the slightest movement off piste.

The lower eye-level is interesting, but actually just adds to my frustration: the weeds are almost near enough to reach, but not quite. (Friends point out this is only a matter of time.) So far the only benefit I can identify is having a garden seat that goes with you everywhere. It invites me to stop in places I usually pass by. These moments of contemplation are often rewarding in unexpected ways – most of them suggesting jobs to be done in future.

UNDER GLASS

Chair-bound in the rain is the moment to be grateful for the conservatory. It has never in its 18 years been so vibrant with flowers or heady with their scents. Aileen is its new groom, and she has coaxed an astonishing assemblage of plants into action. April can give you the last of the winter and the first of the summer together. We only keep the frost out, so nothing is forced into bloom particularly early. But now the long suspense while the heavy-scented jasmine forms its pink buds is over: its white stars are radiant against the rather gloomy foliage of the rampaging 'chestnut' vine, *Tetrastigma voinierianum*. Thank heavens this is in a pot and not in the ground. Even from a 16-inch container it manages shoots nearly 20 feet long.

Prostanthera melissifolia, from Australia, is producing clouds of pale purple, an ideal background for bright miniature oranges. A tall *Camellia* 'Donation', which spends the rest of the year out of doors, has rather small flowers this year – but looks all the more natural and elegant for it. Around it arum lilies are craning their sleek necks.

Clivia has never produced more of its orange trumpets than it has this spring – although their colour is fading now. But regal pelargoniums are just getting into their stride (I specially like the crimson 'Lord Bute') while the pink and white ivy-leaved geraniums are still on the mission they started last year: to reach the roof, using the passion flower as their climbing frame.

A grey olive and bronze *Dodonaea* are the background trees to all this; at their feet foam marguerites, blue *Felicia*, and the very unfuchsia-like pink *Fuchsia paniculata*. It sounds like a cacophony of colour, but I can stand it.

Our pride and joy this week, though, is the most abundant flowering I have ever seen of the willowy drooping noisette rose 'Maréchal Niel'. From its modest pot it scales the weathered pediment of the inner door to the house and hangs out 50 or 60 languid creamy-yellow flowers, cleaning the heavy jasmine from the air with the smoky scent of china tea. Even more potent, but not in such quantity, is the plump dusky-pink 'Climbing Columbia', a rose so clearly scented with Turkish delight that your nose can distinguish the sugar dusting.

❧ July ❧

MONOLITH

I hope readers have not been holding their breath for the next instalment in the Tale of the Standing Stone. In April I reported on the mudbath at the end of the Long Walk here and my intention of creating a menhir for the millennium. (The millennium slant came to us later, I have to admit; but once attached is hard to throw off.)

At that point we were faced with a very horizontal slice of Welsh granite, plucked from the Rhinog mountains in Snowdonia. Its 2 tons had to be persuaded to stand to attention at the precise spot where A and B converge.

Eric Kirby and I have cobbled up many follies in the 25-odd years we have worked together at Saling, but we both felt this was the most momentous, or at least the one likeliest to stand longest – if we could get it to stand at all. Standing stones, after all, are the only things left from our earliest ancestors' efforts at landscaping.

I'd like to say that we dug ditch and ramp, employed rollers, levers and scores of extras, even Charlton Heston for the big scene. The muddy reality was a 3-foot hole in which we shuttered a concrete slot precisely tailored to the foot of the stone. A kindly farmer then contrived a sling of nylon rope (blue) with which his huge loader (yellow) dangled the monolith effortlessly over the slot and lowered it into its extremely permanent place.

The turf is now laid around, the yew hedges planted, and we are left contemplating this ancient stone, a man-and-a-half high, already looking as though it has seen civilisations come and go.

TOO MUCH TO TAKE IN

The third week of May, the ground moist and the sun warm, no frost intervening for the past eight weeks, the garden has reached a pitch of plenitude that almost makes me shout 'Stop!' There is just too much beauty to take in, too many of the loveliest moments of the loveliest plants at once to do justice to a quarter of them. I am hobbling round with a feeling close to panic at the inadequacy of my senses to cope.

There are still magnolias in flower and there is already lilac; wisteria in perfection, enfolding the flushed cream of *Rosa* 'Gloire de Dijon'; yellow asphodel is opening against a blue wall of ceanothus; purple *Abutilon vitifolium* is next to the fading orange of *Rosa* 'Maigold' and the raw scarlet of oriental poppies. Pink tulips and dicentra are giving way in the backlit border to a ripple of gold from Bowles's golden grass, *Euphorbia polychroma* and countless Welsh poppies, punctuated with purple globes of allium. In a glade of bluebells under larches the Judas tree is etched in acid pink. Soft pink deutzia and the white plates of *Viburnum plicatum* f. *tomentosum* 'Mariesii' are overarched by the wide cream saucers of *Rosa* 'Frühlingsgold'.

On a grass bank normally so parched that only cowslips thrive, they are jostled this year by massed buttercups. An old brick wall is entirely veiled in tiny toadflax. The scent of hawthorn and Queen Anne's lace hangs heavily on the air, spiked with the vanilla sweetness of *Elaeagnus*. And against the darkness of pines the slightest breeze sends a golden mist of pollen.

❧ August ❧

UNDERMINED

If any creature other than a sleek, hesitant, snuffly little mole caused such havoc in the garden there would be an outcry. Rabbits, deer (especially muntjac), squirrels and even badgers get a hostile press – at least from gardeners. But Mr (or indeed Mrs) Mole runs around digging District lines at improbable speed, uprooting plants, undermining paths, ruining lawns with scarcely a 'tut-tut' to be heard.

Having just planted 100 yards or so of new box hedge, and given it a trench of good rooting soil in a pretty barren environment, I shouldn't be surprised that the local moles took it for a new autoroute. They tunnelled under the whole thing, leaving its roots hanging like the strip lights in an underpass. In places it caved in; in others the tell-tale sign was brown box. 'You should have used mothballs' was the most sympathetic response to my chagrin.

À LA CARTE

For 23 years (yes, it's that long) I have managed to keep off the subject of food in this column. Yet what garden joy is greater than the first picking of the vegetables of early summer?

Broad beans most of all: tiny things, shirt-button size, their jackets just embryo waistcoats in a different green and their texture faintly squeaky like bluebells. Artichokes so small and tender that you could almost eat the fibrous choke, but still pick them apart, leaf by leaf, for the pleasure of anticipation as the heart is laid bare, to be smeared with mustardy mayonnaise. New potatoes so sweet and firm that their usual relegation to a mere accompaniment is absurd. They grab centre stage. Pale cabbage in its fabric-like folds, tiny cauliflowers, their curds just blanched (raw they are too noisy) and carrots as sweet as apples, but with a quieter snap.

Last night Mrs Trad put all these good things around some fillets of cod with watercress sauce and we drank her brother's dry white wine from far away on the Suffolk border. It was good to be at home.

❧ September ❧

A SOFT SUMMER

I am beginning to think of this as our Scottish summer. We are certainly gardening in the softest conditions: a sprinkle or more of rain every 24 hours has brought the grass to that powerful green that has (I am told, and I am inclined to believe it) an effect on the psyche. Can you get angry, or even excited, surrounded by an emerald world? I am just lulled into thinking that all's well – until another 7-foot sow-thistle brings me back to reality with a start. Even weeding, though, becomes soothing when the roots come out with their hands up.

With no hot sunshine, each flower's lease of life is doubled. Some roses have stayed buoyant for four weeks before succumbing to brown-head. And a curious thing: some that usually change colour fleetingly before they disintegrate have gone the whole way. 'Wedding Day', which after 15 years or so has arranged itself like a bridal train, fanning out into every extremity of an old pear tree, has gradually turned entirely pink, a sort of crushed-raspberry, rising behind the grey-brown purple smoke-bush from old Mr Barcock's Suffolk nursery (RIP). Perhaps this happens in Scotland every year.

WHATEVER NEXT?

As we head for the third millennium, the urge to sum up the past and present and to crystal-gaze about the next century is inevitable. Try as I might, though, I confess to very hazy notions about what will be considered the typical garden of the early 21st century. Contemporary taste is shooting about in all directions, with ecology pulling one way, nostalgia another, and plantsmanship pursuing its own way down the middle.

If you can judge anything by the advertisements in this and other gardening magazines, the pull of the past has never been stronger. *Topiarius* is Latin for a gardener, and seems to be heading that way again. Box has been the plant of the decade so far, in all its manifestations as hedge, ball, lollipop or corkscrew. To go with the box every sort of garden hardware, from bench to statue to paving to conservatory, via pot, pool, fountain and urn, has become the focus of advertisers – so presumably of gardeners' increasingly impressive budgets, too.

THE LONG AND SHORT OF IT

Flowery meads are everywhere these days: grass unmown until after seeding is another of the themes of our time. What is sometimes forgotten is that if long grass needs one thing to set it off it is short grass. Only contrasts gives both long and short their full value.

Mowing a path in the rough is one of the quickest and most satisfying ways to make a garden picture. And you can do it in different places in different seasons, altering the shape and perspective of the garden each time.

I have been experimenting on a rough bank crowned by pine trees overlooking a little pond (the 'Red Sea', to anyone who knows the garden at Saling – except that now, since we had to line it with bitumen, we tend to call it the 'Black Sea'). I have mown two paths each 5 feet wide, and photographed them in different lights. I know that when I look at them in a year or two's time I shall be pushed to recognise that they were in my garden at all.

One garden trick that is beautifully practised at the Prieuré Notre Dame d'Orsan in the Berry is to create a false barrier. They mow a path, then put an elegantly transparent hurdle across it. Of course you could easily walk round it, but the psychological pull-and-push of inviting your steps and then barring them is oddly potent. The simplest contrivance can change a garden mood.

DREAMING SPIRES

I am sure I'm not the only one to have a plant I fantasise about growing, highly desirable but just out of reach. Mine is the echium, the king of the borages, and especially its magnificent Canary Islands species *Echium pininana*.

They were the stars of the show at Glyndebourne this season – at least outdoors. Opera-goers climbing the slope to the north front of the new opera house, through the wonderfully lush and imaginative planting (with such theatrically-leaved extravagance as *Arundo donax*, bamboos, bananas and the castor-oil plant) were stopped in their tracks by the glorious 10-foot echium spires of summer-sky blue.

I had to ask Chris Hughes, the Head Gardener, how he pulled off such a coup. Not without stage management, I was told. They take two years to build up to flowering, from seed sown in autumn in a cool greenhouse, the seedlings planted out next spring at about a foot high. By next autumn their splendid silvery rosettes have risen to about 3 feet high and wide.

At this stage engineering comes into it. Each plant is surrounded by a metal frame, which has to be extensible to support a covering of fleece: over the top in fine weather, all around when it turns frosty or snowy. The plant grows through the winter, so the frame has to grow with it. By late April it is the mighty 10-foot spike, ready to flower. By late May it is in full glory, a blue beacon for all the butterflies from miles around.

Robert Browning must have seen an echium when he wrote: 'Ah, but a man's reach should exceed his grasp, or what's a heaven for?'

PS How the climate has changed. We reached flowering E. pininana *in 2008. Heaven is now properly ripe tomatoes.*

❧ October ❧

LAISSEZ FAIRE

Foresters call it 'regen' – short for regeneration. It simply means seeds of your chosen and desirable plants (or trees) sowing themselves and turning an artificial plantation into a semi-natural one. It is hugely satisfying (and saves lots of money) when it happens generously in the right place at the right time. A lawn of oak or fir seedlings is a stirring sight – to a forester at least.

'Regen' is always going on in gardens – I'm not speaking of weeds – but nearly always, it seems to me, adding a layer of complication the gardener doesn't need. It is exciting (somehow slightly flattering too) when a choice geranium, a dicentra, a salvia and, last year, a yucca volunteers. But how to react when it has put down roots in a satisfying swathe of irises or agapanthus? It is an interloper. It puts out your careful planning, jars the harmony: it must go. But must it? 'A sweet disorder in the dress' is delectable. What a parade-ground mentality you must have for a wayward charmer to give you offence.

This is the story of my gardening life: I don't dig up the wanderer, I enjoy it. Another comes along: a different whim. I would never have thought X and Y could look so fetching together and in no time at all I've lost the plot.

Good gardens are ones where order, harmony and good planning are clearly visible. Great gardens are ones where they are guided by genius and lubricated by perspiration. And gardens where good intentions are set aside to enjoy a spot of 'regen' are, I'm afraid, a mess.

❧ November ❧

DOG DAYS

The French word is *canicule*, the Italian *canicola*. We say, though admittedly not very often, the dog days. Sirius, the Dog Star, is in the ascendant through July and the first half of August. If it is going to get seriously hot it is – it certainly was this year – towards the end of Sirius's ascendancy.

In the centre of France there were three days hotter than 103°F, or 40°C, cooling at night to a mere 95°F or so. Any Texan reading this will scoff: in Dallas last summer the thermometer stayed above 100°F for 50 consecutive days. But the 100°F mark does seem to be critical to the well-being of all sorts of plants, as well as the comfort of human beings. Well below this temperature leaves stop transpiring in self-defence. Our neighbour with a

Jersey herd tells me that grass stops growing at 30°C (about 86°F) whether it rains or not.

In August this year not only did grass look completely dead – the fields an even sandy colour with only deep-rooting weeds, tree suckers and, of course, brambles growing – but the south and west sides of mature oak trees were grilled by the sun. I suppose when leaves stop transpiring they lose their cooling mechanism. If we couldn't sweat we would be in the same predicament. What then makes the difference between individual trees? In a row of oaks some were crisped, others stayed green. And elms under precisely the same conditions seemed not to wilt at all.

Horse chestnuts turning squirrel-brown are a common sight at the end of any summer. Having made their big coarse leaves all in one go in April, with their sticky buds ready for next year, they have no way of refreshing themselves, as most plants do, with new summer shoots. This year, though, one of ours, virtually defoliated in *la canicule*, made what seems to me the extremely rash move of shooting again in September. By mid-September it was actually in flower. I'm afraid the chances of its making new buds in winter to leaf again in spring are slim. Should the coroner return a verdict of suicide?

Even stranger to see was our hilltop pond, whose floating layer of algae turned bright-red in the burning sun, then at sunset – and even by day in the shade of a willow – turned bright-green. The traffic-light effect was so striking that we invited friends to come and watch the lights change.

THE MANNA BORN

This is the best mushroom season we have ever seen in Essex. Every morning a fresh profusion of parasols and field mushrooms and ink-caps has greeted us. But by far the most spectacular are the puffballs, which begin golf-ball size gleaming in the rough, then over the course of a few days inflate themselves into footballs or even bigger. At the mid-size their size, shape and colour are disconcertingly like a weathered skull emerging from the soil. We have even taken to calling them Yoricks.

What is the record weight for a puffball? We have just weighed one at 2 kg (4½ lb). Slicing it into creamy curdy rounds, far too big for a frying pan, with a gleaming cleaver is a strangely sensuous experience, releasing the sweetest of mushroom smells. In the pan they rapidly absorb olive oil and butter, a little garlic and parsley and very little salt to make a sumptuous dish with a texture approaching a pancake. In combination with the more melting parasols they approach the sublime. Ink-caps picked young, on the other hand, rapidly deliquesce on a plate into a pool of jet-black liquid which, with some brown bread mixed in, makes a dramatic – and dramatically-rich – black soup.

What mysterious food. Manna is surely the proper word.

❧ December ❧

PLACE AND PURPOSE

Each time I visit my brother, who lives, paints and gardens in the hills of the Maremma, the southern edge of Tuscany, I feel the sort of primal tug of Italian gardens. What is it about steps and terraces, about gardening with the grain of steep slopes, that appeals so deeply? Partly it is the imperative of conforming to the landscape. Partly it is the very predictability of the main ingredients: silver olive, dark cypress, mounding rosemary and lavender.

In Britain we are seeing a swing away from the purely picture-making, colourist tradition of English gardening (broadly speaking, the school of Jekyll). The first beneficiary seems to be a more structured look, whether expressed in rows of cabbages and corn or alleys of cypresses, orchard rows or straight purposeful lines of any sort. The second is the pseudo-ecological sort of soft planting typified by Piet Oudolf – second because it is much harder to bring off with conviction.

The main casualty will be the mini-landscape of most everyday English gardens, amoeba shapes in plastic ponds and island beds, compositions that depend for their credibility on managing to not see over the fence.

I was walking round a much-medalled new housing development the other day, fascinated and appalled at the same time to see how references to such a ragbag of traditions, in building materials and styles, in fake manors, lodges, farmhouses and anything-but-terraces, are glued together only by roundabouts and rumble-strips – the paraphernalia of traffic.

Some of the gardens are small, others tiny, but almost none, I thought, a sensible and usable shape. They are simply buffers to fill with little trees, bushes and flowers from the garden centre next to the supermarket. Despite lavish structural planting: avenues, cotoneastered roundabouts, public planters everywhere … the prospects for visual coherence or harmony are nil.

Now if someone had dared to call the whole site The Orchard, or The Pinewood, or even Tuscany, and plant it accordingly, both the main directions of modern gardening would have been achieved together. It would be structured and it would have an ecological starting point.

1999

❧ January ❧

BEAR IN MIND

One morning in November the Japanese maples, having held their leaves far longer than usual, finally let them go. They changed colour late too, I suppose gorged with rain and with no cold nights to signal time. Their brief blaze, though, was as wonderful as ever. They seem to generate their own inner light, even on a gloomy day: the yellow, orange and scarlet ones much more so, of course, than the deeper reds.

It seems a pathetically inadequate response to rush for one's camera in the face of such beauty. Better to take out a chair and sit all morning, watch the rime dissolve on the lacy incandescence of leaves, the sun sparkle on the water-drops, shifting the shadows from branch to branch, a leaf falling, then another, on to a lower layer until the combined weight releases a little shower. The pattern of the shower on the grass .... Better to store these pictures as memories to replay in some beauty-less place, shutting your eyes on the Northern line.

We were talking the other day about garden lighting. Apparently it is a smash at Westonbirt: 40,000 people turned up for the show. I am a fan; not for an elaborate set-up putting the whole garden, as it were, in evening dress, but just a plain discretionary spotlight to reveal what is usually hidden: the branch structure of one tree in particular.

It should not be routine: no photocell to turn it on every evening. That just adds to the light pollution. One of the best times to be in the garden is as it disappears in the dusk. Its dawn unveiling, I fear, is a less familiar sight.

THERE COMES A TIDE

The moon gets no mention in *The RHS Dictionary of Gardening*. Nor do lunar phases. Unless I have missed some other reference, the masterwork of horticultural convention skips the whole subject. Gardening manuals of our ancestors, though, were quite punctilious about it. Whether you look it up in Pliny or Thomas Tusser, every garden operation allegedly goes better with the moon in the appropriate phase.

The broadest application of the logic of lunar influence could simply be called tidal. Garden (or farm) operations that relate to growth are best done with the moon waxing towards the full orb. Planting-out and grafting are, quite reasonably, said to benefit from the flow of sap rising. If seeds germinate with a waxing moon it is not absurd to suppose that their initial growth will benefit.

The waning moon, by this argument, is the time for jobs that call for a reduced flow of sap – of which pruning is the most obvious. And I have asked joiners whose work demands perfect timber: they seem unanimous in believing that trees should be felled between the full and the new moon, when 'the sap is down'.

These ideas (and there are plenty more, including many flat contradictions) have more currency today than when the RHS dictionary was compiled. The biodynamic movement is also waxing, and minds that are open to the quieter murmurings of the universe are not likely to ignore something so obviously potent, and so easily charted, as the moon that moves the oceans.

The problem lies in the interpretation. The book I have here, and that inspires these thoughts, is admirably candid about the manifest muddle of folklore. It is a gardener's calendar for 1999 called *Planting by the Moon*. The introductory half of the book is a bizarre mixture of astrology and horticultural common sense. The second half sets out in diary form the astrological year and its possible implications for gardeners – right down to mornings on which it is best to do nothing at all.

THE BOUNTIFUL CAPE

If you are as forgetful as I am about the management of plants leading an artificial existence under glass, you will often be surprised by their flowering out of turn.

I certainly set out to populate the conservatory with agreeable flowering companions. It rubs along nicely through the summer mainly on diverse pelargoniums – wonderfully diverse, as they scramble up vines or erupt in endless bouquets in soft-pink, crimson, white and scarlet.

August is the time when streptocarpus pours forth incredible quantities of flowers, lilac and white, going on into November. This year they were joined by clivias, ignoring their schedule (the book tells them to flower in spring) to put up their clustered orange trumpets, just as we have seen them do in the Cape, among the Cape primroses. At Kirstenbosch there is a shady stream with banks that are memorably painted by this combination.

Indeed with a few exceptions (passion flowers, acacias, oleanders and lots of salvias) the Cape's contribution to this conservatory, from pelargonium on, is paramount.

February

LUSITANIA

It was raining when we visited Portugal in November. The hills of Sintra between Lisbon and the Atlantic, and further north the 500-metre humpback of Bussaco, are famous for their year-round greenness. Atlantic fogs roll round them in most seasons. But in November they were replenishing their tanks.

The gardens of Monserrate at Sintra have been in the news recently. After years of neglect this creation of several English hands (most famously William Beckford's) over two centuries is being restored by the Portuguese government with, it appears, a fairly long purse. The house, Mogul-inspired with touches of Brighton's Royal Pavilion, is being rebuilt, and work is starting on the gardens.

Their most notable feature is Beckford's series of naturalistic waterfalls, prodigious in scale and remarkably convincing. Monserrate has neither the botanical riches nor the sublime setting of La Mortola, with the maritime Alps above and the Mediterranean at its feet. It deserves, though, to be considered its Portuguese opposite number. The long lawn falling from the house into a deep valley dramatises the surrounding forest in a way that only an English eye would have conceived.

At Bussaco the British connection is purely military. On its ridge Wellington won his first serious victory over a Napoleonic army. The many reasons for a visit start with the mist-wrapped hill and its much-loved trees. They were collected, planted and tended by the barefoot monks of the Carmelite convent now dwarfed by Europe's most weirdly wonderful hotel, a Manueline confection of heroic maritime fantasies to make your head swim.

November is scarcely the ideal time to explore these awe-inspiring woods, but one path we took lodges firmly in my mind. From the base of a tremendous *Eucalyptus regnans*, the Tasmanian 'mountain ash', surely Europe's most magnificent, a path follows a brook down a winding ravine. Lined on each side are tall white hydrangeas, their flowers now faded and wan, and white arums, just opening their ivory chalices. Gardening can be picture-making. It can also be poetry.

❧ March ❧

PLAYING WITH WATER

Isn't it called the butterfly effect – the idea that the very faintest motion can have dramatic eventual consequences apparently out of all proportion to the original energy involved? Anyone who takes the same childish delight as I do in playing with water may prefer an alternative version. I call it the leaf in the river.

The other day I was fooling about in an abandoned leet at what was once a gold mine in north Wales, trying to muster enough flow to reach the ruins where once the water drove an overshot wheel powering an ore-crusher. Musing as one does when the hands are busy but the mind idle, I watched a single brown beech leaf snag on a wisp of root from the bank; then two stuck together, an oak leaf, some pine needles, a tiny twig became involved, and already the slim stream was being turned aside. At this point a heavy raindrop would have demolished the incipient dam. But random accretions like this, starting with a speck, are what alter the courses of rivers. Eventually perhaps the boundaries of nations.

I lifted a handful of leaves and twigs from the stream-bed and the pent-up water gushing pushed as much again before it. A minute later and 5 yards further on a watery gleam appeared, swelled, dislodged a few leaves and the process repeated itself ….

I didn't reach the old mill ruins. My stream suddenly disappeared into the ground. But what an afternoon I had, tinkering with primal forces.

EVER-REDDISH

Enjoying the sparkling January sunshine, with the primroses popping, hellebores opening their pale rosy cups, day lily leaves already surging lime-green from the ground, the pearls of pussy-willow and crowns of birches and alders darkening with catkins, a thought struck me. We have no end of evergreens, plenty of evergreys in shades from cypress-blue to the dusty parchment of Jerusalem sage, no shortage – indeed a surplus – of evergolds in holly, elaeagnus and golden conifers, but no shrub or tree with red leaves that keeps them through the winter. I can only think of the far-from-brilliant *Dodonaea* in the conservatory.

The wax-red stems of willow and dogwood prove how valuable an ever-red would be. Any ideas?

ODOURS OF EDOM

Mrs Trad has just put a vase of winter sweet, witch hazel and winter honeysuckle branches in the hall and the scent is worth walking a mile to see – as a Dubliner once said the smell of the Liffey wasn't.

The breath of curry from the kitchen caught me as I was inhaling the midwinter bouquet: a combination so exotic that a perfumer could bottle it as Harem Water.

❧ April ❧

TIME TO PONDER

The wandering American anglophile Bill Bryson wrote somewhere that if he were ever offered a peerage (and I can think of much worse ideas) he would call himself Lord Lather of Indecision.

I remembered his remark wryly as I was pruning vines the other day, puzzling over their twiggy black tangles against the snow. To cut this branch or that, the vigorous shoot with long internodes or the knotty two-year-old peppered with buds that has hardly budged, the timid shoot correctly aligned with the wires or the bold one shooting out of the row at 45 degrees.

At the start, if I let myself, I could stare at each vine for five minutes before chopping. But after half a row the decisions seem less momentous. Eliminating rogue shoots becomes almost automatic; even a cut instantly regretted is soon forgotten in the pleasure of progress – and the certainty that you'll be passing this way again … and again.

There are two ways of working: either make all the cuts and move straight on to the next vine, leaving the disentangling stage for later (or even, perish the thought, for someone else). Or unravel the previous year's complexities as you go, prise the tendrils off the wires and find yourself like Laocoon with the serpents, a flailing prisoner of endless whippy, snaggy, snaking shoots.

The advantage of Plan B is that you can see where you've been, and cut out the real quandaries oneses b' oneses (as my Durham forebears used to say). Yes, you can go quietly potty out there between the silent barricades in the snow.

DOWN SOUTH

So far the piece of Spanish moss I brought back to the conservatory looks unaltered: grey, inert, like a cross between barbed wire and a dishcloth. If I were it, I would be dead of a broken heart, having been stolen far from my element as the adornment of immense spreading oaks to be hung on a vine on a conservatory wall.

Spanish moss is the signature of the Deep South. We were in South Carolina, on a plantation near Charleston where slaves used to weed the rice-paddies along the Sampit river, now massively and almost ineradicably invaded by reeds. The economic activity these days is forestry and shooting: loblolly and longleaf pines in immaculate plantations, the underbrush carefully burned at regular intervals to give quail the conditions they like best.

Around the white-porticoed mansion the 'live' (in other words, evergreen) oaks, *Quercus virginiana*, grow to such preposterous girth and reach that even 50 yards apart they form a moss-hung canopy over the emerald lawns. The brilliance of the grass in January puzzled me until I realised that it is sown afresh in autumn, lives through the winter and dies in the seriously hot summer – hence is never mown. The monumental, dark, grey-green trees in a spring-green lawn are bewilderingly beautiful.

Against the house is a little formal brick-walled and brick-pathed camellia garden with a central fountain. This is a winter house; there is no summer garden. Pink petals are thick on the plants, the paths and beds. An intensely, piercingly scented *Osmanthus* with minuscule flowers lines the path to the front door. Along the drive deer have eaten most of the azalea buds and, oddly, the ground-covering ivy. And that black log among the swamp cypress roots in the serpentine lake is an alligator.

PS See *Darling Buds of May, page 122, for the happy ending.*

❧ May ☙

EVER-REDDISH (CONTINUED)

There was pretty much of a consensus among the readers who kindly wrote, following my March query, to suggest plants with red leaves in winter: there aren't many, and only a couple are guaranteed winter-long. Though there are quite a few more plants that turn ruddy in the cold.

Cryptomeria japonica Elegans Group, that oddly floppy and spectacularly misnamed conifer, is certainly one. Several correspondents wrote about the doorstep plant of Japan, *Nandina domestica*, a botanical curiosity related to berberis but more like a bamboo to look at. The cultivar called 'Fire Power' can turn bright-red in autumn and stay incandescent all winter. Sadly, though, it is a squat little thing beside its genuinely elegant parents.

Presumably it is just coincidence that the other plant most mentioned by readers is (at least until a new taxonomy based on DNA throws us all back into confusion) another berberis of sorts, *Mahonia* x *wagneri* 'Moseri'. I've certainly mentioned this most graceful member of its tribe before, enthusing about its pink and cream spring shoots, lasting well into summer, borne aloft like butterflies on its many slender stems. The red pigment does last all winter, rosy-apple red, though not making a substantial mass.

More substantial, but more of a deep shining copper, is *Mahonia aquifolium* (I wonder about this; its leaves are a different shape and texture) 'Atropurpurea'. The low suckering ground-cover species, *M. nervosa*, with perhaps the best leaves of all, takes on touches of scarlet in the cold.

Photinia x *fraseri* 'Red Robin' has its champions, too. Strictly speaking what is red about it is its spring shoots, not its winter foliage. But admittedly they shoot very early. Others mentioned the reddish forms of phormium, New Zealand flax.

And among perennials in winter, red pigments are more or less a feature of some begonias, of *Heuchera americana* and *Tiarella cordifolia*. But that seems to be about it.

❧ June ☙

A BACKWARD GLANCE

Two weeks of warm sunny weather in early April (last year it was almost equally mild, but rainy) brought on growth and blossom prime for last night's inevitable frost. It was not a hard one: just enough to prostrate the tulips, blacken magnolia petals, scorch walnut leaves as they were starting to unfurl, wilt the proud plumage of *Aralia elata* and leave apparently random scorching in the border. But it set me thinking how the warmer and earlier springs apparently in prospect are probably the reverse of a cheerful outlook for gardeners. The earlier the leaf is coaxed from the bud the greater the chance that a nippy night will cry 'Gotcha!'

Global warming was not an expression they used at the first millennium, but it was certainly an experience they shared with us. I am reading *The Year 1000*, a scholarly, lucid and lively account by Robert Lacey and Danny Danziger of life 999 years ago, based on the Julius Work Calendar of Canterbury Cathedral.

Between about 950 and 1300 AD Edinburgh, we are told, enjoyed the climate of London today, and London that of the Loire valley. (In the middle of this period the Cistercians, a splinter group of Benedictine monks, founded their order and set about perfecting the wines of Burgundy – in conditions considerably more benign, it seems, than those of today.)

I was also fascinated to learn from this little book that the 'hungry gap' before the harvest in August, when that of the previous year was either used up or growing mouldy, drove the poor to eat whatever they could forage. Their bread, such as it was, could include poppies and hemp, and rye on which flowering ergot had produced LSD. The result was the sort of spaced-out village fêtes painted in such detail by Brueghel the Elder.

It helps to bring into focus the revolutionary importance of the potato, when it arrived from America 500 years later, to remember that our ancestors had to wait until after midsummer to bring in an edible harvest.

NAME THAT PONG

Rummaging around with my bare hands in the undergrowth in April, as the explosion of sheep's parsley and its jungle friends induces a mixture of panic and ecstasy, I find one plant whose touch sets off the sensation of summer. The rank pungency of hedge woundwort, *Stachys sylvatica*, that dead-nettle so fleet of runner that (at least in damp places) it could cross a motorway in the rush hour, has more evocative power than the honeysuckle of warm June evenings.

Looking round for a way to describe this clinging, unmistakable smell I hit on Sauvignon Blanc, picked half-ripe by a none-too-hygienic vintner. A couple of years ago we were struggling to define wine smells by reference to plants. Now the boot is on the other foot.

❧ July ❧

BUDGE OVER

The summer bedding is all ready to go out: cosmos and tobacco, marguerites, white mallows and dusky purple salvias. But where? The borders have closed up; hardly a chink of open ground volunteers.

This is a moment for resolution. My self-sown favourites must give way: poppies and sweet rocket, love-in-a-mist and columbines, violas and alliums are in for strict editing. Alstroemerias invading from their proper billet half a bed away, flopping boughs of Jerusalem sage, over-exuberant vinca and *Epimedium* are for the chop.

Flowery cheerfulness after midsummer depends on the prodigal persistence of plants that have only a short summer to enjoy. Room must be found.

NIGHT WATCH

A country gardener who can drag himself indoors before dark on a clear night in May or June is no gardener at all. I might have said before midnight: in the lingering dusk, and with any hint of a moon, your eyes adapt to perceive shapes and your ears grow stalks.

Once the commuters, tractors, mowers and strimmers have turned in for the evening, all is quiet until the pub closes and its car park empties. It takes half an hour for peace to return to the lanes, but by then you can hear a worm burying leaves. We have no insistent background night noises like the crickets of Italy or the frogs of France to baffle our ears. The little clatter of a fountain does no more than structure the silence.

This year the moonlight patrol reveals an unprecedented snail population. Very quiet, our snails. Heaven knows what it is like in the dark of the borders: the box hedges are encrusted with them and the paths crunchy underfoot.

In early May it was nightingales: to descant on their song is just to prove how lamely words limp after music. Last night it was courting hedgehogs who made most noise: something between a snuffle and a snort repeated excitedly and endlessly – I think only by the female, wheeling about to face her circling suitor snout to snout. A second feller nipped across the lawn, then tactfully backed off – or so it seemed to this voyeur.

The night garden is marked out into zones of fragrance. As you move from one to another scents blend, but one is usually dominant. In May here the vanilla sweetness of *Elaeagnus umbellata* dominates, until an azalea adds a sharper note or honeysuckle insinuates its emotive breath.

You cross thresholds of temperature and humidity too, not always easy to account for. It is colder in the shallow valley in the arboretum, warmer and damper (and darker) under a spreading tree. But sometimes a chill patch is as unexplained as a ghost. I move from seat to seat in the vastness of the dark, more alive than one can ever be amid the distractions of the light.

WHY NOT HERE?

We have tried planting them deep and tried them shallow. We have tried gravel, clay, rubble and even water. But *Romneya*, those most ethereal white poppies of the American west, won't grow in this garden. Our best effort was a diminutive clump, yellowish in leaf rather the proper glaucous green, facing west at the foot of a sandy bank. It flowered sparsely and was dead in five years.

Up the road, in Great Bardfield, the painter John Aldridge had them pushing up through his terrace, and even the brick floor of the cellar, inside the house.

Graham Stuart Thomas in *Perennial Garden Plants* does acknowledge that they are 'tricky to divide and best established by means of well-rooted pot plants'. Tried that. 'Any deep and somewhat retentive soil' describes ours to a tee. Perhaps someone who is being elbowed out of their living quarters by rampant *Romneya* could give us some further instruction.

EUROTUNNEL

Your English and your French mole keep different timetables. I learnt this from Jeremy Bremridge of the Professional Gardeners' Guild. While French moles, I was told, work a six-hour cycle, checking the earthworks at six, noon and six, ours do four-hour shifts, more like naval watches. The times to meet face-to-face with an English mole are eight in the morning, noon and just before tea at four o'clock.

Euromole time is therefore noon, and gardeners who can steel themselves to it should stand stock-still, spade in hand, within range of a fresh molehill (decapitated in preparation) at the appointed hour. Stillness is essential.

I leave it to you to decide what to do when the little gentleman in the velvet waistcoat pops his head over the parapet. But happily there is a less violent alternative. We are testing a 'sonic device': a torch-like object, a foot or so long buried vertically in the ground, whose batteries produce an intermittent buzz at a pitch moles are supposed to dislike. So far, six weeks on, they are still discouraging ünterlopers from entering restricted areas.

Napoleon's mother had a favourite expression that perfectly covers the situation – and many others: '*Pourvu que ça dure.*' (It needs a heavy Corsican accent for full effect.) Translation? 'Fingers crossed.'

PS It took more than that. See March 2000, page 134

❧ August ❧

DIRECTIVE NEEDED

Among innumerable delicate questions of European culture (and on which no doubt Brussels will soon issue a 'directive') the colour of your asparagus, green or white, is one of the more troubling.

The French regard thick creamy-white stalks, earthed-up in the sandy soil of Cavaillon, the Loire, or the Sologne, as the proper thing. Their artificial appearance must have appealed to the 19th-century creators of *la cuisine classique*, when everything had to look like something else.

The Spanish not only seem to agree about the colour, they frequently distance their gross white digits even further from nature by canning them – a certain way to bring out their inherent bitterness.

In Italy it depends where you are. As Jane Grigson points out in her admirable *Vegetable Book*, Venetians prize the white asparagus of Bassano while the Milanese prefer it green, from Varese near the Swiss border.

I have not done a hand-count, but I suspect the British on the whole agree with the Milanese. Green asparagus has more flavour, is less bitter, and is certainly far more beautiful than white. To earth it up and blanch it seems a waste of time, almost a perversion.

I was talking to an organic asparagus-grower the other day in the market in central France where she stood behind trays of the white stuff, delicately purple-tipped. Did she ever, I asked her, allow nature its way to the extent of cutting green asparagus? 'Oh yes,' she answered, 'but it's already gone ten. You must come first thing if you want it green.' Ah, the mysterious laws of supply and demand.

Further discussion, though, produced another possible explanation for the supposed superiority of the denatured variety. It produces less of that characteristic smell.

ELUSIVE BLUE NOTE

I don't suppose there is soil much more acid anywhere than in part of our wood in France. The pH drops well below 4, even to 3·5. One plant that loves these extreme conditions, oddly enough, is holly. Oaks grow well there but birch seems short-lived and even the heather is unenthusiastic.

When I took soil from here, then, to fill three old stone troughs to grow hydrangeas, I expected the sort of electric blue that makes you look with alarm in your driving mirror. The chap to read on hydrangeas is Michael Haworth-Booth. His *Effective Flowering Shrubs*, though nearly 50 years old, is still the Hydrangea Bible. His account of the hybrid lacecap he named 'Blue Wave' is enough to send anyone racing to a nursery: hardy, reliable, wide-spreading, late- and long-flowering, and blue as a summer sky.

Not, however, in this soil of mine. They are flowering magnificently (though much earlier than Haworth-Booth says. They started in May). But their colour range is mauve to lavender, with the outer ray-florets closer to white.

I can, of course, and probably will, experiment with aluminium sulphate, the standard recipe for 'blueing'. But in soils as acid as ours the available aluminium should, I'm told, already be at a level lethal to most plants. Have I been sold 'Mauve Wave' after all?

Frustrated by hydrangeas, I am minded to turn to artificial means to play the blue note. One of the enduring images of the dreamy garden of Ninfa, near Rome, is the almost surreal blue orchard, where the trunks of the trees are stained copper-sulphate blue by being sprayed many times with Bordeaux Mixture.

Mixing slaked lime with copper sulphate makes it soluble so that it sticks to the leaves. The recipe was apparently invented in Bordeaux as an all-purpose vineyard spray. It remains in use because copper in solution is an effective destroyer of both harmful fungi and bacteria.

Its authorised use in the UK these days is limited to treating potato and tomato blight, peach leaf curl and bacterial canker on fruit (or I suppose any) trees. Its mildew-fighting properties could of course tempt you to turn your roses blue, too. This seems to be against the rules. But the blue orchard is something one could look into.

DARLING BUDS OF MAY

Perhaps the least sensational floral event of the year has been the flowering of the Spanish moss – trophy from South Carolina – in the conservatory.

Other bromeliads may make you gasp and rub your eyes, but Spanish moss is not given to flamboyant display. The *RHS Dictionary* (where you will find it under *Tillandsia usneoides*) is mildly excited about its petals: '9–11 mm, pale-blue or chartreuse green, narrow'. Yes, green for a day or two, but chartreuse is coming on a bit strong, and the whole aspect of this most mournful plant in flower scarcely changes. It just looks untidier than ever.

Excitement comes with germination. Suddenly, in the water tank below the *Tetrastigma* (itself not the most hilarious plant) where it hangs, fresh threads of grey-green appear. A young *Tillandsia* is born into all the hurly-burly of epiphytic life.

✻ September ✻

IN THE BOX

I wonder how many gardeners are calling this the Year of the Snail. Not that slugs have been (how do I put it?) sluggish, but my mention of snails in July seems to have acted as an invitation. They have shinned up the stems of lilies, thalictrum … all sorts of tall plants that they might as well have felled at ground level. But then their feast would be shared in the common pot. Recently I have seen snails high up on poplar trees.

Am I just being fanciful in seeing a link between the snail surge and the current fashion for box? More box has been planted in more gardens recently than for many years. At Chelsea it was *archi-chic*. Balls, pyramids, corkscrews, hedges and whole parterres are the (very expensive) dernier cri. And apparently it provides just the sort of quarters snails like best.

ACTS OF ADMIRATION

In July we spent a nostalgic afternoon in the tiny Fry Gallery at Saffron Walden with its summer exhibition of Edwin Smith's garden photographs. Edwin Smith was the last master of black-and-white garden photography before we were all swept away in a polychromatic tide.

He illustrated Peter Coats's *Great Gardens* in 1963, Edward Hyam's *The English Garden* in 1964 and *English Cottage Gardens* in 1967. He worked with a big 'bellows' camera taking half-plates, the quality of which remain impressive. His great gift, though, as it seems to me, was to capture views, and often intimate details, in a way that influenced garden appreciation for at least a generation. His 'acts of admiration', as he called them, whether of majestic French garden architecture, Italy's splashing fountains or a glimpse through an open lattice of a cottage garden seem to define the mood that led to the conservation movement. The Garden History Society was founded in 1965.

The Fry Gallery is a little gem, the only permanent collection of paintings by the Bardfield School, artists of the 1940–60s who lived in north Essex, including Edward Bawden, Eric Ravilious and John Aldridge. (John Nash lived further east, near Ipswich.) It stands at the entrance to the mysterious Bridge End Gardens, a high-Victorian creation teetering on the edge of survival, but for those afflicted by garden nostalgia an essential visit. May Edwin Smith's shade protect them.

PS Bridge End Gardens have been restored, are open to the public, and are well worth a visit.

BORECAST

Gardeners and sailors are weather-forecast addicts. Sailors get a regular, responsible, comprehensive and comprehensible service from the BBC. But the rest of us have to put up with utter rubbish, with 'expert meteorologists' systematically talking down to us as though we couldn't distinguish a westerly from a bar of soap.

Why do we have to put up with muddled thinking in excruciating English? Why not a clear, predictable, region-by-region forecast? Yes, the weather in these islands is complicated. All the more reason, then, to talk about it in an adult, organised way. If news-writers wrote the weather forecast at least we wouldn't miss a passing reference to our own region because we had nodded off with boredom.

❧ October ❧

WALLS WITHIN WALLS

Sometimes you see a simple garden idea that you would love to borrow (or indeed steal) but which you just can't apply to your own patch. For years I have loved the garden of Gloria Birkett's Sussex farmhouse for her inspired plantswomanship. But the idea I am tempted to try to copy is a wall straight across the front, only 6 feet from the house, perhaps 3 feet high, to form, as it were, one big window box to the whole facade.

I suppose the original purpose was to keep the pigs at arm's length. The effect is to provide a double shelter for the wall plants and anything growing in this long, narrow south-facing alley. I'm convinced some of the plants think they are in a conservatory. Echiums, forsooth!

The front of the house is hardly visible for tender shrubs, vines and, round the door, of all desirable things, *Rosa bracteata*, the 'Macartney' rose. It has dark, shiny, roundish leaves, cistus-like pure white flowers and hips that form as the petals fall, their leafy bracts still surrounding them. From inside the house, you look out through the vines directly on to a near-barricade of exotic leaves and flowers.

I have thought long and hard about applying the same idea, building a waist-high wall, to our French farmhouse. It would certainly improve both a rather stark facade and the open view. But the French stymie themselves from ever really indulging in wall plants. Every French house has shutters, and shutters do not mix (or rather do mix, much too closely) with wall plants of any kind.

EAST, WEST ...

It has been years since we have spent all August at home. I'm not sure why we slipped into the lemming-pattern of going away at the same time as everyone else. School holidays may once have been the reason, long ago. But this year we weighed the thought of queues and jams against the tranquillity that settles at home in August, a silent telephone and an insignificant post, while the vegetable garden reaches its productive climax. There was no contest.

It is about the third week of the month that the garden perceptibly changes gear. Roses are ready for a second or third flowering. The Michaelmas daisies are just breaking cover. By early September new groups of colours have radically changed the garden picture. Two of my favourites at the moment are both tricolour, and both involve salvias. One is the lush carmine of *S. involucrata* 'Bethellii', in its second year a yard high and wide, mingling with the palest-cream flowers of the hybrid musk rose 'Moonlight', and the daily-increasing blue of *Caryopteris* x *clandonensis*.

The second is *Salvia uliginosa*, its tiny flowers September-sky blue, with the two roses that make the coolest and most touching picture together: pink (hybrid musk again) *R.* 'Felicia' and unbeatable *R.* Iceberg. The pink theme is repeated down the border in unconstrained outbursts of pale-pink *Anemone* x *hybrida* backlit by the low sun.

We still have the sedums, nerines and the main pack of the blue, white, purple and mauve daisies to come. And meanwhile the old crooked apple tree of 'Ellison's Orange' is offering sweet crunchy refreshment.

ROT AT THE ROOT

Most of the hedge that will eventually enclose the standing stone we planted last year, giving it (as it were) its private chapel, is growing splendidly. It is just the apse, curving to enclose this barbaric altar, that is letting us down, as yew hedges tend to do. The reason is usually bad drainage. I found it hard to credit this, though, when the 3-foot high plants started browning in the heat and comparative drought of July. You expect plants to drown in winter when it is wet. But it is rarely that simple.

It took me a while to work out that the yews here, planted in an 18-inch trench, are slightly downhill from the rest. Winter rain had drained to their roots and presumably drowned those at the bottom of the trench. While the topsoil remained damp, the plants looked fine. But in summer, they found the deep roots they called on for supplies were dead. This is how bad drainage can kill by delayed action. The moral, of course, is to encourage deep rooting with deep drains.

DARKNESS AT NOON

[*Britain saw a total solar eclipse on August 11, the first since 1927 and the last until 2090.*]

One thing about the eclipse everyone seemed to agree on: the birds would fall silent. One that didn't was our green woodpecker. It flew around in circles, making even more of a racket than usual.

Another prognostication, though, came brilliantly true. Shafts of light hitting the ground under trees and bushes became little white crescents. They gave the garden a sudden Moorish feeling.

❧ November ❧

CORAL CAULIFLOWERS

There are too many apples this year. A steady rain of them has been going on for two months. It is not entirely a good idea to grow the trees in a lawn you mow regularly, however beautiful their blossom, their summer shade and the glowing fruit that has now transformed them into Tiffany lamps.

Fruit of all sorts, in fact, is revving up the colour-content of the garden just now, from rose hips to viburnums (*V. opulus* 'Compactum' droops with gleaming scarlet berries) to the fishbone cotoneaster scaling the house wall. The white-variegated cornelian cherry, *Cornus mas*, is the prettiest picture with its plump red fruit. Before a leaf has turned, the garden is being warmed with colours of ripeness and filled with the fatness of autumn flowers.

How thickly the Michaelmas daisies grow, denser than any earlier flowers. Their expanding clumps (memo: dig up, divide, reduce, give to friends) are elbowing and burying tired summer plants. *Sedum spectabile* is the other really solid one, almost like coral cauliflowers filling the border. We planted a single line of *S. spectabile* 'Brilliant' along the foot of the conservatory's brick wall 20 years ago and here it is again like clockwork: brilliant.

We are debating who gets the prize for the longest-running show. The downside of months-long performance is that you get used to it and no longer notice. I'm afraid this happens with the we-never-close shrubby yellow potentillas and not-quite-red penstemons. Hydrangeas keep being interesting by changing colour. But I think this year's vote is for the lanky purple *Verbena bonariensis*, standing to attention while all else flops, and beside it that glorious giant grass *Stipa gigantea*. The evening sun behind it has given us daily pleasure since June.

THE FUN PARK

When we first moved to Essex in the 1970s, the Henry Doubleday Research Association was a humble enough affair. Its founder, Lawrence Hills, was a visionary whose time was about to come, but the HDRA garden in the old town of Bocking (comfrey was its main theme) didn't even begin to foreshadow the splendour of their recent return to Essex in the walled kitchen garden at Audley End. I am sure the number of visitors to Audley End has zoomed up since the 10-acre walled garden was reopened.

The history of Audley End was not without mishaps, from Benedictine Abbey to Jacobean mansion, until in the 1760s Sir John Griffin unleashed Lancelot Brown on the domain. Over the next 100 years, with the Neville family following on, every genteel, neat and ingenious turn of gardening fashion found its echo at Audley End.

I admit to an unworthy thought as I walked around recently between the parterre and the Temple of Concord (don't hope for shelter: it was designed without a roof), between Lady Portsmouth's Column and the Tea Bridge with its Elysian Gardens, before admiring the cascade and water turbine, the Pond Garden with its otter pool, grotto and torrent, and finally the splendid walled garden. The phrase 'Georgian fun park' came into my mind. It has before, I admit, in establishments where, in Byron's phrase, 'wealth has done wonders; taste, not much'. Now that they are cloaked in majestic trees, their textures lichened and mellowed, the patina of time flatters extravagant follies. Once, let me admit, I thought the crazy eclecticism of Biddulph Grange, with its chinoiserie, Cheshire Cottage, sphinxes, and all the rest, was a wonderful relic. But maybe its importance, and that of similar magpie creations all over Europe, is really to serve as a warning.

Don't get me wrong, I love Audley End. The serenity of the mansion in its lawn beside the placid Cam is one of East Anglia's finest sights. But despite, not because of, the uninhibited spending of Georgians and Victorians.

PS Gardens and house, run by English Heritage, are more visited now than ever. The house even has working 'servants' to goggle at.

A MINORITY VIEW

If the human race is divided, and I'm sure it is, between those who worship the sun and those who think a little of it goes a long way, the split is decidedly uneven. I am in the latter camp. Could we rain-worshippers and cloud-freaks muster 10 per cent of the population? I doubt it.

Society runs on the assumption that sunshine and heat are good in themselves, and their absence a calamity. Where would the airline industry be without the annual urge to go anywhere where it is uncomfortably hot to wear clothes? I am all for sunshine at the beginning and end of the day, to bring radiance to the raindrops. The moderate warmth of a January sun on its short course low in the sky is an unmixed blessing. But our ancestors evidently shunned the summer noonday sun, and so do I.

The builder of this ancient house was a wise man. He pointed the corner of it due south, to bring the morning into the rooms facing south-east and the evening into those facing south-west. At noon the light enters obliquely: an ideal arrangement.

INVASIVE BEAUTY

I mentioned *Salvia uliginosa* with enthusiasm last month: a willowy five-footer with racemes of sky-blue flowers that detonate patchily over a long period. I imagine its (very welcome) flourishing is another result of global warming – or, to be less apocalyptic, recent warm winters. But I did not realise quite how flourishing it is until I recognised strange little dark-green hairy-leaved seedlings in a brick path as its offspring – scores of them. Or until last weekend when I saw what amounts to a hedge of it in a spectacular kitchen garden in Hampshire. It looks set to join the Japanese anemones as a major feature of late summer. Even, who knows, as a significant weed.

❧ December ❧

TOURISTS

An excursion with the IDS to Touraine in October (D stands for Dendrology, the study of trees, as in rhododendron, the 'rose-tree') – although the wonderfully heterogeneous members of this Society (which is truly International) include people knowledgeable about every class of plants, every nuance of nature and every cranny of history.

We spent a morning in the botanical gardens at Tours. I had never realised that Tours contains such a treasure: not just rare trees of record size (growing on drained marshland, hence amply watered) but every department, down to tender climbers, well grown and displayed in a way that makes botany clear even to a simpleton like me.

The dendrologists swarmed over everything, crying out in many tongues (but mostly Latin) as they filled their notebooks and cameras, clustering round recognised experts to debate the identity, provenance, hardiness or merit of each rare specimen. The director of the garden employed a device I have never seen before to make his commentary heard: a loudspeaker mounted on an airport-style luggage trolley. We were, as the French say, ravished.

There were other gardens and parks of great beauty, notably La Fosse near Vendôme, one of France's three or four senior, 200-years-in-the-same-family arboreta, magnificent in maturity; and at the opposite extreme an arboretum-from-scratch, a bare field of tiny trees redolent of hope and aspiration, but nonetheless fascinating to true dendrologists. Everyone had a view on how to plant, feed, protect, arrange and label them.

NEAT AND BEAUTIFUL

I seem to have learned a good deal about box hedges in the past two years, last year having planted a whole new French-style parterre, and this year discovering a colony of snails many thousands strong in our old hedges in the walled garden here at Saling.

The appeal of box as edging to paths and beds is so strong that I had never looked for a further reason for planting it. But a kind reader in Exeter has referred me to William Cobbett for enlightenment. We tend to think of Cobbett as the political pamphleteer who foreshadowed Hansard, as an adventurer in America, as historian, a conservative radical member of parliament and author of the still very readable *Rural Rides*, a view of the English countryside and its agriculture in the early 19th century.

Then, like so many intelligent and energetic people in maturity, he settled down to gardening. He was 66 when he published *The English Gardener*. It is a clear and practical manual, and makes plain that box hedges were considered the only way to keep earth from the (slightly raised) beds of flowers or vegetables from falling out on to the gravel paths. Box 'will act like a little wall to keep the earth out of the walks'. It should be clipped in winter and again at midsummer. 'And if there be a more neat and beautiful thing than this in the world, all I can say is that I never saw that thing.'

PENNY-PINCHING

Hands up those who are digging, or planning, ha-has. I thought not. They have always been one of the fastest ways of burying money – even if you have a garden to protect from a deer park.

Yet earth-moving, for those with room to swing a digger-bucket, is one of the great bargains of modern times. It can never have been so (relatively) cheap since the days of slaves. What a digger, even a mini one, can accomplish in a day is formidable. Changes of level, in other words, always a major asset in giving a garden character and definition, no longer belong in a dream world.

I was even given a money-saving tip for ha-ha builders recently. The cost of the trench has come down, but the cost of the wall to support the upper side keeps going up. The tip is to build the wall with wire cages of stones; the sort they use to stop landslips on mountain roads. You just pile them up: no mortar, no mess. You can earth them over or plant them – they are there forever. I'm not sure, on the other hand, where to find them in the Yellow Pages.

PS The word is gabion.

WISH 2000

Trad's last page of the century should surely contain some profound sentiment or ringing cry to arms.

Do I have a final wish for the Millennium? Oh yes indeed. It is to find the same names two years running in *The RHS Plant Finder*. If only we could relegate taxonomic fidgeting-about to history. Let's draw the line under 20th-century names and never change them again.

2000

❧ January ❧

PRACTISE TO DECEIVE

Our County Gardens Trust put on a pair of lectures at its recent AGM which set the grey matter surging about. Anthea Taigel, a conservation officer for the Garden History Society, covering eastern England from Dover to York, is a busy lady with an astonishing grip of her abundant material. The title of her talk was 'Rescued or Ruined', and her proposition – or part of it – that while conservationists will always prefer the gentle, natural processes by which gardens slowly change and evolve, there are times when something radical is called for. This is an age that thirsts for novelty. The modern visitor is not always content with revisiting a garden and enjoying its slow growth and seasonal flux. He wants surprises.

She used the Duchess of Northumberland's much-flagged new garden at Alnwick as an indicator of the future. The capacity for change is being built into it: the notion is garden crossed with theme park. Visitors will come back again and again to see a different show each time. I can't wait.

The second lecturer, Fiona Cowell, has made a deep study of Humphry Repton which gave resonance to the theme. Repton famously took over from Brown as the principal landscaper of England. Fiona, who has restored the 18th-century grounds of The Priory, Hatfield Peverel, Essex, showed that for all his elegantly expressed principles Repton was first and foremost a pragmatist, a fixer without too many scruples. He offered the maximum effect for the minimum effort. Wool-pulling was the height of his art, and his gardens theatres of illusion. What fun, I thought, as I came home bursting with plans to cozen and deceive.

TEA AND LEAVES

The best books are the ones that make you want to get up and do something there and then: no delay, the thought is irresistible. Not something that has been on your conscience for weeks, but a whim that will not be delayed.

I've mentioned Molly Chappellet here before. Her book *A Vineyard Garden* is about California, and gardening on a heroic scale in a land of buckeyes and giant boulders. Her principle is: 'If you can lift it, bring it indoors.' It has just galvanised me to use the after-tea dusk to collect fallen leaves (no forklift truck needed) and bring them into the bright light of the kitchen. Leaves from 30 or 40 trees, bushes and plants that disintegrate gradually in November.

They are spread out now on a wicker tray, still gleaming wet, in colours from beige to black and vermilion to verdigris. Outdoors, however lovely they look in pools under the trees, one never sees them in such sharp focus. The different ways they change colour (evenly, blotchily, in patterns along or between the veins) are characteristic – why, I wonder?

Naming them is better than Trivial Pursuit. The prize for the best clear yellow goes to the Caucasian maple, *Acer cappadocicum*, with our native field maple a good runner-up. For red, at least this year, *Acer mono* from Japan, with the orange-red of *Berberis thunbergii* not far behind, juicy with its masses of little red fruit. The trophy for the most original goes to the grey poplar, *Populus* x *canescens*, whose leaves remain white underneath while turning jet black on top.

Here, it is always the last week of October and the first of November that set the pigments ringing, along with such lovely little back-markers of the year as cyclamen, *Saxifraga fortunei* with its tearful white flowers, and the sparkling white (better even than the pink) nerine.

MORE ON METSPEAK

When I wrote in September about the slipshod and condescending weather forecasts we have to put up with, I received a shower of letters. In fact the 'pulses' (where did they get this awful expression?) are still arriving.

I have been watching some other countries'TV forecasts, looking for better alternatives. Those on CNN are comically vague. South Africa will be dry, central Africa wet, India patchy … that sort of thing. A German channel I hit on the other day, though, was I thought exemplary. It started with a satellite shot of the whole of Europe so you could see where the weather was coming from. Then it superimposed the technical stuff, isobars and so on, for a few seconds. Then it had graphic indicators of the likely outcome in rain, wind, and temperature over 12 and 24 hours. All this without anyone prattling about clouds bubbling up.

Our island forecasters, of course, don't seem remotely interested in anything happening across the Channel (or even the southern part of the Irish Sea). Their preoccupation with Scotland may be understandable, but they rarely mention London.

Prescribing a better radio treatment is harder. My inclination is towards the completely terse and factual. More like the shipping forecast in fact. You know when to listen because you know when your bit is coming up. Need it ever take more than five or six words to tell you whether to bother with your umbrella?

❧ February ❧

QUANDARY COPSE

There is a rough bit of the garden here (one of plenty, I'm afraid) where years ago, seeing only elm saplings and suckers, I planted scattered yew and box. I had no idea whether the elms would grow or die (they have done both) but a notion that one day the two most biddable evergreens would give me a solid foundation for making something new, elms or no elms.

The copse thickened over time (especially with ivy, which made it look respectably furnished; a good green backdrop). As the bigger elms died I planted a score or so of beech saplings, thinking that their bright winter golden-brown would go well with the deep greens. This winter we have had a laborious clear-out of elm suckers and an ocean of ivy, and the combination of green and brown on a sunny day is a joy. The question is what next? How do I keep it pretty much like this as a winter feature, without beech and yew shading out the box and each other?

The yew is not a problem. We can cut it ruthlessly – and why not into balls or pyramids or towers? The beech is the puzzle: clipped beech keeps its winter foliage, as the young plants are doing now. Shall we clip these trees, the tallest now 15 feet? Just by cutting off their branches, hoping they will become roughly cylindrical with new shoots, or by coppicing them at ground level, or indeed both?

The copse looks so pretty today, with lithe young beech branches interlacing among the evergreens, that I hesitate to intervene. But this, like so many garden situations, is a passing phase that needs a decision taken and a contract drawn up for future development and maintenance. It is something to ponder while falling asleep.

⚘ March ⚘

WE'LL HAVE TO HUMP IT

Can you bear another word on moles? So far all my efforts to deflect them from the sensitive parts of our French garden have been in vain. One of my 'sonic devices', a battery-powered subterranean foghorn sort of thing, is surrounded, almost buried, by molehills. Now my Sunday paper has declared the whole idea a con. I was had.

Readers' suggestions, though, continue to give me moments of hope. Tortoiseshell cats, I am told, have been known to lay out the bodies tidily. Ours are clearly the wrong colour. Children's plastic windmills are reputed infallible – and look very fetching with a matching gnome. Other infallible remedies we are urged to try are mothballs or anything smelly (such as sardines and their oil) in the tunnels, chewing gum, and the old gardener's dodge of planting caper spurge. (Did it work, old gardener?)

One member suggested buying the cheapest little transistor radio, tuning into Radio 1, wrapping it in clingfilm and burying it in the tunnel. My sister even tried it. And if smells and bells both fail, the latest suggestion is a half-full bottle of water standing in the molehill to dazzle them with reflected light. Despairing of attempts to either distract or catch them I'm afraid I have just administered what I hope will be a once-and-for-all dose of pink poison gruesomely mixed with sections of wriggly worms. But I know I'll be seeing more and more humps of beautiful potting soil. Perhaps that is the best way of looking at it after all.

BELLES OF ST CLEMENTS

At last we seem to have learnt how to grow citrus trees in the conservatory – or at least two citrus trees: Meyer's lemon and the tiny calamondin orange. In past winters they have looked mopey, dropped leaves, and their fruit barely ripened properly. I put it down to our cool regime: we only keep the frost out. It may be partly because we have had only a token winter so far, but this year they have been the prettiest things, weighed down by their bright crops, overarched in January by silver-grey fronds and pale-yellow puffs of mimosa.

'Puffs' is awful, isn't it? But in botany-speak the flowers are 'globose'.

The lemons are delicious. So delicately acidic and scented that you can suck them without pain; small, smoothly golden, their rind thin, their juice abundant. I marinated a smoked trout in it last night. The tiny almost-globose oranges are not exactly gastronomical. Last year we candied some. If they had been great we would not have a jar of them still. But they are a wonderful colour; they smell good – and the next crop of flowers smells divine.

The secret of turning Essex into Arabia? A fertiliser modestly called Winter Food for Citrus Trees. It bucks them up with an impressive list of trace elements. I never thought I would be hankering after an orangery. Indeed I am not. But a lemonery – there's an idea.

❧ April ❧

THE WELL DOCTOR

The well doctor has just come up from his final inspection. I even went down the well in the bo'sun's chair myself. Our failing well has been an increasing worry for ten years. All sorts of sages have had a look and shaken their heads. Then I had a brainwave. The Yellow Pages. There was The Well Doctor – and rather a lot of money later the patient is spectacularly cured, its yield up from a mere 150 gallons of water an hour to around 1,200: a triumphant spurt.

It must be an ancient well. It is hard to see how there could be a dwelling here without it – and the records of this one go back to Domesday Book. Most Saxon manors in Essex are on the sites of Roman villas. There is no evidence, but the Roman Stane Street is only 2 miles away.

It could have been dug at any time before the Tudors, it seems to me. But its construction baffled the well doctor, who has seen hundreds. The shaft is 6 feet across and built of flint and mortar, 30 feet deep. The usual method is to build a circular wall and undermine it while it sinks; then build some more and continue till the wretch digging at the bottom of the hole nearly drowns. This wouldn't work, the doctor figured, with a rubble wall. So they must have dug the hole and built up from below. Quite a job.

More intriguing still, below the water level is a barrel-like wooden lining of thick narrow planks, joined with beautifully forged nails. Presumably this is to keep the sand down here from caving in. The wooden walls were a serious impediment to going on down, their diameter a shade too snug for the precast concrete cylinders that are the modern counterpart of circular walls. It took days of underwater chiselling – a next-to-impossible job – to make space to lower eight circles of concrete and laboriously undermine them in the old way: an extra 6 feet of depth. And *mirabile dictu* we were once more in the water table: a perpetual self-filling pond.

Happy as we are to have the water, I am more intrigued than ever to know how long 30 feet had been deep enough. The secret lies in the age of the barrel. A small section has gone off to Oxford for radiocarbon dating.

SINISTER EVENTS

Reports of the French storms of 26 and 28 December brought back memories of the winds that shook us in 1987 and 1990. It was not so much the statistics. Who can begin to imagine 300 million trees? It was the stories of whole apple orchards in Normandy uprooted, landmarks felled, indeed landscapes destroyed (the all-too-vivid French word is *sinistré*) that made one's heart sink. Any summer garden-touring to France this year will be like visiting a bereaved family.

Last week we set off to see the much-reported desolation of the Bois de Boulogne and the park at Versailles. A vast amount of clearing up has already been done, but the wreckage is still awesome. At a rough estimate I should say perhaps one in five or one in six of the mature trees in the Bois have been destroyed: many of them still leaning on their neighbours or lying in heaps of utter confusion.

The puzzle for gardeners, especially in such immaculate gardens as the Bagatelle, is what to do about tree stumps lying at 45 degrees with enormous root-balls attached? You hope, when you saw through the stem of a leaning tree, that the root-ball, released, will thud back into its hole. What do you do when a two-ton disc of soil and roots remains stuck at a jaunty angle, half a footpath pulled up with it?

However many thousands of trees came down at Versailles, the sense of confusion there is only local. Le Nôtre used tall forest trees as the infilling of his *bosquets*, usually surrounded with tightly pruned *allées* of red-twigged limes, which glow ruddily in the winter sun. Hundreds of the tall *bosquet* trees have been uprooted or smashed. Some here and there have broken through the *allées*, but amazingly it seems not one of the hundreds of statues, vases, urns or fountains – all snug in their winter overcoats – suffered a direct hit. From the main terraces overlooking the great canal and the orangery, the main east-west and north-south axes of the stupendous plan, the overall scene is scarcely even ruffled. Versailles is so vast it can take the punishment.

Of other parks and gardens I have heard even sorrier stories. The lovely Courances, south-east of Paris, a sublime study in trees and water, is apparently grievously wounded. And I'm told the unique arboretum of Balaine near Moulins, France's best 18th-century collection of the then-new American trees, has been all but wiped out.

✂ May ✂

SAN FANTASTICO

Unqualified as I am in the technicalities of show-judging RHS-style, with all the rules codified in a handbook, I was excited to be asked to join the panel of judges at San Francisco's Flower and Garden Show in March. The venue for this annual event is the Cow Palace, the vast hall built just south of San Francisco in the days when you could still smell saddle-leather on Market Street. A delicate nose, indeed, may just detect an agricultural background to the sweet flower smells at the show.

Spring was late in northern California this year, after six weeks of constant rainy days (which they'll be glad of later: the reservoirs are full). Our spring is so absurdly early that there was hardly any difference in the state of growth here and there (where you are on the latitude of Tunis). So it was very much a spring show, with all the sharp colours of early bulbs and blossom.

The gardens we were judging (Rosemary Verey is their favourite judge; alas this year she was not fit enough to go) could be roughly divided into the indigenous, the derivative and the fantastic. The derivative gardens were the least impressive category, particularly the ones that tried for an English look. Modern English gardening is all about control (unless the Chelsea Flower Show contradicts me later in the month). Older ideas stressed muddle – or at least a more indulgent attitude to wayward plants. Somehow both points were missed and the parodies were not quite funny enough to win the judges over.

It was the gardens that drew on California's own landscape, flora and funky sense of design that were most original, and most fun. One pretended that cymbidiums, in a wonderful variety of colours, were the wild flowers in a redwood grove around a ferny cascade over mossy logs. Perhaps in this case fantasy triumphed over reality, but the picture was beautifully composed, and the orchids were scintillating. Another garden recalled the faux-Mexico look of a Los Angeles suburb with a little yellow adobe house. Its doors and windows were secured (a necessary precaution, I suppose) by marvels of snaking wrought ironwork, while the planting had the bravura eclecticism of Roberto Burle Marx: a no-holds-barred palette that makes you reach for the sun block.

Most fantastic was a virtual opera-set for *La Bohème*, billed as The Streets of Europe, where All Life is Lived. The buildings, fountain, market stall, pavement café and the explosion of pot plants were a marvel. The problem the judges found was accepting it as being a garden at all.

The outright winner on almost all counts was a subtropical fantasy, made possible by the glasshouses of the Berkeley campus, whose various palms (I won't attempt their names) jostled round a sort of beach shelter constructed of sea-worn beams and a great sail of white muslin. Its roof was a jewel tray of gleaming little succulents, its floor smooth pebbles. The only bright colours were in the kalanchoes and such on the roof.

Why did it work so well? A simple plot, restraint, texture, proportion … one falls back on abstracts. Was it truly a garden? I expect people have asked that about Derek Jarman's famous patch of beach on Dungeness.

CHATSWORTHY

It is bewildering (but don't think I'm complaining) to watch the headlong onrush of spring. On only ten nights so far this century has the thermometer here at Saling Hall registered lower than freezing point; the coldest night was a mere -2°C (28°F). One couldn't say it has been balmy, but one sunny day has followed another, with an already worrying shortage of rainfall. At this rate the East Anglian Tourist Board will soon be talking about the attractions of the Dunmow Riviera.

Not that the early spring is confined to the South East. An afternoon at Chatsworth in mid-March proved that, once again, latitude has little to do with it. That glorious garden was positively chirruping with spring. Inevitably the focus was on the glasshouses with their superlative camellias. (What other word can you use about plants 150 years old and the size of forest trees?)

The great camellias (*C. reticulata* and *C. japonica* 'Alba Plena') form the central climax of Paxton's immensely long display case for wall fruit. The one quality these camellias lack, perfume, is supplied by *Osmanthus* hard by. On either side the perfectly-fanned peaches in blossom against the white wall were as exquisite as Chinese silk wallpaper, especially where the trunk and branches have been painted white with the wall, leaving the flowers and emerging leaves strangely disembodied.

It is 50 years since the present Duke and Duchess of Devonshire moved in to Chatsworth to maintain, adapt and improve the palace and its park. It enters the 21st century as the magnificent example of best ducal practice it has always been, available to all for inspection and inspiration. How lucky we are.

❧ June ❧

BLINK AND YOU'VE MISSED IT

We are at the moment when tiny early leaves are beginning to fleck the skeletal winter garden with green, and the woodland plants are frantic to flower before they drown in green shade. Blackthorn is flowering as though the hedges were full of snow. How can there be so much of a bush you don't notice again until the time of sloes? Blackthorn is supposed to bring with it a cold snap, the 'blackthorn winter', alias 'peewit pinch' because the poor little peewit apparently starts her nest in nippy weather. *Brewer's Dictionary of Phrase and Fable*, my first resort when faced with such an idiom, makes a (rare) mistake by confusing it with the 'Ice Saints' in mid-May, when late frosts can be even more devastating.

This year blackthorn seems less precocious than everything else in the garden, and at Saling has coincided perfectly with our massed amelanchiers; mounds, now, of pink-tinged white that close-to match the blackthorn in intricacy of a million tiny petals. This is my desert-island bush, the amelanchier; the annunciation of spring and the fiery farewell of autumn. We planted a score of them 20 years ago and have never regretted it.

Brilliant against this background are kerrias, magnolias, chaenomeles, flowering currants, mahonias (still), pieris, and at ground level anemones, violets, scillas, pulmonarias, bergenias, daffodils, hyacinths, primroses and wallflowers. Each is a sharp, shocking, independent outbreak of energy from bare ground or bare twig; nature incoherent with excitement, and looking on I am panicked by what I am missing in the rush. 'Hold it,' I want to say; 'wait till my senses have registered everything.' There is time in the other seasons. Not in spring.

❧ July ❧

EAST IS EAST, AND WEST IS WEST

In the east of England we mostly garden in a certain way, with certain hopes and expectations, based on our soils, our distinctly moderate rainfall and (at least historically) our relatively intemperate climate. Which of course has always made me long to do some comparative gardening, as it were, in the west. And finally I have a chance, within sight of Cardigan Bay, in the ruins of an old gold mine (Wales had a gold rush, too, in the 1840s) now deep in mature woods.

Sixty inches of rain is a dryish year in Snowdonia. There are frosts, of course, but rarely deep or sustained cold. The soil, mostly fractured granite and peat, is exceptionally acid. The woods, and the ruined mine buildings, uniform slate-grey, provide shelter and substance. It is not hard to imagine you are in the Pacific Northwest or Japan.

It was a visit to Crûg Farm Plants that got us started. This magic nursery, overlooking the Menai Straits, seems to invent more and more desirable plants as it goes along. Or rather as the Wynn-Joneses explore the Far East.

We were smitten the moment we walked into their walled garden, the very opposite of ours in Essex, spacious, straight-pathed and box-edged. This was like a big container stuffed with exotic plants, few of which we could name. And it reminded us instantly of our roofless mine building, a fraction of the size but a ready-made plant box.

We started with much-loved plants that have never survived long in Essex: *Euphorbia mellifera*, *Solanum laxum* 'Album'. Then we started cherry-picking the Crûg collection. An old mining tunnel, overhung with ash and oak, issues near the ruins: a deep, dark grotto ringing with water-drops that form a gentle stream at its mouth. Here with fierce glee we planted the forbidden Himalayan magnolias, eucryphias, the Chilean firebush *Embothrium coccineum*, *Oxydendrum arboreum*, a few rhododendrons (this is not going to be a big-flower garden) and gunneras in the swampy ground where ferns and kingcups cluster round the entrance to the tunnel.

Absentee gardening is far from ideal. We will have disappointments, and plenty of brambles to pull up (they come out with huge bunches of roots in this open soil). But it will be something cool and soothing to dream about. And one day, long after I'm gone, there will be great pink magnolia flowers high among the oak, ash and birch.

SCENTS AND SENSIBILITY

Some garden scents can float on the air as an unnoticed background until you suddenly become conscious of them. The gentle honey of wisteria carries a long way, but you can walk beside cascades of it scarcely aware that it smells at all. The prevailing temperature and humidity seem to be the deciding factors.

The wisteria claims a zone to itself, but not nearly so wide or pungent a zone as the *Elaeagnus umbellata* which is now filling the wilder part of the garden with the smell of Australian Chardonnay. 'Buttery toasty vanillin oak' is what Oz Clarke would no doubt call it. Vanilla, certainly. And wine-like headiness that makes me seek out some sharper, more astringent smell to clear my head. The Scotch rose, fresh, citric and penetrating, clears the pipes – but only so long as you hold it to your nose.

HALF-FULL OR HALF-EMPTY

I had a passionate rejoinder from a reader when I referred to the Ranelagh Gardens in Chelsea as a 'weedy bank'. 'No! You are wrong. The gardens are something to be proud of, not fussed over, not ordered, just a peaceful … sanctuary from the general nightmare that is London.'

I'm not sure. To some (probably most) of us the essential garden pleasure lies in order and tidiness; we turn to nature for the beauty of untrammelled growth, with the fittest coming out on top. With the smell of dead-nettle still on my hands as I write, I have a pretty clear idea of how much control I am looking for.

The ideal for each of us lies somewhere between fusspottery and letting everything rip. I walk round a garden and see only plants; you see only weeds. I'm told that the county organisers of the National Gardens Scheme, dedicated to finding gardens good enough to feature in its Yellow Book (so successfully that it becomes a bestseller every year) frequently have to field complaints from visitors scandalised by a weed in a border or a not-yet-cut hedge. Jeeves would put it down to the psychology of the individual. And Jeeves would be right.

❧ August ❧

RECOLLECTION IN TRANQUILLITY

Everybody at the Chelsea Flower Show this year, whether in rain or sun, must have come away with thoughts about change and the passing of time. The old marquee, austere but redolent of John Major's England, village cricket and spinsters on bikes, used to cast its spell over the whole show. Exhibitors this year who found the new hard-edged backdrop to their gardens less sympathetic than the mellow canvas will presumably be bringing taller trees next year. Certainly fastigiate oaks served Cartier and Clifton Nurseries well.

There was clearly a buzz about where gardening is going. There has been time now to let it all sink in. In retrospect Chelsea was a wonderful performance, with a sense of renewal everyone seemed to share.

My own impression was that there is less consensus than ever about gardening fashion. On the one hand there is a powerful lobby for 'good taste', the colour green, symmetry and masses of clipped box. With some exhibitors it retreated into downright nostalgia, others had more original ways of playing the same cards. Certainly the hardware merchants bank on it. It is clear from all the purveyors of teak furniture, statues and faux-stone urns that we still miss garden architecture, with its historical references and connotations of status. (We apparently prefer a hard seat to a soft one, too: I counted one hammock and not one deckchair.)

The bold modernism of such as Christopher Bradley-Hole attempts to break this spell. It would be fascinating to know how many visitors feel they learn useful lessons from these non-traditional gardens. If *Ground Force* is a guide, there should be a big constituency.

For me the two most memorable gardens, which tied for the elusive Trad Award, were the re-creations of a beach and an old mine. The sterility of a beach is a powerful image at Chelsea. A few sea-worn timbers, a hemp rope half-buried in sand and limpets, a whiff of brine and a hidden wave machine made from an old mower brilliantly evoked the sea; in nature the total antithesis of a garden. The result was to make the unexceptional planting round its little cottage strangely poignant.

A stream running towards you down the Rock Garden Bank is one of Chelsea's hoariest clichés. Yet somehow Her Majesty's guests at Leyhill used the idea in their abandoned industrial landscape so skilfully, with such fidelity to a vision, that it seemed quite accidental. It might always have been there. Perhaps it still is.

Neither design nor horticulture were important elements in either garden. They were stage sets, evoking very specific moods, recalling hundreds of humdrum corners of our islands with discipline and almost passionate purity. Is this gardening? Now there's a question for a philosopher.

SI MONUMENTUM REQUIRIS ...

Our Australian sculptor friend, Len Evans, has just been finishing the limestone figure he has carved for our hideout in the centre of France. As the sculptor's apprentice I have learned, over weeks of chiselling and grinding, something of the bare rudiments. But I am still awestruck by the huge head that Len has conjured from the original block. The secret? As he says, you just cut off those bits that don't look like a head.

The siting part was as delicate in its way as the carving. Formal gardens make it easy. They have straight axes: you have the weapon of inevitability ready to hand. But in what you might optimistically call romantic landscape, the goal is to give the illusion of inevitability on a canvas already busy with incident. Everyone has a different idea. The decision relies on complex calculations, stimulates debate and calls for masterful decisiveness.

The first factor is the vantage point or points it will be seen from, which of course will change with your use of the site, and with the growth of vegetation, unless the whole place is to be kept bald. Another is the light. Ideally the sun should cast the most telling shadows at the most appropriate times of day. With an urn or any round object this is not a problem: all angles are the same.

The scale is important, too. While we were carving the 8-foot-high stone, just outside the barn, it made even the big barn doors look paltry. It needed distance from the eye to be taken in as a whole, somewhere at a culminating point, preferably a lofty one .... We placed it, finally, at the corner of the pine wood 200 metres straight ahead from the house, its face half-turned towards the sweeping view – the way our own heads are most often turned.

Aussymandias (I'm sorry, that's his name) and we now share the view of valley, château, and the first foothills of the Auvergne. But he'll be there forever.

❦ September ❧

SHAPES AND SHADOWS

You haven't really experienced a garden until you have slept in it. Seen it, that is, in light fading to extinction, explored it at night with hesitant steps, and watched it come awake to birdsong at dawn.

A romantic notion, perhaps, but one that came over me while I was staying with my brother in the hills of southern Tuscany. It was the landscape, and a map-like view of the coast and islands from 30 kilometres away and 500 metres up, that drew him and his wife here, to a ruined stone farmhouse, ten years ago.

A decade has been enough, to my amazement, to create a garden, now virtually mature, that tackles a classic Italian site on a steep hillside, using the classic Tuscan plant repertoire, in an unmistakably English style. Rather than emphasising the slope with full-frontal terraces and flights of steps, the painter's paths and steps hug the hill, seeming to sidle without effort from one level to another between steep banks of rosemary, lavender, cistus, euphorbias, sages, yuccas, irises and low roses. They come to rest on small lawns shaded by olives, by wide bushy oaks, by arbutus, bay and Judas trees, by fine-needled Aleppo pines and dark columns of cypress.

Each irregular landing has a raison d'être: a pergola for roses or vines, an arbour with a seat, a gleaming pool, a grotto or simply a rope hammock slung suggestively between shading trees. The effect is effortless – a great deceit, because every plant except the oaks has been installed, nurtured and above all watered without fail until it has acquiesced and become part of the landscape. This is the strength of the plan: oaks are the soul of Tuscany, brandishing their crooked boughs and dark leaves in every view. Oaks link the garden to the landscape, obscuring the transition. And the swell of the hills, near and far, even repeated distantly offshore in hazy islands, is echoed in the garden in swelling mounds of rosemary or lavender.

The colours of spring and summer are soon gone in Tuscany. By July it is shapes and shadows and spaces that are important. And of course pots. Pelargoniums, pale or dusky, are vital as highlights, while in the shade hydrangeas are heavy with huge flowers.

The sun goes behind the western hill, but still lights the distant coast. Gathering darkness tricks and deceives. Groping down steps at night may sound eccentric. But I found a hammock, and the garden told me its secrets.

Saling Hall in Essex has been my headquarters for 40 years. Much of the diary records the pleasures and problems of its 12 acres of garden and park. My study window is bottom right, looking down towards the duck pond.

Salvia sclarea var. *turkestanica* or (to give it a more primitive name) 'hot housemaid' is a biennial welcome for its soft colour (not its smell) wherever it seeds itself. The kniphofia across the path is a happy accident.

Top: The tender climbing rose 'Maréchal Niel' flowers above the conservatory door as early as February. **Above:** By April the conservatory has to compete with the garden outside. Prostanthera, clivia, pelargoniums and little calamondin oranges are all in play, under the watchful eye of Zeus.

Top: St James's parish church is benign witness to the seasons in the walled garden: in September, Michaelmas daisies and the turning leaves of *Koelreuteria paniculata*. **Above:** In the centre of the garden, under an iron pergola, stands the figure of Flora, goddess of flowers.

Top left: A gothic gateway leads from the walled garden to the church. **Top right:** I write little about my kitchen garden, content to munch its produce. The lobster pots help to keep off the insatiable pigeons. **Above:** The walled garden's very approximate symmetry is best judged from the vantage point of the attic.

Clipped box bushes crowd on a bank above a little pond and cascade, in an oblique reference to Japan. The Japanese original is planted with evergreen azaleas: absurd, I think, when pink-spotted with flowers. Box closes the gap with Europe. In any case the azaleas are tender here.

Two more little ponds in a sheltered hollow constitute the water garden at Saling Hall, densely planted with irises and ferns, primulas and such big-leaved plants as skunk cabbage and rodgersias. Low winter sunshine dramatises the fountain jet and fallen leaves.

Saling Hall again: a pond known as the Red Sea reflects the white trunks of Himalayan birches (Hillier's 'Jermyns') on a promontory. Beyond it the Temple of Pisces, with two carp playing in the pediment, surveys the long central glade of the arboretum.

Top left: Nature moulded the obelisk we brought from Snowdonia to mark the millennium. **Top right:** Sir Roy Strong's Shakespeare monument at The Laskett in Hereford reflects a different sort of monumental sentiment. **Above:** Spring in the arboretum, with Judas trees in bloom, is my favourite time and place.

Show a French gardener a tree and he will reach for his pruning saw: wayward nature is not for French gardens. In England even pleached lime trees like these in the front courtyard at Saling seem to speak with a continental accent.

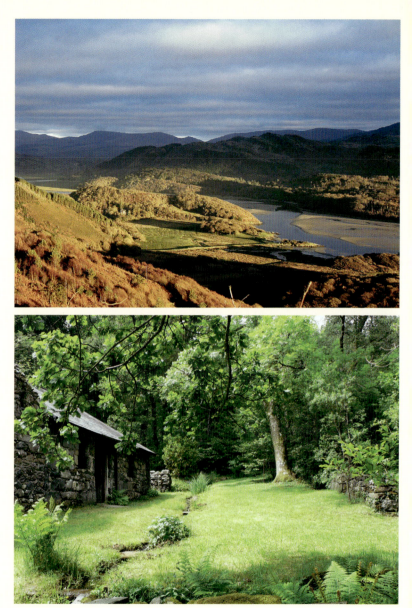

Top: My woods in North Wales overlook the estuary of the River Mawdach, now silted up but once a busy harbour building ships and handling minerals from the mines. **Above:** Our own little stone cabin in its perfunctory sketch of a garden was once the office of a short-lived gold mine.

Tuscany and deepest France. **Top:** My brother Brian knows the secret of gardening in Italy: make your planting look inevitable; use lavender and rosemary like an addict. **Above:** Our farmhouse in the Bourbonnais was open to more interpretations, but in the end the courtyard decided a parterre was the only option.

I have watched the creation of this neo-monastic garden, the brainchild of two Paris architects, since its birth in 1992. Le Prieuré Notre Dame d'Orsan in the Cher was an offshoot of Fontevraud Abbey. Its garden is a modern fantasy that has influenced gardeners in France and England – including me.

Top: Autumn, you would say. But this is the April colour of Japanese maples in the garden of Villa Melzi at Bellagio on Lake Como. **Above:** Lessons in simplicity, texture, restraint and relevance in Tom Stuart-Smith's 2008 Chelsea garden.

The total scene-change of the seasons is a privilege of the high latitudes of the temperate world. These views across a pond are from almost the same spot at Saling in July **(top)** and January **(above)**.

TO BOLDLY GO

Christopher Lloyd's new book, *Garden Flowers*, demonstrates all that is best about our greatest garden plantsman. No one else can do practical advice so pithily. No writer can touch him in curiosity, diligent observation, hands-on experience and crisply expressed judgement.

Lloyd uses words such as sleazy, sloppy, sordid and slovenly about plants and planting with relish. He is a true critic in a field where most writers are either purblind with enthusiasm, or content to concoct blurbs. To apply his judgement to my own garden, I fear, is to expose its dowdiness, not to mention its lack of flair or discipline.

Since Christopher Lloyd revved up his palette, turning over the rose garden at Great Dixter to the strongest statements of summer, to cannas and dahlias, hedychiums and gladioli and everything bold and brazen, we who still fiddle timidly with pastels have been exposed as mealy-mouthed and bourgeois.

Looking along our own borders in midsummer I see crowds of white and lavender, pale-pink, grey, blue, tawny and touches of yellow. The phloxes are white and mauve, acanthus purplish, *Ceanothus* x *delileanus* 'Gloire de Versailles' and its natural companion *Clematis* 'Perle d'Azur' grey-blue, Japanese anemones pink and white, day-lilies soft orange, artemisia grey, penstemon and monarda both what I believe is called garnet (another low-voltage colour), yuccas ivory and *Macleaya* grey and pale corn-colour. They are all what Lloyd would call safe, or 'gentrified', flowers.

My problem, as Lloyd makes me well aware, is that I am not critical enough. Not competitive enough, either: the concept of better, let alone best, is alien to my easily-pleased nature. I look for, and find, some virtue in everything except goosegrass and bindweed. Proper gardeners, I know, discard nonentities ruthlessly. Lloyd knows the difference between a goose and a swan.

❧ October ❧

CORNUCOPIA

We have not needed a sunny summer to ripen an unprecedented quantity and variety of fruit in gardens around here. One kind neighbour gave us some sensationally sweet and juicy white peaches from a tree in the open. Cherry plums are weighing down their branches.

Apples and pears are going to be in serious glut. Wineberries are glowing deep-scarlet and for a week or two we were experimenting with mulberries.

Black mulberries, to my mind, have always been more remarkable for staining anything they touch than as dessert. But when one morning we saw four moorhens climbing, or at least clambering about in, the small tree near the moat, we were moved to harvest the fruit ourselves. In taste it is inferior to a good old blackberry. But combined in a fruit salad, especially with melon, its mild sharpness is very pleasant.

As for white mulberries, though their tree is bigger and its leaves prettier (and reliably glow yellow in autumn), we had believed the books that say the fruit is tasteless. Alone, yes. But it is beautiful, cream ripening to pure white, and its sweetness complements the acidity of raspberries perfectly. One of the best fruit bowls of the summer was a mixture of the two with the dark, sweet, almost currant-like berries of *Amelanchier* x *grandiflora* 'Ballerina', which got better and better as they ripened to over-maturity – apparently (but exceptionally) unnoticed by the birds.

In the cherry plum department we are blessed with three quite different trees, in an area which seems foggy even to botanists. The wild *Prunus cerasifera* has pure-white blossom in March, plain green leaves and, if you are lucky, sweet-acid scarlet fruit. Another tree looks almost identical, but its fruit is purple, less acid and more sugary.

A third, a lucky seedling beside a silvery willow, has light-bronze leaves (a lovely combination with the silver in spring), pale-pink flowers, and this year hundreds of bloomy pale-purple plums hanging among leaves with the same bloomy look, mottled green and bronze: a picture I have never seen before and would never have imagined. It is somewhere near W J Bean's description of *Prunus* x *blireana*, but single-flowered and much prettier. If any nursery would like cuttings I'd be happy to supply.

PS It has been propagated (as Prunus *x* blireana *'Saling Hall') by Reads Nursery in Norfolk. www.readsnursery.co.uk*

✿ November ✿

MOVING ON

Of all the adornments our house has acquired over 30 years, the one that gives me most repeated pleasure is a painted glass panel over the door from kitchen to conservatory. The painter, Jane Gray, asked us to choose our favourite flower of each season. For winter we selected the Corsican hellebore, for spring a crown imperial, for summer blue agapanthus and for autumn a white Japanese anemone, a flower at once ravishing, reliable and perverse – and named after someone called Honorine Jobert.

From my desk I am looking out at a jostling crowd of her radiant spidery flowerheads lining the low brick wall that runs away at right angles to the house, topped by a pleached lime hedge. The same plants used to fill the bed below my study window, growing so tall that their white moons filtered the light falling on my papers. But then they took it into their head to migrate, moving through the grass and under a path to take up a new position on the west side of the wall – where I thought they probably found more moisture than against the house.

But it can't be moisture they are after, because now they are duck-diving under the wall and growing well in seriously dry and shady conditions under the pleached limes. If we have to draw a conclusion it must be that this most seductive flower, the very emblem of the end of summer, is a flibbertigibbet, one day basking in cultivated ease, the next running off with the tinkers.

❦ December ❦

INTO THE BLUE

Overheard at Wisley: 'Surely a member of the RHS would never paint anything blue?' 'Blue' came out in the appalled tones of Lady Bracknell saying 'a handbag?' What on earth, I thought, was wrong with blue? Had there just been an outbreak of it on *Ground Force*?

The colour blue, though, is an exception in gardens. Flowers that are really blue, rather than purplish or mauvish, clear cerulean like certain delphiniums, like *Salvia patens*, some gentians or *Meconopsis*, are rare and truly precious. Garden woodwork and metalwork, doors, gates, benches and such, are more usually, and more sympathetically, painted in something more retiring, less eye-grabbing, than a primary colour.

The big blue in a garden, though not as often as we would like, is the sky. And perhaps most commonly after the sky, certainly most eye-grabbingly, it is the swimming pool.

Why is the aquamarine geometry of a pool such a visual anathema? Under Mediterranean skies, in certain contexts, it can be thrilling. The answer has everything to do with light. Swimming-pool blue is harsh and discordant under milky skies, among soft colours and modulated tones. It overwhelms everything around it except substantial walls or, preferably, hedges, as light-absorbent as possible. Yew has no peer around swimming pools: first to hide them, then to relieve the eye from the searing colour. The late David Hicks painted his pool black with dramatic effect. I have seen a pool in Provence painted terracotta, which blended with the water to create an interesting tawny grey. A member of the RHS would never have a blue pool, surely?

SWEET AUBURN

Thanks largely to the Church Commissioners, we have at last succeeded in swapping our 50-year-old wooden village hall for a spanking new one. Its bright new brickwork inevitably gives a slightly Tescoid impression, which I have been trying to soften and alleviate by the surrounding planting.

I have used only the quiet plants of the countryside as the matrix, in a typical field hedge with specimen oaks and ashes; continuing, in fact, the existing vegetation. To shade the car park I have used a dozen of a broadly upright form of the common field maple, *Acer campestre* 'Elsrijk'. On a broad, low mound of spoil I have put a substantial clump of Scots pine to make a future landmark. And as 'foundation planting' round the walls a very simple mixture of rosemary and lavender, with box bushes planted at random to be topiaried in future into whatever forms take our fancy. The only outbreak of flowers will be the annual spring snowstorm of a double white cherry planted in memory of a former chairman.

What I would really like, though, would be a sculpture to symbolise the spirit of a little village, 1,000 years old at least, soldiering on in a world that has turned its back on the small settlements of the countryside.

CALLING TIME

What do gardeners think of the annual plunge into daylight-unsaving time? I suspect there would be a clear division between professionals, who find getting up in the dark the worst part of the short winter days, and amateurs, who resent having afternoons cut short.

Early November can bring the most harmonious colours of the whole year as the leaves go down in glory. At this moment I am still not sure whether the heavy downpours this year will have put out the fire or just postponed it.

Whatever the majority view, it seems absurd that it should be swayed, as it is, by the Scots on the grounds of their hours of daylight – which are even shorter than those we southerners suffer. The Scottish parliament, after all, can vote itself whatever time it likes on the clock. Down here in the South East I'd rather be in sync with the rest of Europe. But only, I hasten to add, over the time of day.

2001

❦ January ❦

DE PROFUNDIS

The fountain is drowned, the pond in the water garden three times its regulation size, and all the big-leaved plants that gave the little declivity its jungle character in summer are lying flattened under a brown litter of swamp-cypress twigs shredded by the gale.

The light is struggling, too. A dirty fleece of low clouds is spitting intermittently. But there in the gloom, on a pale, thin stem curving up from the water, is a gem-like purple flower. And another. A purple that seizes the struggling light and concentrates it; that gives a focus to this desolation. *Iris ensata* chooses a strange moment to recall the spring with a second flowering, as though responding to its cousin the gladwyn (or gladdon) *Iris foetidissima*, now so pregnant with its orange beads that its pods bend to the earth.

I love the gladwyn. Its dark-green sword-leaves (gladiator has the same root) are unfailingly burnished and smart. As its seeds ripen and their pods dry and crisp, the pod raises its head and opens its three segments to mimic the three-petalled iris flower, offering up its crowded gleaming berries to the appreciative birds.

There are so many that I fill the pockets of my windcheater and dribble them on to the ground in any shady forgotten corner, under a shrub, at the foot of a tree, in the angle of a wall (I don't limit my sowing to my own garden, either). Its flower may be modest, even dowdy. But is there an easier, better-tempered autumn ornament?

A DUMMY RUN

Most gardeners are focused firmly on the present and the near future. The Society's librarian, though, is a philosopher too. Brent Elliott has some fascinating things to say about where our gardening ideas come from, and in particular the way styles of gardening are recycled, but never exactly. 'Every original style', he wrote in an article in last summer's issue of *Garden History*, 'is simply the dummy run for a future revival; and every style is better the second time round.'

I am not convinced about 'better'. But the concept of styles and influences is deeply embedded in gardeners' (and especially garden historians') minds. What, in the first place, is an original style? Every gardener since Adam has seen the work of previous gardeners. There is no escaping their influence: our ancestors conceived the language of gardening which we cannot avoid speaking. On the other hand there is a great deal of difference between imitating an idea and letting it play on the subconscious until an apparently new idea emerges. Which is surely what we mean when we say 'influence'.

Is the aim of garden-visiting to make carbon copies or to stimulate the imagination? Presumably a bit of both. What is rare, though, despite the current culture of the makeover (who on earth coined this appalling word?), is the clean sweep; the garden done entirely from scratch.

Most people's plans include at least part of what is already there. In small gardens a single old plant may be decisive, nudging the design one way or the other. A chance tree in a small garden (few people cut them down, even if the planners allow it) can inhibit any rational design at all. Style, in other words, whether original or 'second time-round', is almost always compromised. Perhaps what we are really talking about is taste.

THE BRIGHT SPEED HE HAD

I don't know what possessed the government to drop the clear identity of the National Rivers Authority (NRA) and rebrand it the Environmental Agency. But just see how it has muddied the waters.

As I understood it, the job of the NRA was to keep the rivers flowing in their beds. Rivers included every form of watercourse, however paltry in summer, that played a part in draining sodden land. Farmers were enjoined to dig and trim every ditch every year. Trees, branches, rubbish, silt and even leaves had to be cleared. The faster water could get away the smaller the risk of unpredictable floods.

Nobody works any more on the farm where I take my daily walk.

The stream bed is invisible under brambles and sallows. Trees are left where they fall. During the recent rains the water took an easier way: straight across the fields. The scene is repeated on thousands of farms where ditching is a thing of the past. Mechanised hedging, whether by farmers or local authorities, makes it worse by leaving trashed vegetation in the ditch. Those old boys with their spades and bagging hooks were doing an essential job.

❧ February ❧

AH WELL

A wise romantic wouldn't put his heady notions to the test. I wrote last April about our well-deepening operations here at Saling, and how we found an oak well-lining 10 yards down which I fondly imagined might be medieval, or maybe even Roman.

The results are just back from the Oxford radiocarbon dating laboratory (or Accelerator Unit, to give it its proper name). They give them in percentage of probability. To summarise, in the most likely bracket of 95·4 per cent probability the odds are 2:1 that the date is around 1800, 1:2 between 1670 and 1780. (The house was rebuilt in 1699.) So much for great antiquity, then.

It is tempting to see a more general result of our well-deepening in the almost constant rainfall since we took this expensive step. All I can say is sorry.

BLDG REGS

The only part of this house that would have the remotest chance of withstanding a major explosion is the footings of the conservatory. By a strict application of the building regulations we were obliged (this was 20 years ago) by the district council to pour concrete foundations 1 metre deep and 50 cm thick, for a mere 2-foot wall supporting a structure made almost entirely of timber and glass.

At the time I was fearful for the safety of the house, whose brick walls have stood for 300 years on no more than a wallplate: an oak beam laid on the ground. Sure they chose a good gravel site. But what would all this digging and all this concrete do to the antique equilibrium of the place? I reassured myself as far as possible by keeping the two structures separate. No mortar ties them together.

I was reminded of this by my daughter, who is building a little conservatory in her London garden. Many tons of soil have been lugged out through the house, and many tons of aggregate and cement lugged in, to satisfy a building inspector. Did he really have the right, let alone duty, to demand 1-metre footings?

Rather late in the day I telephoned the Department of the Environment to find out. No. Conservatories of less than 30 square metres (323 square feet) are exempt from building regulations, provided they are separated from the house by a door and the roof is at least 60 per cent glass.

ALL LIT UP

Not everyone, for sure, was going to make the trip to Tetbury in December to see trees lit up. I did, having business in Westonbirt's marvellous new Great Oak Hall. Happily there was a lull between the downpours, and a party of us set off on the mile-long trail winding through a mysterious world of floodlit and spotlit trees. The Forestry Commission has resisted the temptation to use such Disney terms as Fairy Forest or Winter Wonderland, but in the strictest sense they would be justified.

In a word, it is a masterpiece. Magnificent, even moving, as Westonbirt's giant groves can be in summer, I was unprepared for the vision of immense oaks, planes, pines, hickories – it scarcely matters what species – painted with light from a palette of colours running from crimson to pale-violet, green or a wash of gold.

Some trees are lit as individuals. A spreading, writhing crown 60 feet above your head, each limb infused with scarlet as though it had been dipped in blood, is an awesome sight. Some are lit as groups: a dozen tall Japanese maples are coloured light-gold; their twigs and remaining fruit forming a lacy cloud unmistakably maplesque. The maple's growth-pattern of repeated forks is so distinct that even at 50 yards it needs no caption. Elsewhere, Westonbirt's low red mounds of dogwood, *Cornus alba* 'Sibirica', are lit to glow from within the brush of bright twigs, while above them, ghostly white, hang the tattered topsails and topgallants of a veteran Scots pine.

You will have to wait until next December to see this magical sight again. Perhaps, if enough people are enthused, it might play for longer next season. And while you are there you can see the oak hall, wrought from huge Gloucestershire timbers as men-of-war once were. How it disgraces the Greenwich dish-cover. How those vast canopies etched in colour are imprinted in my mind.

❦ March ❧

COLD DUCK

The snow was like a festival. Newspaper columnists wrote about little else for days. All were in favour: this was a novelty they approved of. How clean – and under this unaccustomed sun, how bright. Joining in the spirit of the thing we spurned the duck pond and went to Somerset House to skate. I have rarely enjoyed a queue so much: in that noble yard you could imagine yourself in the St Petersburg of the 19th century.

The snow timed it perfectly, too. It fell on sodden ground, then froze to protect it. Had the freeze come first it could have done far more damage, and lasted far longer.

I was amused to see a friend brushing it off her winter salad plants – chicory, rocket, mâche, spinach – to pick a few leaves for lunch, then brushing it gently back over them to keep them snug from the cold wind.

Alas, though, the freeze did for our veteran Aylesbury duck. It must be ten years since a neighbour dumped this rather inelegant white bird on us. At the time we had two call ducks, white, tiny and as trim as they were raucous. The newcomer made firm friends with them, and when a fox caught one napping became the constant companion of the other. That disappeared, though, a year later, and since then the large white (we never gave it a name) had the island to itself, occasionally entertaining a squadron of mallards or a pair of Canada geese for a day or two.

When the pond started to freeze our friend left the island for an overhanging bank where ivy-covered branches were keeping the frost off the water. A rash move. We took food in the afternoon, while there was still a patch of open water. Next morning, though, there was no open water, and no duck to be seen. A few feathers on the ice suggested another visit from the fox (ban hunting? The fox doesn't pity the duck). Then I saw a vague white mass under the snow-sprinkled ice. I'm afraid the duck dived for cover and couldn't find the way back up.

TOKYO REPORT

Not long ago I was taken to task for suggesting that English gardening lecturers should steer clear of Japan for fear of polluting one of the purest forms of garden art.

They haven't, and they have. Polluted it, that is. The Okura Hotel's *Tokyo Report* for last December carried an article called The New Japanese Garden.

The picture could have been taken on any bourgeois patio in the world: white metal furniture, white window boxes, red geraniums. The argument of the piece was that the subtle restraint of real Japanese gardening takes too much time (in a busy golfing life, perhaps). 'New gardeners', says the article, 'enjoy the splashes of colour and variety of flowers.' Indeed they do. The modern world and pure Japanese taste sit awkwardly side by side. Is there a more hideous city on earth than Tokyo, for all its wealth?

It is clearly too much to expect the Japanese to stick to their own way of gardening, to deny themselves the variety we so enjoy. But sadly variety is just what the world loses when everyone borrows ideas from the same magazines and buys plants and furniture from the same suppliers.

✵ April ✵

ROYAL PLANTER

History (largely in the shape of the French) has made Morocco the most accessible of the Islamic countries in almost every sense. Any gardener who suffers from SAD (infallible indicator: snowdrops leave you cold) should investigate the possibilities. Some 1,500 miles due south lies a land where the summer bedding is coming into bloom under the laden orange trees, and the way to the ski lift lies through valleys of almond blossom.

Marrakech is a city of gardens in a state of renewal. Noticeboards in each public garden (and they are many and large) proclaim '*Prochainement* …', 'Coming soon … redesign, replanting, refreshment'. Palms, oranges and olives are the recurring themes; usually in classically formal layouts. Less expected are the roses, many thousands of them, and the lavish use of annuals jumbled in a chaotic mix of colours and sizes and scents.

All this activity, apparently, is due to the young king, Mohammed VI, and his desire to make his country shine. It is evident far from the centres of towns, too, in the startling sight of new avenues heading off apparently into the desert. We were told that King Mohammed is seen early in the morning jogging through the vast palm plantations stretching round his favourite city.

NOTHING VENTURED …

Can we begin to consider the olive tree hardy? Think of the implications if the answer is yes. The black pencil cypress presents no problem. So the two elements that together create the coveted look of Provence and Tuscany would be ours for the planting. Not of course the sunshine that blesses them further south.

But sunshine or not, an olive is arguably the ultimate small-garden tree: evergreen but semi-transparent, giving a light shade, grey glinting silver, good on one trunk but better still with several stems, and infinitely amenable to pruning and shaping. And if one olive is good, two are better – and a whole grove devoutly to be wished.

The grand spreading tree in the Chelsea Physic Garden was always thought to be an aberration. At one time the credit for its survival went to Battersea Power Station just across the river. But recently I have seen several thriving in other parts of London. The late John Codrington grew one on a wall in Rutland. Are there others further north?

We planted one on the west wall here five years ago, thought we had lost it when it was cut back by its first winter, but now look up into its still slim branches with growing pleasure. (We keep a spare in the conservatory.)

A mature olive tree in well-drained ground will survive down to -15°C (5°F). But mature is the operative word: deep roots, stout growth and ripened new shoots. It is not clear which cultivars are the hardiest: two that are recommended (self-pollinators, too) are *Olea europaea* 'Aglandau' and 'Cailletier'.

A wild olive is inherently less lovely than such cultivars: its leaves are shorter, roughly oval, and dark-green on top. It may well be the safest to start with. Gardeners in our warmer counties should really have a go.

CYCLAPERSONS

It is surprising how cyclamen put up with being mowed, but I can't believe they like it. The problem is where they have self-sown into the lawn, far from their official billet under an apple tree. This is *Cyclamen coum*, the February cyclamen from the Caucasus with its round leaves, maroon beneath, and its tiny purple-pink flowers. I've just been forking it gingerly out of the grass, tracing the long pliant leaf stalks back to feel with my fingers for the little nut of a corm an inch down. I am putting them in, flowers and all, under pines where fallen needles kill the grass; unconventional timing, but needs must. There are already autumn ivy-leaved cyclamen there. Their problem is just that: ivy leaves, which look so similar that weeding out the runners takes intense concentration.

DE MINIMIS

Minimalism. What does it say to you? An empty yard. A stark trellis. A single plant lit to throw its shadow on a wall? *Faites simple* was always the golden rule of style, in gardening as in every art. But minimalism is about something more deliberate, more challenging, more impudent perhaps than mere simplicity.

These thoughts came as I was reading Christopher Bradley-Hole's book *The Minimalist Garden*, one of last year's bountiful crop. Many of its images are powerful; some extremely elegant. But the strongest impression is that minimalism is not for those on minimal incomes.

Here is lavish use of stone; daring doings with concrete, large spaces left void; all with the confidence of fashionable designers and skilful builders. Minimalism on a budget somehow doesn't play so well.

❧ May ❧

DOWNSCALING

Nobody else knows how many plants you have killed. You can feel foolish about lots of things you have done in the garden without having to live with the glaring evidence. My current folly is not easy to hide – nor to replace. I planted climbing roses in places much too small for their natural vigour.

Perhaps it was the forked tongue of the catalogue. More likely it was just my breezy nature. I put *Rosa* 'Gloire de Dijon' on the 9-foot wall of a cottage and am having to live with shoots behind the gutter, in the eaves, pushing up the tiles and reaching out to grab the jumpers of passers-by.

It's no good just pruning them hard. It only encourages the brutes. A great green shoot explodes from any draconian pruning cut and heads straight for the eaves without any attempt at flowering. The option of cutting them right down, digging out the roots and moving them to more spacious quarters (where? The taller walls are all full) means no roses at all. Replant disease surely strikes if you replace one rose with another.

If all else fails read the instructions. Or at least consult the authorities. David Hessayon's admirable *The Rose Expert* has a tempting suggestion: the 'easy-care method'. The plant is cut to half its height with secateurs 'or a hedge-trimmer'. Why do I hesitate? Because something tells me the roses' reaction would soon be dislodging tiles.

I took my problem to Wisley. The Members' Advisory Service was sympathetic. The advice, in brief, was to discourage the plants with pruning in spring and summer. Cut anything too vigorous back, and then cut it back again until the excess energy is curbed. Leaving the old spindly wood will, if anything, help curb vigour. This is certainly what I'm trying, starting with pretty radical pruning this March, to be followed up when need arises.

What about digging out my mistakes? Could I put less athletic roses (I was thinking of something like the single scarlet R. Altissimo, or the pink R. 'Bantry Bay') in the same soil? It depends on how long the roses have been in, I was told. Up to about four years the soil shouldn't be too sick. A good dig and a measure of new soil should mean a clear start. But surely with a top hamper like this the roots must already reach the centre of the earth?

PUMPING OUT

How I wish my diary could deviate from the subject. But the soaking is still with us. I had not quite realised how soaking until I walked to a walled corner where no one goes in winter and found my shoes awash in submerged moss where lawn should be. It takes the run-off from the drive, the wall blocks its drainage, and there is nowhere for the water to go. Somehow I had to pump it out.

I took my problem to the man who sells pumps. I want a tiny one, I said, to put in a hole I shall dig for the purpose to dry out the ground. A petrol-driven pump would be too powerful. It would instantly empty the hole – and what would I do with a gushing pipe? I need a small steady flow. Mr Pump had the answer: an electrical pump no bigger than the handle of a tennis racket run off a small 12-volt car battery. It is called a Spirex Amazon.

I dug a little sump in the swamp, pierced a bucket with holes to line it, clipped the battery to the pump and watched the water level gradually sink. Then I realised that all I needed to do was to attach the pump to a long enough hose to reach a spot marginally lower (a drain happily not far away) to start a siphon. All the pump had to do was to fill the pipe and I could put the battery back in the car. Gravity is doing the rest.

SPRING: AN ODE

If I haven't mentioned the conservatory for a long time it is because not much is new. It's in a routine – but a wonderful one to live with, and at this moment heaven.

Jasmine has just filled it with its high-cholesterol perfume. It tends to coincide exactly with 'February Gold', the most potent morale-boosting yellow of any daffodil. Perhaps it's the headiest moment of the year: outside the crocuses, early daffs, finger-high irises and stooping hellebores. Also our climbing – or maybe only scandent – snowdrop, *Galanthus elwesii,* which emerges every year 18 inches up a box pyramid.

And inside, pink camellias, orange clivias, blushing jasmine and glowing lemons. All too briefly our Australian mintbush joins in with a constellation of brilliant little rosy lilac flowers. Pelargoniums are fattening up to flower. The lawn needs mowing, raking, feeding ... we're off!

❧ June ❧

THE PREVIOUS APOCALYPSE

There have been moments this spring when the apocalypse almost did seem now. The foot-and-mouth holocaust of friendly familiar animals, the rivers bursting their banks, the earth itself unusable slime, the daily news of incompetence and hypocrisy in public affairs brought on a feeling of impotence I last felt exactly 25 years ago.

But then it was drought that made the earth unusable, and the plague over the land was Dutch elm disease. A pyre of animals is a more moving sight, to be sure, than a great tree suddenly losing the will to live. But in the summer of 1976 there was a sensation of near-despair. The countryside was suffering terrible harm and we were powerless to help.

What brought this to mind was the final collapse of two spectacular relics of the elm disease. The village of Great Saling was distinguished for the reputed champion of all the spreading smooth-leaved elms of eastern England: a tree recorded in 1841 as being 114 feet high and by 1976, when it died, 36 feet in circumference. The stump has stood on the village green like an archaeological relic until now. Twenty-five years is as long as it takes for a vast hulk of elm to decay: its roots no longer buttress it; final collapse is imminent.

We kept one memorial elm in the garden, too. A mere 16 feet around, this one, but the 20-foot stump we left standing, planted with ivy and Virginia creeper, was monumental enough. For a year now this has been leaning at a more and more threatening angle, guyed only by strong cables of ivy. This month it fell (speeded, I guess, by the rain).

Twenty-five years ago we felt that the landscape would take centuries to recover: that Essex – and much of lowland England – would look flat and empty all our lives and our children's lives. But far from it. Where the elms lined the roads and fields, seemingly irreplaceable, oak, ash and willow have grown prodigiously. We are comforted by trees again. The earth recovers.

BLUE POPPIES, BLUE STOCKINGS

I would be surprised if you have forgotten your first sight of the Himalayan blue poppy, *Meconopsis grandis*. It is one of those moments in a gardener's life that open new vistas of beauty – and covetousness. My first sighting was at Jack Drake's nursery at Inshriach near Aviemore. I suppose the sun sometimes shines on this wonderful place, but my memories of it are always of rain, soft and straight, drenching the beds of primulas and lewisias and gentians and *Nomocharis*, and giving the meconopsis the subtle gleam of raindrops on their golden fur that no other plant quite matches.

Of course, the searing sky-blue of their simple flowers is the first eye-catcher. But then every part of the plant excels in beauty. 'Bristly' rather than 'furry' is the proper description of the soft covering of the emerging leaves, often continuing up the stems and enveloping the fat pod-shaped buds. When the flowers open they are demure as young ladies used to be: faces downcast at the precise angle that reveals and yet conceals. Raindrops cling to the silken petals like pearls to the bosom of an odalisque … but I must not allow myself to wax too botanical.

If these ravishing creatures of the Himalaya and the highlands have a problem it is their identities. There are more or less perennial ones, more or less beautifully blue ones, ones with broader or narrower, furrier or less furry leaves arranged in different ways at the base and up the stems.

❧ July ❧

POET'S CORNER

The last thing I expected to find in the middle of Sherwood Forest was a palm tree. Newstead Abbey, the ancestral home of the Byron family, until the poet sold it to someone who could afford it, boasts a splendid row of Chusan palms, which I saw bursting spectacularly into bloom at the end of May. *Trachycarpus* flowers, for those in any doubt, appear like great slabs of scrambled egg emerging from cellophane wrapping.

Newstead now belongs to the City of Nottingham, which does remarkably well, it seems to me, to maintain its enormous and extremely ambitious gardens in the heart of what was, and still partly is, Sherwood Forest.

At the end of the lower of two huge lakes (the poet's great uncle used to stage mock naval battles on the upper one) a thunderous cascade crashes down into a considerable Japanese garden, not so much fine in detail as impressive in maturity, with monster maples and a katsura tree which must be worth seeing in autumn.

The former kitchen garden, which shelters, among many fine things along its walls, the row of Chusan palms, is now a formal, and perhaps not exactly inspired, rose garden. Much more interesting is the massive surviving formal garden from the early 18th century.

Historical résumés are always telling us that the Landscape Movement left us hardly anything of the taste of Queen Anne's time in the gardening line. Yet here it is: in the form of impressive symmetrical earthworks, broad terraces with grass banks overlooking a sheet of water 300 feet long by 100 wide. Though the planting tells us little of the original plan, the scale certainly does: the upper terraces, affording prospects over the surrounding country, the kitchen garden and the abbey, must be 750 feet long.

The enthusiastic Victorian owners, the Webb family, had only to plant a 700-foot herbaceous border along the north terrace to bring the design bang up to date. The crinolines of one age would have looked as perfect here as the bustles of a century-and-a-half before. The border is still blooming. How the four gardeners employed here by Nottingham City Council cope with such grandiose imperial notions is the greatest wonder of all.

NUTS IN MAY

My fingers are tingling as I type with the aftermath of a morning pulling nettles. Not only nettles, happily; but they are the weeds your hands remember.

The difficulty, as always in mid-spring, is coming indoors at all. Was this year exceptional in the bounty of hawthorn and Queen Anne's lace, making every wayside a garden and filling the air with that smell that gets the juices surging, and is such hell for poor wights with hayfever?

Here it was certainly exceptional in skipping late frosts altogether, going on raining until it was safe for the sky to clear and the temperature to rise without the customary complications. Such smooth progression without setbacks added to this year's boundless water supplies to make growth positively embarrassing.

We tend to leave mental spaces, so to speak, round our plants. Places to tuck in treasures, to fill with annuals, even just to step in to reach things you can't get at from the path. Where are they now? Access to the backs of borders was barred long ago. One can only imagine what seedlings are rocketing up. Already the two bryonies, those elegant serpents of climbers, are announcing their success by waving from the top of whatever bush they chose as their climbing frame. Bindweed is sure to follow.

Did you ever wonder about nuts in May? In the nursery rhyme, that is. What nuts could ever be ready to gather in May? The answer to the riddle, it seems, is that nuts is a corruption of knots, and that knots were posies of flowers.

Plums in May seem almost equally unlikely. But my eye was caught yesterday by a scarlet gleam high in the wildling plum tree I have mentioned before, the one by the moat – and there they were. It is a wonderfully fructiferous tree, with dusky leaves the colour of which registers on *The RHS Colour Chart* in the greyed red group as 182C, but suffused with green to give an overall brownish look, beautiful beside a silver willow.

I am delighted to see *The RHS Colour Chart* reissued. It gives one a comfortingly scientific way of identifying colours. The trouble is, of course, that we no more have enough names for colours than we have enough names for flavours.

❧ August ❧

FALSE ALARM

There was an unnerving article in last September's Journal about a new box fungus of such potency that it threatens all the box hedges, the parterres, the dinky little pompons, the cloud hedges – all the pretty horticultural contrivances from nature's most malleable plant.

This spring a yelp of fright went up from Saling. Our most-photographed feature is the bank of what are fashionably called clouds clipped over the past 25 years by Eric Kirby with ever-growing ingenuity.

In March they started to die. In part, that is, but enough to scare us silly. I noticed that the dead leaves and shoots were principally in hollows and crevices where fallen leaves had lain, sodden, winter-long. Hoping that this, rather than an imported fungus, was the proximate cause, I sent samples of dead wood to Wisley. As I cut it, though, my spirits rose. Down at the base the old bushes were sprouting new growth. These were not exactly at death's door.

There was a pause while the scientific staff went to work. The spores of

Cylindrocladium take a while to incubate. *Volutella*, a relatively benign fungus, was found. Three weeks later came the all-clear: no *Cylindrocladium*. Meanwhile with fingers crossed we had cut the infected bushes back to good new shoots, sprayed them with copper fungicide, fed and mulched them heavily and given them a foliar feed for good measure.

I see now how the bushes were weakened. A quarter-century of clipping, on a gravelly bank, with feeding neglected, leaves a plant with few reserves. Accretions of wet leaves gave fungi an open door. It won't happen again.

ELEGY

I wrote last year that we were looking for a sculpture to stand outside our new lottery-funded village hall. One or two galleries responded suggesting a grand commission. But the funds, alas, were consumed in the building. An objet trouvé, I thought, was our best chance.

Then Robert Lowe, our village's resident gypsy headman (resident for longer than the 30 years we have been here) came up with an idea. A plough. He produced a beautiful object, whose crouching, springing lines vaguely suggest a hunting animal. Nothing could symbolise the quietly strenuous 2,000-year history of a farming community better. It stands on a brick plinth as a proud reminder. The schoolchildren, of course, all ask what it is.

✹ September ✹

RING O' ROSES

A new horticultural abomination is spreading among us at alarming speed. It is called the roundabout. Its worst proponents are the French. No one who has had to drive in France in the last year has been spared the sight of *rondpoints fleuris*. Indeed I am now considering a coffee-table anthology of outstanding examples. You can help. I will send a bottle of excellent champagne to the person who sends me (via *The Garden*) the picture of the funniest *rondpoint* (or indeed roundabout). I'm the sole judge. I should tell you, though, I already have the one just outside Nantes with a spaceman beside a flying saucer among the clutter of arrows, one-way signs and '*Vous n'avez pas la priorité*'. How many crashes, one wonders, result from these gratuitous distractions?

Britain seems to have nothing, so far, so wholeheartedly naff as the best of the French municipal efforts. The Essex authorities allow sponsored gardening on roundabouts with a loudly distracting sponsor's sign. (At least you learn whose products to avoid.)

Nothing here yet compares, though, with the efforts of towns (Beaune was the first) that plant a whole vineyard on one *rondpoint*, build a press-house on the next one and a cellar on the third; the whole naffed-up with hanging baskets – and in spring, of course, naffodils.

THE LION AND THE BEE

The Strongs, Sir Roy and Julia Trevelyan Oman, manage to combine a high public profile with private discretion. One might imagine that a couple so creative in the public arena, he in museums and history, she in theatre design, might go home to Hereford to put their feet up.

Having just seen their garden (a visit keenly anticipated for years) I can say that up is the last place they can ever put their feet. The Laskett is a thinking, building, acquisitive visionary's garden. It is also an incredibly hands-on, every-leaf-and-petal-counts, garden of super-refined detail.

What can I say to describe it in a diary note? It takes the art of the vista, of deliberate manipulations of the visitor's eyes and feet, to a new level. The signposts are statues, urns, fountains, topiary: a conventional vocabulary but entirely personalised. A wonderful range of objects – antique, new, ingenious, but always decorative – often in the 'house colours' of light-blue and/or yellow, each commemorate an event, a person or a memory.

The paths, alleys, hedges and avenues that form the structure are as original as the artefacts they bind together. Even more absorbing, though, is the plantsmanship that manages to thread through this formal garden important collections of apples, lilies, snowdrops and a vast variety of unusual and choice plants.

Who does all this? The Strongs, with four days a week of devoted help from a neighbour. Yes, it's humbling.

OUR FOUNDER

It was at the Strongs that I first saw the Tradescant plaque which is now produced by Haddonstone for the Museum of Garden History. This figure of a Tudor gardener in high relief survived on a wall in Gardeners' Lane, between Upper Thames Street and the river. The date 1670 was just discernible, although the poor fellow's face and other details had suffered over the centuries.

The original plaque is now in the museum, but the carvers at Haddonstone have given their version the features of John Tradescant the Elder from the portrait held in the Ashmolean Museum: beard and splendid whiskers and a twinkle in his stony eye. He stands with spade and trowel, elegant in hat and cloak, doublet and trunk-hose; a horticultural homunculus with an illustrious past.

AROMATHERAPY

The scent crescendos as the light fades and the air grows humid with night. By 11 o'clock it is almost too much to bear in our little Temple of Pisces under the cascading branches of a weeping silver lime. The air is a bath of intense sweetness, more enveloping even than a field of broad beans in flower, with a sharper edge, purer than phlox, sweeter than tobacco flowers, with a citrus content that points to orange blossom.

Our Australian friend Len Evans is almost overcome. There are no lime trees in the gum-scented Hunter Valley – or only the kind that bear limes. As we sit on the temple steps in this aroma bath, sipping wine the taste of which is quite extinguished, Len says only Riesling must smells like this. (The juice of Riesling, that is, before it ferments.)

I am left wishing there was some sort of olfactory equivalent of *The RHS Colour Chart* for pinpointing the nuances of our most powerful sense. Honeysuckle has a different power. It seems to reach back in the subconscious to the barely-remembered Junes of adolescence. Lime blossom is scent at its most commanding, full-frontal, impossible to ignore or analyse. No wonder perfumers love it. In the tisane trade they say it calms and sends you to sleep. The drink, maybe: not the tree at close quarters.

If a lime-junky had the space, the trees to plant for the longest season of flowers and scent would be *Tilia platyphyllos* for late June; *T.* x *europaea* for early July; *T. oliveri*, the lovely Chinese silver lime, for mid-July; then *T. cordata*, our native small-leaved lime, for late July; leading up to the climax of *T. tomentosa*, our silver lime, and its weeping cousin *T.* 'Petiolaris' at the end of July and well into August. Last in flower, into September, would be *T. henryana*, a Chinese tree with extravagantly red-fringed young leaves.

❧ October ❧

TIME AND THE PLACE

By a happy chance I bumped into Anna Pavord in the middle of a Prom concert on Radio 3. Not literally, but she was the speaker while the musicians went out for their half-time shandy. She was speaking, engagingly, lucidly, and two-thirds convincingly about the element of time in gardening.

I hope I don't misinterpret her, but her point was that gardening is as much about patient anticipation as it is about the final (of course it never is final) picture. Obviously there are many different rhythms: your courgettes come and go while your Japanese maples inch forward. But a great part of gardening pleasure is the acceptance that one season builds on another. Memory and anticipation are both constantly engaged.

It followed, naturally, that she is none too keen on 'makeover' gardening. An abrupt and total change of decor to her is the abnegation of horticulture. (So long as it's quick, who cares where it comes from, or is related to, or how long it lasts?)

And yet. If change (you can call it development if you like) is a significant part of gardening pleasure why should one insist (or even prefer) that it happens slowly? I can't hear one of Repton's redbook clients saying 'Hang on, old chap, that's a bit sudden isn't it?' I imagine the moment they flipped the flap and saw the proposed *cottage orné*, the glimpse of water, the balustrade and the hollyhock border they were asking if it could all be up and running for little Sophia's coming out next July.

Yes, we love the slow ripening of the seasons and the gradual maturing of a cherished plan. But there's always a corner of my mind projecting away, scanning the Journal for neat dodges (in Mr Salteena's irreplaceable phrase) that we might find a place for. It was Repton (again) who said 'my axe is my pencil'. The culture of the makeover is certainly not horticulture. But you can't exclude excitement altogether.

HARVEST TIME

Late summer is the time to stay at home. We haven't spent the whole of August at home for years. There are always reasons but, if you are lucky enough to cultivate a country patch, this is surely the time when it rewards you most bountifully.

Above all it is vegetable time. I grant you our kitchen garden is eccentric. Andrew Marvell would have felt at home: 'stumbling on melons as I pass, ensnared with flowers ...' except that the melons are courgettes and squashes, the latter flinging out 6-foot tentacles at the sight of a passing ankle. Where the surging jungle of cucurbits stops is more or less marked by a row of tall white and red dahlias; then sweetcorn in an infantry square; then the spreading grey rosettes of artichokes, which always vaguely remind me of sea anemones, as though a fretty grey frond could hook you.

The two sides of the kitchen garden are officially and very obviously divided by a central path, which by August has become an avenue of heavily seeding, bowing and swaying purple orache. Encourage this stuff (it is reputedly edible) and it will fill fields. We simply hoe most of the seedlings (easy to spot, because purple) but leave them to grow way above head height down the central path. At their feet surge and billow equally self-sowing nasturtiums and blue borage. By now, as the orache leaves are taking on a hint of autumn orange, the shoots of the squash (I didn't mention its bright-yellow upturned trumpets) are lunging across the path amid the orache, nasturtiums (did I mention marigolds?) and juicy milk-thistles that appear overnight.

The right side of this perhaps slightly bohemian garden is getting gappy now as we eat the potatoes, the spinach, the Swiss chard with leaves almost approaching banana size, the carrots and leeks and cabbages and salads. A patch of Michaelmas daisy heeled in here and somehow overlooked is flowering anyway. The golden rod is not supposed to be there either. But the row of roses, for picking, has at least some official standing.

Never have we had such a season for figs: a dozen at a time. 'Brown Turkey' is not the sweetest or juiciest variety (no match for the little golden figs of Italy) but where a *Tropaeolum speciosum* is infiltrating its micro-leaves and scarlet flowers among the fig's great dusty lobed leaves (they were the first clothes, when you think of it) I almost laugh with pleasure at nature's impromptu arrangements.

WATER MUSIC

Half-barrels with phoney pumps, concrete lion's masks and spitting plaster Pans: water 'features' are half the stock-in-trade of garden centres these days. A dribble of water certainly animates a garden, a patio or a conservatory. The tricky part is the sound. 'Suggestive' is perhaps the politest word for the steady tinkling of most such devices. In the resonant space of a conservatory it can be a minor torment. After years of experiment, I've come up with an answer.

The water circulates through a tap and falls into a substantial tank. The trick is to break and vary its fall. I have perched a big-leaved fern on an old chimneypot beside the tank so that its fronds filter the fall. The sound is hesitant now, like drips from stalactites in a grotto. We can all relax.

The fern, by the way, is *Woodwardia radicans*, grandchild of a fernlet Christopher Lloyd once gave me. His master-fern stood on a table in the great oriel window at Great Dixter, filling the whole bay with its 10-foot wingspan.

❧ November ❧

YIN AND YANG

How often do you see a new garden idea so successful that you go home looking for somewhere to fit it in your patch? About once a month, in my case, which has bred a certain reserve in an otherwise totally magpie nature.

But here is one I can't get out of my head. Our neighbours in Essex, Len and Dorothy Ratcliff, do more gardening in less space than anyone I know. I do worry slightly when they plant trees about 18 inches apart. But I can't fault their sense of style, or the way they divide and fill the limited spaces round their house.

This year they installed a semi-transparent space-divider of two seemingly unlikely elements: iron and grass. They built a simple and open fence of widely-spaced wrought-iron strips painted black and linked at the top with black crescents. Under it they planted a row of *Stipa gigantea*, the grass which by June has flowered in long oat-like heads of shining gold on waving 6-foot wands. Black and rigid, golden and always in movement, yin and yang, the elements are perfectly matched, the effect utterly memorable. And the stipa is still in flower in October.

❧ December ❧

SEASON OF MISTS

Boats in the High Street in October. That was no way to go into autumn. Although we had precious little sign that autumn was even on its way. The last week of October or the first of November is usually the best time around here for bright colours in autumn leaves. This year the maples were still green – indeed growing. The borders were thoroughly tousled.

Tall big-leaved trees, horse chestnuts for example, had most of their upholstery blown away. But that was all. The seasons go on hold when the rain buckets down. How glad I am of the conservatory – and the toolshed – roof.

Plants under glass are charging ahead too in the warm days and nights. The gumdrop scent of Meyer's lemon in the conservatory seeps into the house. Cape primroses clearly like shady moisture; they are going full tilt. Nerines are at their long-lasting best, sparkling pink above the primroses' blue and white. Dipladenias are the longest-flowering climbers so far: both the pink and white kinds have been opening their 3-inch-wide flowers for six months or so and show no sign of stopping. Perhaps it is merciful they are not scented.

But their flowering record is under challenge. A kind friend this summer brought us a new passion flower, a true original, alarmingly vigorous, with astonishing numbers of yellow flowers that remind me, especially in bud, of 'lemon-peel' clematis, *C. orientalis*. Its garden-centre label gives little away except its name, *Passiflora citrina*, and the need to keep it in full sun, which is not happening. Wisley tells me it is a newcomer, introduced from Honduras or Guatemala only in 1989, and may stay in flower as much as ten months of the year, skipping only January and February. It will be a relief if it stops growing then, too.

Outside, the late star of the borders is a 6-foot chalk-white daisy now known as *Leucanthemella serotina*. Perhaps because it is merely green all summer this tall but not lanky aristocrat gets overlooked. It takes all summer for its stems to become strong enough to stand up to September gales and October rain. But it is worth the wait for its noble purity in the darkening garden.

DO WE NEED BOOTS?

Some of us in the South East have been able to draw some uncomfortable conclusions by comparing this autumn's floods with the last batch. True the rain was concentrated in different places. Maybe a different kind of rain, too. But it has also become clear who keeps their drains and ditches clean and who doesn't.

Some farmers on relatively high but flat land had a shock last time when the water failed to drain away. There was expensive ditching done last summer. But unless the next recipient of the water had a clear-out too, and the next and the next right down to a comfortable flood plain, or even the sea, the extra flow from upstream was bound to cause trouble to a new set of unfortunate victims.

Smug on the summit of the Essex alps (altitude: 299 feet) we are not flooded, at least not from neighbours' land. We are merely digging drains in parts of the garden that have been dry for most of 30 years. 'Do we need boots?' visitors ask. I wouldn't risk a decent pair of shoes in the garden here for the foreseeable future.

CRARAE FOR CHRISTMAS

And for my Christmas present? Thank you for asking. I'd like a donation to Crarae in Crisis. I was deeply upset to read in October that the appeal for the gardens of Crarae in Argyll is apparently bogged down well short of its target of £1.5 million, and their fate is in the balance. To me Crarae has more magic than almost any garden in these islands; its Himalayan cascade is simply unforgettable. Had someone come up with the wheeze of labelling it 'lost' ten years ago it would be famous today. Loch Fyne, after all, is no more remote than Cornwall.

Time is running short. Crarae in Crisis at The National Trust for Scotland tells me the money is needed before the end of January 2002, or it will be thumbs down for this unique place. So there is just time to help.

2002

CORNUCOPIA

Copia is or was the Roman goddess of plenty. I am sure there were many altars to her – though I have never heard of a temple. She has one now; a temple complex indeed. It is the new American Center for Wine, Food and the Arts (Copia for short), opened in November in the heart of Napa, capital of the valley of California's most celebrated wines.

I went to the opening not knowing what to expect: 18 months before there was only the site, right downtown yet cradled in an oxbow river bend facing wild woods. Now, 18 months and $50 million later, there is a visionary building housing teaching theatres, kitchens, art galleries and one of America's best restaurants: Julia (Child)'s Kitchen. On the river side musicians play in a grassy, green amphitheatre. On the entrance side 3 acres of formal gardens are dedicated to what Jeff Dawson, their curator, calls 'the edible botanical world'. Nowhere, to my knowledge, is gastro-horticulture so comprehensively studied. All the fruits (grapes of course included), the herbs, vegetables, salads that will grow in the benign climate of Napa are put through their paces – in conjunction with a first-rate kitchen and critical tasters.

The garden plan nods to Villandry in its formal asymmetry, with wide paths and productive beds. But Villandry is about patterns of colour; Copia about patterns of taste. Berries, nuts, olives … everything is for tasting. If a grape is said to resemble blackcurrants or red peppers or apricots, there are the associated plants growing side by side. Seed selections are sown, tested, resown from the same plants and tested again several times before being grown in production beds.

I have the list of beds and their first contents in front of me. How to precis a catalogue of 35 50-foot squares, each with a different theme? Imagine, shall we say, half of Vincent Square laid out to fruit and veg, the planes replaced with fruit trees, and Gordon Ramsay installed where the Lindley Library is to test the produce. And with part of Tate Modern on top for good measure. Welcome to the Napa Valley ….

MOON MINION

We came home to moonlight. Moonlight so bright that even garden colours showed. But no detail; the full moon was lighting a fine mist that soft-filtered a view of spectral brilliance. From upstairs the garden looked like an underexposed watercolour, its forms – and its faults – reinterpreted in a highly legible shorthand.

It has been the same through two weeks of increasingly high pressure and the onset of frosts. The barometer needle, on 144 millibars, looks as though it is coming loose. The moon has waned from the full orb to a grapefruit segment – seemingly without losing wattage. No wind to drift fallen leaves. Bats and the leisurely owl make the only moves.

But what a tiny minority we country-dwellers are. They are putting streetlamps along the main road 2 miles away, presaging who knows what illumination to come. The loom of Braintree is low on one horizon – at 5 miles away low enough for trees to screen it. But most of us now have to accept nights in which natural darkness never descends – and the heavenly bodies move unnoticed.

TRIUMPHANT IF IT'S DEAD

Octogenarian iconoclasts commonly have good aim. Few, though, are as true as Deborah (Duchess of) Devonshire whose little book of reprinted articles – *Counting my Chickens* is the title – was rushing out of switched-on bookshops at the end of the year.

She knows her gardeners. 'Something strange', she writes, seems to seize 'otherwise normal folk' going round other people's gardens. 'Although they have probably travelled miles to their treat, they show themselves to be really only interested in what they have left at home. People who haven't got gardens of their own can stand back and delight in the big picture of someone else's work, but the real gardener fastens on some small plant, pleased if it doesn't look too well and triumphant if it's dead.'

❦ March ❧

THE MOST EXPENSIVE TREE?

Horticulture is not the best advertised of Hong Kong's pleasures. Indeed the new conservatory in Hong Kong Park came as a complete surprise as I took the green short-cut between the glass and silver towers crowding at the foot of the Peak. Hong Kong Central is far better-known for the competing corporate egos manifest in its spectacular buildings than for its botanical gardens, aviary, zoo – and now this splendid conservatory in the manner of Lloyd's building in the City of London: viscerally functional with plumbing and naked structure as decor.

There are no plateaux on the way up the Peak; the conservatory climbs the hill, against the tumble of its internal cascade, divided like the Eden Project into climate zones with worthwhile collections of succulents, palms, creepers, bamboos and ferns spilling over a chaos of artificial rocks.

Rocks are the lawns and the hedges of Chinese gardening; they take care of every transition. The market in artificial rock has not seen such heady times since Napoleon III filled his Paris parks with alps and cascades. The Hong Kong Park waterfall is a beauty: a 50-foot swoosh over a cliff of man-made rock, a great blade of water glittering as brilliantly as the skyscrapers around it. Between two of these I rested under a mighty banyan tree with a story to tell. A plaque beside it records that it was planted in the old barracks on this spot in 1870. Preserving it when the neighbouring tower was built in 1979 meant retaining a cylinder of earth 12 metres across and 10 deep, at a cost of 23,890,227 Hong Kong dollars (about £2 million). Conservationists, take heart.

❦ April ❧

DOME GONE

The gale sneaked round the thatched barn to attack our biggest strawberry tree – so broad and substantial a feature that I had never imagined that part of the garden without it. It decided the route of the path, the shape of a little sheltered circle of lawn, and the disposition of 50 other plants. Its dense dome of glossy foliage must have started swaying in the gusts until the trunk could take no more. It shattered at ground level, to spreadeagle on azaleas, a *Mahonia* x *media* 'Winter Sun', a scarlet quince and all sorts of woodland herbs, and leaving a *Robinia hispida*, the one with soft-pink June flowers which is more a climber than a tree, without support.

I mourn it for itself, its venerable grey-brown stringybarked trunk and its wonderfully generous gleaming leaves, and for its defining role in the garden. When the clearing up is done (which won't be until the ground is considerably less squelchy) we shall inspect the gap from every angle for a longish while before making commitments. Or just possibly decide that there isn't a gap at all.

People have already looked out of the kitchen window and said how good it is to see the soaring pink stems of a Japanese birch that was hidden before. Most of the plants the arbutus shaded will rejoice.

A BRIEF ACCOUNT

Do supermarkets presage a gardening revolution? Looking at their cellophane bags of mixed salad leaves – half a dozen different lettuces, mâche, cress, chicories red, green and frisé, and rocket, even more chic than chicory – I anticipate allotments breaking out in positively Italian colours this summer. It will be high time. Our winter salads – and indeed our summer ones – have remained almost as boring and predictable (and vinegary) as they evidently were in the reign of the first Elizabeth.

For this we have the evidence of Giacomo Castelvetro, who wrote a *Brieve Racconto* of Italian vegetables, fruit, salads and herbs in the vain hope of changing British ways. It was finally translated and published (by Gillian Riley and Viking Press respectively) in 1989. Though not anticipating the rocket vogue in all its glory, Castelvetro gives the perfect description of a mixed spring salad, 'the most wonderful of all. Take young leaves of mint, those of garden cress, basil, lemon balm, the tips of salad burnet, tarragon, the flowers and tenderest leaves of borage … young shoots of fennel, leaves of rocket, of sorrel, rosemary flowers, some sweet violets, and the tenderest leaves or hearts of lettuce.'

But don't dress them the English way, 'washing them heavens knows how, putting the vinegar in the dish first, and enough of that for a footbath …'. The secret of a good salad is plenty of salt, generous oil and little vinegar, hence the Sacred Law of Salads:

Salt the salad quite a lot,
Then generous oil put in the pot,
And vinegar, but just a jot.

HOW VERY KIND

We have some extraordinarily generous readers. Just how generous I had little idea when I said that for a Christmas present I would like a donation towards saving the gardens of Crarae. The National Trust for Scotland promptly received, among many others, one anonymous gift of well over £100,000. The initial target of £1.5 million was exceeded well before the April deadline. Crarae is safe.

Which of course makes me more bashful than ever, with a birthday coming up, to mention the critical appeal for funds for the Victorian Bridge End Gardens at Saffron Walden, Essex. Nothing could be more different from highland Crarae than this urban period piece – except in being a garden (that flexible word) with a price on its head.

❧ May ❧

AND IN THE RED CORNER

Red borders are not the easiest – for the same reason that they photograph badly: the colour red absorbs the light and tends to disappear as it dims. There is a celebrated example at Hidcote Manor Garden in Gloucestershire, but did you ever see a really tempting picture of it?

Perhaps I am perverse, then, to be planning a border around a red theme for the front of this house. When visitors arrive here they invariably seem to ignore the first garden space, the house-front, draped with vines, floored with rockrose and rosemary, daphne and alstroemeria, to make a dash for space two, the walled garden. The red border idea is to persuade them to linger, to take in the roses on the churchyard wall, the immaculate pleached limes, the duck pond view, the stone figure of Tradescant the First ....

I am tempted to let fly, Lloyd-style, with no matter what colour that has any red in it. Think of flaming crocosmias and the acidic purple of *Geranium psilostemon*. The extremes could always be suppressed if there is an outcry. I'm not at all sure, though, that with a palette ranging from orange to magenta my border would ever be taken as red.

FAIR GAME

There was a pheasant in one of the pelargonium pots in front of the house this morning when I drew the curtains, and another on the churchyard wall. Fat contented birds both of them, spending their days strutting or ambling about the garden, certainly in no fear of me, although surprises still send them up with that raucous rattle that is one of my favourite country sounds.

This is their sanctuary, where they are welcome to stay, out of range of the angry weekend guns. I've never understood how driven birds can be described as 'sport'. Sport is hunting: stalking or lying in wait for an enemy, or at least vermin whose depredations need checking. The canny woodpigeon is a worthy adversary. He knows the calibre and range of your gun at one glance. The grey squirrel too: you need a light foot and quick reflexes.

Now I read that a Smithfield restaurant is serving up grey squirrel stew my hopes are rising that the little destroyer is in the firing line at last. Or do you suppose someone will start farming them for the table?

❧ June ❧

THISBE'S CHINK

Why is everything much more interesting, intriguing or important seen through a hole? The peephole appeals to something pretty basic in all of us. Think of Pyramus and Thisbe. Its manifestations in the garden are doorways, framed perspectives, moongates … and *claire voyées*. Clairvoyant is current in English; *claire voyée* maybe less so. It means a window or transparent screen devised deliberately to give a tempting glimpse of something not immediately accessible. The feet cannot just follow the eye, as they can at a doorway. Which makes the view only more desirable. Such is human nature.

I have just made a *claire voyée*. Or, less portentously, cut a hole in a hedge. We planted a yew hedge 25 years ago around our new swimming pool. It was mature, dense and almost ancestral-looking in ten years; by 20 it needed what we call the 'National Trust cut': to the bone, front and back in successive years – with a good feeding into the bargain. Cut right back even yew becomes transparent. I saw a pleasing cameo through the branches and cut them away to form a circular aperture about a metre across. Now you can see a statue of Bacchus and a white mulberry tree while you are towelling yourself, and I am scouting for the next opportunity to introduce a glimpse of one part of the garden from another, otherwise unrelated.

A MYTH IS AS GOOD …

A month without rain. A marvellous sun-soaked month with little wind. A textbook spring unfolding, a little hurriedly perhaps, while the boggy bits at last dried out ....This was horticultural heaven.

Anticipating a spring like last year's, when we took our gumboots off only to go to bed, we made an early-April dash to Italy. *The Enchanted April* (did you see the film?) is an enduring myth: Tuscany waking up to the sun in touches of glowing colour and wafts of suggestive scent. The airfare revolution now makes it nearer than the West Country. This year not only distance had shrunk: difference was negligible too.

What are the elements of an enchanted April? Lilacs and their perfume, light-blue and deep-green masses of rosemary, the cool rigidity and sumptuous petals of irises, quinces in quiet flower, the bright shock of Judas trees. In the Maremma woods, the oaks barely wakening, the floor was jewelled with deep-pink cyclamen and white anemones. Then pale-blue anemones and acid-yellow spurge, and deep-blue bugle, and dusky-purple orchids. Which of these elements is exotic here? Of the garden plants that make the Tuscan spring none is impossible and only perhaps mimosa, French lavender and germander even difficult. This blessed isle.

❧ July ❧

CHELSEA GOES WILD

Hotfoot (or rather wetfoot) home from the Chelsea Flower Show bursting with ideas. Pride, too, since Ken Livingstone, the guest of honour at the press lunch, pointed out that the RHS has more members than any of the political parties.

Ken is exactly in tune with the new relaxed Chelsea mood. The greening of London is high on his agenda. 'Encourage the cabbage white', he said, and told us that his famous interest in newts is matched by the mayor of Moscow's passion for bees.

Which year was it that a dandelion or buttercup first appeared in a prominent display garden? Steve Wooster the photographer remembered recording some (and nettles too, and even a bramble) on a Haddonstone ruin back in the 1980s. Now the buttercup is almost the emblem of the show. Or rather of the gardens. There seems to be a bigger and bigger gap between the horticulturally refined cultivars in what I still think of as the 'marquee' and the return-to-nature character of many of the garden medallists.

I have doubts about wildflower meadows myself. In what sense can they be called gardens? There was a charming slice of Japanese landscape this year, grassland full of day lilies, which it was hard to include within the definition of a garden. The Celtic Sanctuary, on the other hand, by clearly being a work of art, needed only artfully disposed stones, thorn-trees, grass and wild flowers to qualify.

Roger Platt's winning garden for the National Gardens Scheme won the Trad Prize on sight. It expressed the current rustic-nostalgic mood in first-class plants and planting. And it gave a strong sense that there was more beyond, in glimpses of a path, a greenhouse, foxgloves over a fence. And more to come: plants still in bud – including a lovely moss rose right in the front. Perhaps it is this sense of pleasures in store that a wildflower meadow lacks. 'And next week?' you think.

❦ August ❦

HOME AND AWAY

Two fascinating lectures at the Hatfield House Garden Festival in June. The Duchess of Northumberland on her new showpiece garden at Alnwick and the botanist James Compton on his recent plant-hunting in the northern Argentine Andes.

What wonderful contrasts there are in gardening. The Duchess, petite, animated, confident, radiating excitement for her huge project: one million on lighting, another million (or two) on fountains, the Wirtz family designing cloud hedges and hornbeam tunnels on a scale not seen for a hundred years. Northumberland may not be Disney's next destination, but I can see the Alnwick garden becoming the northern riposte to the Eden Project.

James Compton, next on stage, tall, spare and slow-speaking, lives in a different world. He told us of the trackless wastes west of Tucumán, of woods peopled with parrots, bright with scarlet fuchsias and begonias (note *B. boliviensis*, flowering from May to November and no problem to grow). Hearing an explorer back from a far-off country of which you know next to nothing fills you with questions. His slides light up your mind. Here was a guanaco, a sort of immense llama, standing out like a monument in the brilliant mountain light. And here was a perennial cosmos and an intensely perfumed verbena I shall grow as soon as I see them in *The RHS Plant Finder*. What a contrast in styles; what a contrast in stories.

Meanwhile a tip for controlling long grass, as practised at Hatfield and useful to anyone planning a flowery mead (as seen at Chelsea). Scatter the seed of *Rhinanthus minor* (yellow rattle, or shacklebags if you come from Dorset). It is a parasite on the roots of grass, slowing its growth to the profit of your colourful additions. Its little flowers are pleasant in June, followed by its brown seedheads. Certainly the long grass at Hatfield (like everything else there) is under control.

SOFT TOUCH

This has surely been the longest spring in history. Wimbledon is here and still no summer. But then we've had no cold since February. The months merge in one long saga of meteorological moderation and immoderate growth.

Where are the spaces we had allocated to annuals? As usual, luxuriously overgrown by their perennial neighbours. The convention of growing them in separate quarters is based on long experience – however frustrating to a magpie gardener who likes to plant shrubs, herbs, roses and annuals in cheerful variety but technical disorder.

There are tidy perennials that keep within their bounds. Phlox seems to me a model of upright character. Delphiniums will not wander. Nor do salvias or hostas or penstemons or hellebores or day lilies aspire to take over the garden. But acanthus is an empire-builder. It advances steadily with its formidable dark mound of magnificently sculpted leaves to fill your ground with powerful deep roots. Alstroemeria is a sinister underground invader. Clumplets spring up from running roots yards from where you planted it and years later, to flower and disappear, leaving a late-summer hole. All you know is that the underground network is planning more breakouts next year.

Japanese anemone is a gypsy, exhausting one campsite and moving on – probably into the roots of your roses. And that is not to mention the plants that offer you seductive seedlings: this year incredible numbers of pale-blue *Geranium pratense* (what splendid leaves), alliums and euphorbias.

Common sense provides plenty of answers. Avoid invasive plants. Dig up, clean and replant your border regularly. Be ruthless in reviewing its contents. But sentiment says no. It sympathises with seedlings, and trusts convicted criminals. I know what visitors think: this man is simply too soft-hearted to run an orderly garden.

PS Why did I think phlox can't wander? It takes time, but in light soil it pops up yards away.

❧ September ❧

RING, RATTLE AND CLANG

What sort of garden looks best in the rain? We have certainly had plenty of opportunity to find out in the past few months. One with shelter is the obvious answer. Appreciation and contemplation are much easier without a drip down your collar. Shelter can be relative, as in a wood compared with an open field. It can be incidental: you happen to glimpse a garden from a window, or even a passing train. Or it can be deliberate, the main motive, the very reason for the garden's existence and plan.

This is what the Japanese do to perfection. They sit snug under a roof on silky mats with paper screens to deflect the draughts as the rain anoints, then polishes, then seeps into the landscape. Around them aucubas glisten, maples nod and bamboos bow, while the rivulets of rain form into preordained pools in the moss.

And the gutters. They ring, rattle and clang like a rain-driven band. A bronze hopper collects the water from the shining eaves. From the hopper, instead of a downpipe, a chain of copper hoops leads the water to a gurgling basin.

If the gardeners of one group of rain-prone islands can devise such games to play with it, why can't we? The European way is to pretend rain is an aberration, to stuff it into a drain unseen as soon as possible. Show most Britons the beauty of raindrops on a pond and they shudder and ask for tea. We have a very serviceable rain-viewing house at Saling: a tiled wooden building overlooking the little hollow of the water garden. There is a table and benches. A single fountain jet rises from the pond to tease the maple leaves 10 feet above and keep up a quiet splash that excludes most of the intrusion of cars and planes.

Sitting in this house is idyllic in sunshine; private and meditative in rain. Perhaps I should add a gong and joss-sticks to satisfy sensation-seekers.

WITH A MISSIONARY'S ZEAL

Roy Lancaster's lecture after the Society's AGM in June was a welcome chance to see what our most eloquent plantsman grows in his own Hampshire garden. His cadences of wonder and delight, seasoned with anecdote and science, are seriously seductive. He has the capacity to make me plant a buttercup.

When he shows you one of the first plants of *Rosa chinensis* var. *spontanea* in cultivation, blazing cream and scarlet (as seen from his son's bedroom window), his north wall dripping with *Itea ilicifolia*, his porch almost blocked with *Camellia* 'Spring Festival' and his garage submerged under *Hydrangea seemannii*, I feel the urge to plant them all.

One of the most exciting was a Chinese climbing honeysuckle flowering for the first time here, with flowers that open white and change to cream, then apricot, then flame-orange, all appearing sequentially along the spray. *Lonicera calcarata* is its name. It was collected on Mt Omei in western China and given to Roy by its collector, Mikinori Ogisu, one of the most remarkable men in Japanese horticulture.

You could call Ogisu a one-man NCCPG (National Council for the Conservation of Plants and Gardens) – but more accurately NCCGP: his life's work is conserving garden plants. I have his masterwork in front of me: *History and Principle of the Traditional Floriculture in Japan* by S Kashioka and M Ogisu, published in 1997 in a remarkably good English translation. Seizo Kashioka was an industrialist, born in 1907, who witnessed the transformation of the Osaka district from country to enormous city. 'Everything', he said, 'was at the cost of the greens that coloured and nourished my childhood.'

In 1978 he met a kindred spirit 40 years his junior, the horticulturist Mikinori Ogisu. Together they started an iris garden with a million plants, of 1,000 cultivars, adding rare rhododendrons, hydrangeas and *Phlox subulata* until today 4,000 species and cultivars are represented. In Europe this would be admirable; in Japan it is unique. As for their book, we have nothing like it here. It records 33 of Japan's favourite groups of garden plants in deeply appreciative detail: not just their botany, but their history in cultivation, how they have customarily been grown, even how they have been critically admired by artists, breeders and flower-arrangers. Plants include, as you would expect, maples, irises, wisterias, hydrangeas, but also grasses, and even the epiphyte *Psilotum nudum*, which has obligingly sported into 120 different forms for our entertainment.

The plants are often illustrated by paintings, sometimes by paintings of their admirers in their gardens. Each group of plants has a diagram showing the number of selections in cultivation rising (and often falling) between the year 1600 and today. Any history of European gardens, oddly enough, would also date the study of plants in detail from the same time – the days of Tradescant the First.

❧ October ❧

THE E WORD

Have you ever wondered why the national gardening style of this country is known as 'English'? Having just spent a week in Scotland and the North of England I am none the wiser. Certainly there are ways of gardening more commonly found in Scotland than in England. Growing wildly exotic plants on an exposed western shore is one. But the elements of what we call Englishness in gardening are all present, in fact magnificently at home, in Scottish gardens: herbaceous borders, mixed borders, cottage gardens, water and rock gardens, woodland gardens and serene sweeps of lawn from a mansion to its lake.

The last, the landscape style, is the one foreigners most often refer to as English. It is attributed largely to Capability Brown, who was born in Northumberland. Had he been born in Roxburghshire, would we call his style Scottish? No, because most of his work was done in English parks. But it was never confined to south of the border, nor, come to that, east of the Welsh border. Rather than fumbling with the embattled E word, then, why don't we simply call it the British gardening style?

My goodness, though, Scottish conditions can suit it. This has been a miserably wet summer in the north, as in the south, but gardens at the two stylistic extremes, the formal and the jungle-like, were both surpassing. We found what to me was the perfect traditional border on the grand scale in the walled garden at Floors Castle at Kelso: 100 yards or more of a blue, white and silver scheme, the softest of symphonies under fluffy clouds, faced across the path by the same length of agapanthus. This was among a number I could cite, at Floors (in different colours) and elsewhere. And the plantsman's garden, naturalising rarities in a regime of just enough control, is everywhere on every scale, from the drama of Crarae, now safely in the hands of The National Trust for Scotland, to my particular favourite, the intimate, intellectual Cluny House at Aberfeldy.

There was certainly one garden that no one could call English. The walled Hercules garden at Blair Atholl was made in the 1740s, while Jacobites were still active, as perhaps the first attempt at high horticulture in the Highlands. Its grey walls are enormous, as much perhaps to keep out the wildlife as to profit from the sun. They enclose a valley of ponds whose potential for curling was certainly not wasted, with files of fruit trees planted down the slopes, presumably to minimise frost damage, and broad borders under south-west-

and east-facing walls, now planted again with the food and flowers they were built to shelter.

À LA CARTE

Each year presents the same dilemma: go away in August and you miss the big moment for vegetables. This year the effect was intensified by a long, slow growing season. There was not a tomato worth the name until August. (More mysteriously this was also true in the shops: wherever they came from we could not find a properly sweet tomato of any kind.) Then suddenly glut, especially of courgettes, where a daily pick is essential if they are not to become marrows. What to do with yet another basket of courgettes? The Saling answer is courgette soup (cook in milk, mush in mixer, add fresh mint), refreshing hot or cold.

❧ November ❧

ON THE DOLE

Consider the poor conifer. Few things have lived on earth so long. Long before the dinosaurs they had evolved designs that work so well that nothing needs changing. In their vast forests they had scarcely met mankind – until suddenly there were steamships and botanists and their tranquillity was over.

For a century or more they were celebrities: pursued, pampered, collected; the height of fashion and the subject of enormous investments. They were made to march over mountains and stand about in gardens. Then, almost as suddenly as fame had arrived, fickle fashion turned its back on them. Gardeners discovered they grow too big and age badly; foresters that they are rotten at biodiversity. Whether you are a Leyland cypress, a Sitka spruce or a sweet little sport destined for a rockery, things are not what they were.

What went wrong? Surely there is a market these days for good strong simple design. Nothing could be more purposeful than a spruce, advancing annually by a long upright shoot and a ring of spokes. A glance around the Chelsea Flower Show in May, or the show plots at Westonbirt last summer, finds few conifers venturing outside a hedge. Savagely picturesque the veteran pine may be, monumental the *Sequoia* or original the *Cunninghamia*; they do not have the modern garden look.

Would things change if new ones were discovered? If Roy Lancaster, say, were to find forests full of new designs or a nursery to go mad with a breeding programme? I doubt it. A few have found niches where their originality, their productivity or their fortitude will keep them going as valued members of plant society. But to an aspiring young conifer turning up with its CV I would have to say that jobs are hard to find these days.

PS But a new one does have a market. The Wollemi pine, introduced from Australia in 1994 and launched at Kew Gardens in 2005, sells at high prices.

A SECOND WIND

'Gardeners give up after August.' So it seems at least to a nurseryman who finds that Michaelmas daisies no longer draw crowds. I rang Wol Staines at Glen Chantry nursery at Wickham Bishops in Essex to check the name of the lovely lilac-blue thing that has just joined the pink Japanese anemones in the border. '*Aster* "Little Carlow", probably,' he told me. 'No mildew, stands up straight. But no one wants asters these days.'

Can it be because they are just too complicated? Too many names with slight differences that scarcely seem to matter? That they have a reputation for wandering, for needing to be dug up and divided, for harbouring mildew? Are they associated with melancholy, with days drawing in, with other border plants in undisciplined autumn retreat? Surely this is just the moment when new recruits are needed: fresh faces in a jaded garden. We welcome the return of roses from their summer break. Colchicums, cyclamen and nerines ravish us with their clear-skinned innocence. And asters produce their stars like an unexpected bonus from tidy green clumps that have been quietly furnishing the border all summer.

Yes, there are blowsy asters, mildewed asters and asters that have cheapened themselves with the buddlejas on railway embankments. But I am looking out at the tall *A. laevis* 'Calliope', the same clear lilac-blue as *A.* 'Little Carlow' on strikingly dark purple stems, in perfect partnership with the splendid yellow *Rudbeckia* 'Goldsturm'. And at ground level the bright little stars of *A. divaricatus*, its wiry stems almost black, scramble over the shining leaves and snowy flowers of *Saxifraga fortunei*. Gardeners who pack it in in autumn, or who plant only for summer, are missing a great deal: flowers that take their time coming, but revitalise the garden until it is time for us all to hibernate.

TABLES TURNED

Some debates will go on forever. Nature versus nurture is one. Designers versus plantsmen is another. Either discussion (are they by any chance related?)

grows sterile when it degenerates into the statement of opposing positions. All the interest lies in their interplay – which of course changes over time as people, or plants, mature.

Take the Japanese maple I planted 20 years ago as a minor attribute of a rocky cascade into a little pond with Japanese pretensions. The design was my priority; I took great care with the size and shape of the water, the bank, the disposition of the rocks, the flow of the stream. I even visited Japan and sat in contemplation in monastic teahouses.

The maple has flourished like the biblical wicked. The soil, shelter and for all I know the splash and the reflections in the water have been enormously to its liking. What was pond with maple is now maple with pond: the designer's intention is reversed. What should the designer do: cut down the tree or rearrange his priorities?

December

FAR BETTER NOT

The end of the year means resolutions, and resolutions decisions. We all have areas of our gardens we gloss over. We know they are tired and in need of replanting. Now is inspection time: time for clear-eyed and unsentimental appraisal: the blue pencil for mistakes.

The longer you have lived with your garden the harder it is to look at it afresh. We are territorial creatures. We make a corner of the earth our own and pad round it until it suits us like a dog settling in its basket. The old blanket feels best.

Could this border or that bed be better, fresher, more happening in spring or autumn? Yes, but only by removing an old familiar focus? I habitually temporise. 'Far better not', the mantra of a Victorian statesman, is a powerful voice. But look at the plants we have available to us; the advice, the inspiration, all those magazines ....

Don't be like me, ambling down to the plant centre at Easter to see what they've got left over. Happy Christmas.

2003

❧ January ❧

VOLVO *APPIATTITO*

In late October 150 dendrologists (students of trees, from the Greek *dendron*, as in *rhododendron* = rose tree) met in Brussels for the 50th Anniversary of the International Dendrology Society (IDS). Belgium is where the society was founded, by a posse of Belgian and Dutch nurserymen – the world's most experienced. Now it has 1,500 members from 50 countries, the current president being Australian. Hardly a nurseryman among them today though: these are amateurs in the purest sense.

It rained on our parade. It rained on our picnics, our eager huddles round rare or venerable trees, our notebooks and dog-eared copies of Hillier's *Manual of Trees and Shrubs* (the Wisden, you might say, of the tree-world fanatic). But trees thrive in rain, so dendrologists pretend to. Until, that is, the wind gets up as well – as it duly did.

The best autumn-leaf colours work even under low grey clouds. Does anyone know by what alchemy their pigments generate such inner light? Standing under the burning filigree of a Japanese maple you are warmed, your face flushed, by its orange and vermilion fire. At Herkenrode and Kalmthout and Hemelrijk, in some of Europe's noblest galleries of trees, we were warmed through and through.

The one surviving IDS founder is Dick van Hoey Smith, whose arboretum Trompenburg in Rotterdam is the source of such striking additions to the repertoire as golden, purple and cut-leaved beeches in narrow upright format: notably useful trees. He told us how the pioneer of flowering cherries, Captain Collingwood Ingram, just retired from the army, had complained of boredom to the famous plant-breeder Williams of Caerhays. 'Cross rhododendrons, dear chap,' said Williams; 'you'll have 20 years of joyful anticipation and only one day of disappointment.'

We had a day of dismay when a much-trailed westerly came up the Channel on schedule to toss trees about and fell powerlines on both sides of the water. Each time we learn lessons. Don't trust a forked tree and beware grafted trees; the wind finds the weak spots. At home it did: we lost four trees, and large parts of four others.

When we rang Belgian friends the next day to see how they had fared the worst news concerned the Lancasters' car. Roy and Sue had parked their Volvo at the gates of the National Botanic Garden. When they came back they found it squashed flat by a venerable sycamore. 'At least', said Roy, 'it didn't waste anything rare.'

EXIT THE YEAR

After that gale thick drifts of wet leaves and broken twigs have put paid to any lingering beauty in the borders. Even the pale emerging flowers of *Mahonia japonica*, promising the scent of lily of the valley, are violated, scattered on the ground with leaves and berries and tousled stems, as though the year had left in a hurry, no time to pack, slamming the door behind it.

Time to get back to bare earth and make provision for spring. My first affirmative act after the clear-up was to buy pansies and wallflowers: hardly original, but then spring does not need redesigning. Last April at Hadspen in Dorset I was inspired to be bold with tulips. Nori and Sandra Pope plant big clumps of them announcing the colours to come along later in other flowers in the same places. Would that I were that colour coordinated. I have got as far as 'China Pink', yellow 'West Point', red 'Dyanito' and 'White Triumphator'.

GREEN DIGITS

Does sharing your New Year resolutions make it more or less likely that you will keep them? Mine nearly always concern record-keeping. Make notes. Write labels. Take pictures. But this year I am deploying a new, a positively futuristic weapon. I'm going digital.

To anyone with a word processor a digital camera is the best gardening, or rather garden-planning, aid since paper. A camera that needs no film, always primed, is already pretty good. A foolproof one is better: the only decisions whether to zoom and whether to flash. Better still: no processing, no envelopes of expensive mistakes to collect. Better yet: the power to crop, enlarge, even to alter the colours if you think you know better, and to print the result. Best of all, as I discovered when I clicked on 'Camera Info', a precise record of the date and time each picture was taken, and the details of its exposure. Labelling is just making an electronic file. Attaching captions, plant names – or come to that I suppose birdsong – is scarcely more complicated. And filing and indexing, the heavy decisions and major time-takers in any garden picture collection, are rapid and easily redone when you change your mind.

There must be a catch. The colours fade; the computer crashes; all is lost. Not yet. If it goes on raining like this I shall soon be desktop-publishing an illustrated Trad's Diary.

PS It took five years.

❧ February ❧

BEAUTY DRIVE

D o we gardeners believe that what we do is in some way inherently virtuous? I suspect we do. I have a notion that gardening is considered praiseworthy – and not just because fresh air is good for you and digging stimulates the circulation. We admire a flower or plan a flower bed, we mow the lawn or prune a rose and feel morally justified – even a touch smug, as though we had just done our good deed for the day. It is more than just a matter of doing no harm: because our minds are in Beauty Drive, they are somehow attracting, collecting or communicating a Force for Good.

Or so we used to think. Until art took off in another direction, leaving beauty a stranded orphan; no longer even 'relevant' – let alone good. The Modernism of the 20th century set out purposefully to snub beauty – certainly feminine beauty (think of Picasso's *Demoiselles d'Avignon*), and by extension natural beauty too. Where is the virtue, then, in the outworn bourgeois preoccupation with creating and enjoying beautiful places and things?

Since art included unmade beds in its scope I am doing my best to be ironically post-modern. The beds in the walled garden are going to stay unmade until someone nominates them for a prize – or until I get round to making them, whichever comes sooner. I hear from Keith Tyson, the Turner Prize winner, that the randomness of chance adds meaning (if I have the right expression) to art. Does weather qualify as random? It used to be organised, up to a point, by a system called The Seasons. If they have been corrupted by a virus, as it appears, does it add another layer of irony to the heap or free me up to go back to making beds? As I glow with the effort I shall at least feel a little stab of virtue.

STARTING OVER

Three in the afternoon and the outlines of the garden are already disappearing in the thick grey air. The landmarks: wall, pleached limes, poplars and cedar are dark shapes. Skeletal anemones in the border under the wall and *Rosa* 'Mutabilis' pressing one faded pink flower against the window are the only things in focus. A street light emphasises the gloom. I am going through back numbers of *The Garden*, startled by summer's colours as I turn the pages.

This is project time. Trees that crashed in the October gale have opened up new prospects. I never dreamed that a healthy metasequoia would snap in the wind, but the one in the middle of the water garden came apart halfway up, at 30 feet or so. When I saw its torn top next morning I was baffled. What had happened to the rest of it? The wreckage of other trees was all too visible, but 30 feet of Chinese dawn redwood seemed to have blown clean out of the garden.

What, though, was that new tree on the other side of the pond? It was the top half, precisely vertical, dropped plumb into the ground 7 yards from its base and looking happy to grow there. It was a sad business cutting down the stump: pale sweet-smelling wood. Will it burn well, I wonder, or will it spit? The whole water garden needs re-editing around the mournful stump at the water's edge. Out come the catalogues. Happily Ken Akers, who is a whizz with ponds, still lives next door. His advice was key 20 years ago.

RISK AVERSE

You worry about a sick plant. You finally get round to sending a sample to the long-suffering pathologists at Wisley. And back comes the prognosis with a note: 'no treatment is available to amateur gardeners'. Or in some cases professional gardeners either. So what do you do? No treatment, no plant. You sadly cross your old favourite off the list and double your security patrol round the glasshouse, pots, borders – everywhere bugs can lurk.

We were warned in *The Garden* of April 2000 that by 2003 most of the pesticides we know would be banned by European regulations. And lo, it has come to pass. It was for the manufacturers, not the regulators, to pay the high costs of testing for effects on the environment, to standards set by the EU. For most horticultural products the potential market was just not worth the expense.

The cynical view is that here was a heaven-sent opportunity to simplify the range and make bigger batches of fewer chemicals; hence more profit. Those who believe the Euro-agenda is largely driven by big business can add this to their list of evidence. But to blame big business alone is unfair. Who is really driving the agenda that wants to eliminate risk of all sorts from our lives? We can hear our own voices, clamouring for more and more safety precautions of every kind, every day on the radio. An accident? There's a villain somewhere. A disaster? We'll have an inquiry to decide where to send the bill.

❧ March ❧

MUD AND LATIN

Gardening's own Action Man is back on the air again. His name is Chris Beardshaw, and he comes by helicopter, botanising over Cumbria at 1,000 feet before bouncing down to help a householder transform her garden into a combination of Levens Hall and Tresco.

Action Man's previous programme was *Hidden Gardens*, a notably well-researched series on gardens which (if scarcely hidden – or indeed lost) needed a bit of unearthing. He is not a man to talk without striding about and jumping off walls. The question is what does flying do for gardening? It gives you the aerial view of course. It makes you think Big Budget. But it also makes me fear the BBC is despairing of the mere terrestrial stuff. You can sense the producer ticking off a formula for Making Gardening Interesting. A chopper to attract younger viewers. A presenter on springs to keep them watching. A stately-home garden for the Big Time. An Average Plot for applying the lessons.

The average plotter in the Cumbria programme (the theme was evergreens) was left with several hundred pounds worth of incipient topiary in a pretty wild mixture of shapes and colours: red phormiums, for sure, and I think yellow choisyas. Did the effect remind me of the glowing colours of winter moorland seen from the helicopter? Not precisely.

It is sad if television should ever really see gardening as a boring muddy affair complicated by Latin names. I prize our Friday evening gardening slot (though I wish it were either before dinner or after it). We have our authentic gardening adventurers – even if what they get up to in Yunnan may not merit sending a camera crew. The essence of gardening, though, is close-up work, and yes, it is slow.

ON THE WARDS

How is your winter-flowering cherry looking? And your spring-flowering ones for that matter? Japanese cherries are in a bad way round here; not apparently for any one reason, but for several.

I reported last year on the death of a great white cherry, *Prunus* 'Taihaku', the most vigorous and generous of trees, which at 15 years of age, having grown and flowered as per the description, made no winter buds and was firewood by spring. It was followed to the woodshed by a *P.* 'Shirofugen', a magnificent, late, pale-pink cherry with such a wide and low-flying wingspan that it was the favourite place to photograph little pink babies, apparently floating like cherubs on Tiepolo clouds. One day fluffy clouds, the next dry sticks.

With no other suspects around I blamed waterlogging. Our *P.* 'Shirofugen' was old for a cherry; perhaps 70. Trees, too, get less and less adaptable as they age. But winter-flowering *Prunus* x *subhirtella* 'Autumnalis', to my mind the trooper of the tribe, began to look sick. So did *P.* 'Okame', which lights up late February with single bright-cerise flowers by the ten thousand. Similar symptoms appeared on both: the flowers and flower buds shrivelling into limp brown remains. The leaves died too, and turned yellow or fell off.

I wish I had less reason for referring to the pathologists at Wisley as my most helpful friends. 'Not fireblight,' they said, when I asked. '*Prunus* doesn't catch it.' This is blossom wilt (*P.* 'Okame') and bacterial canker (*P.* x *subhirtella* 'Autumnalis'). 'The disease is encouraged by a damp atmosphere.' Yes. 'There are no fungicides available to the home gardener for the control of blossom wilt.' See last month. Happily they look better now – but what will springtime bring?

In any case I shall break out the Bordeaux Mixture, the bright-blue copper spray. If I cut out all I can of the cankers, then apply it liberally three times in late summer, it might help to control the residue. I am not too sanguine, but what is there to lose? At Ninfa they spray the fruit trees blue all over and the effect is phantasmagorical.

CHATLINE

The blackbird that frequents our yard is getting friendlier. Before Christmas I was convinced he was eating moss; pecking it from between cobbles and actually swallowing it. Eager for knowledge I found a birdwatchers' chatline on the Internet. Was this a special sign or portent? 'Why do blackbirds uproot pansies?' was one question, which received the reply 'To get tae the wee beasties beneath.'

Perhaps the moss is the veg to balance a diet of beasties. My blackbird (we are friends now) let me come within 5 feet to make sure he ate his greens. Then the other day when I was clearing fallen leaves from the little cascade nearby he hopped down into the shallow water, came within easy reach, and took an elaborate bath, shaking himself enough to shower me. Am I specially lucky, or do all gardeners have such sweet companions?

❧ April ☙

COLD BUT NOT DEAD

When William Robinson was a young man in Ireland he took revenge on his employer, the story goes, by leaving the greenhouses open on a cold night. What you would now have to call 'this alleged incident' came back to me the other morning when I found I had left the top light of the conservatory open. At breakfast time it was icy. And the just-opening buds of my favourite rose were hanging down, seemingly blasted by frost.

As far as I am concerned *the* conservatory rose is *Rosa* 'Maréchal Niel', a sort of indoor *R*. 'Gloire de Dijon'. Flowering in February it complements the already amazing long run of this essential rose (which was in flower in December). January is the only month deprived of tea scent and dense-packed petals like most intimate skin. 'Maréchal Niel' is pale butter-yellow, whereas 'Gloire de Dijon' is buff-yellow warmed with pink and orange.

The Maréchal has grown in a pot here for 20 years, ignoring the books that say it needs open soil. It is leggy (a tendency of 'Gloire de Dijon' too) but I need its legs to keep its flowers high above the hall door, where they show their hanging faces, a dozen at a time.

They were not frosted. Their stalks were touched with brown, they hung their heads even lower than in their usual bashful deportment, but they opened and mingled their scent with the output from this year's most exciting new recruit: white winter-flowering *Buddleja asiatica*. Not that *B. asiatica* needs help in spreading perfume. How did this wall-fountain of elegant white flowers, long and narrow from among grey leaves, not come our way before? In one year from a cutting it is a 10-foot plant heavy with honey and already alive with bumblebees.

THE OLD ORDER

Lord Aberconway, who died in February, was President of the RHS when I joined. He was a robust figure of the patrician school of gardeners who have now largely been superseded by less personal institutions. As a recruit I was puzzled, I remember, by the word 'puddle' that kept punctuating his immensely knowledgeable discourses on the plants at Bodnant. Puddle, I soon learned, was his, and The National Trust's, Head Gardener at their great North Wales garden. To possess a head gardener at all I thought impressive. To inherit one was even more so … but to inherit one who in turn had inherited his role from his father – as Charles Puddle did – seemed almost miraculous.

That was the world, though, that produced the great English garden, whether in the 10,000-wallflowers tradition or the private Himalayas of rhodoland, where plants never cultivated before were treated as domestic acquisitions, their new Latin names shortened to a familiar 'arborea' or 'obtusa'. Not bad names for gundogs either.

The creations of the new century are going to be tame in comparison. Or are they? They may be more collaborative than competitive, but the Eden Project is not exactly timid, and pusillanimous is not the word for the new cascade at Alnwick. The main difference may be that today's projects have to appear public-spirited from the start, whereas the term in Lord Aberconway's time was noblesse oblige.

May

SUCKERED

Did it ever occur to you that it is not the human race that exploits plants but the other way round? Nor me, until a friend gave me *The Botany of Desire*. Not every plant is so wily. A handful, though, have us by the short hairs, or so thinks Michael Pollan, the author. Pollan is perverse, or perhaps alternative is a better word. He sees the plants' point of view.

The Botany of Desire (just reprinted in paperback by Bloomsbury) traces the history in cultivation of apples, tulips, potatoes and marijuana, four plants that correspond with man's desires for, respectively, sweetness, beauty, control over nature and intoxication. The immense success of these, and other, plants that man has cultivated and multiplied is an evolutionary triumph – for the plants. How smart they have been to spread their genes so widely, and the smartest part is that they have used mankind to serve their needs.

We all know that our cats are using us, watching our habits and feelings to bend them to their purposes. To that extent human desires are as much a part of the natural history cats inhabit as weather, mice, catmint and catflaps. What we find harder to realise is that plants steer us far more powerfully. They invent and produce substances we want or need, from calories to stimulants to sheer irresistible beauty; they tempt us to exploit them as a way of exploiting us.

They did it to the bees long before we got involved: a bee is simply following the plant's instructions when it clambers down the chute into the flower and covers itself with pollen. So, says Michael Pollan, are we when we choose the sweeter apple, the blacker tulip or the marijuana plant that grows fastest and packs the most exciting effects. In evolutionary terms, they are the winners.

BEFORE THE SWALLOW DARES

It has been summer without leaves for the past two weeks. The whole garden in warm sunshine with no shade is slightly bizarre, a walk round a bit of an anticlimax: no leaves, few flowers; the cast seem to have missed their cue. It certainly tests the structure, as designers call the parts permanently on show and the ones that summer clothes in what at present seem improbable amounts of growth. There are parts of this garden I am not feeling proud of at present.

Rather unfair, then, to visit a garden for the first time in these conditions. I noticed in our March issue, though, that the garden of the old vicarage at East Ruston in Norfolk invited inspection on a special RHS day. I had heard great things, I had to visit Norwich and the sun was shining. I went, and came away dazzled.

North Norfolk and the Isles of Scilly are not two ideas I had ever associated before. But at East Ruston Alan Gray and Graham Robeson are turning geography on its head. What a wimp I am, I realised, not to grow tree ferns, agaves, acacias, palms, bananas ....They credit the benign North Sea, a mile away across a prairie. I am inclined to credit good gardening, drainage, shelter and level-headed risk-assessment.

The project is massive: 20 acres already hedged, alleyed, walled, terraced, bordered and bedded with immense formal swagger and what looks easy plantsmanship. And 12 more in development. Surely the name is ironic: anything less like an old vicarage garden than this is hard to imagine.

My mind turned to Devon and Rosemoor, where we had been a fortnight earlier on another sunny day. There was no sense there either that this was the wrong moment. The lovely landscape, nestling in the woods, and the sheltered shrub borders were prime in the gentle sun; the trees more beautiful than in summer. Best of all in March was the most cheerful winter garden anywhere, alight with barks in all shades of pink and orange, yellow, jade and white, with golden leaves and rugs of white and purple heather. But in everything, even in paths under construction and big trees on the move, there was the same sense of living in an age of enterprise, when great things can be achieved – a sense only new-minted gardens can give.

❧ June ❧

GENTLY NOW

This is not precisely a complaint. Who could complain when the garden is so fresh and such fun, firing on all cylinders, more happening than at any time of the year? Or any time in living memory. The trouble is it is all happening at once.

Spring is always an assault on the senses – dozy as they are after winter. For months the nose has been pleased to sniff viburnums, thrilled to have *Mahonia japonica* and winter honeysuckle as treats, and has almost forgotten what the garden in growth smells like: the great head-filling fragrance of the ground and its whole population starting into life.

Now all the senses are in play, including the sense of time. Everything conspires to speed it up; especially 24-hour war news on television. Everyone says time hurries as you get older. (It does.) But not every year does spring pile all its most powerful effects into a crash-course three weeks. Bulbs that expect to be braving cold winds and nights have frazzled in the sun. At this rate my favourite daff, 'February Gold', will hardly be worth its space. It was over in ten days. Nor is it intended to overlap with my other favourite, the two-flowers-to-a-stem, falling-outwards clumps of 'Thalia'. Let alone such latecomers as pheasant's-eye narcissus.

Under one sheltering gable we have a group of shrubs I devised to detonate in a spring sequence. First goes *Staphylea holocarpa* 'Rosea' with its little spikes of double bellflowers, the inner bell white, the outer pale-pink. Leaves come later so the effect is pure and dainty. *Clematis* 'Apple Blossom' is a near-perfect match. It careers up the gable behind and flops down on top (pointing the way to this plant is like persuading teenagers). Then it is the turn of *Viburnum carlesii*, which usually waits, with its leaf-pairs opening like the beaks of hungry nestlings, until the staphylea is done before opening its carnation-scented clusters. Not this year. And, last in line, *Spiraea thunbergii* has almost caught up too.

MUNCHJAC

The tulips I planted in long grass a few years ago had faded away. While it lasted the effect was delicious: fantasy wild flowers gleaming scarlet among the grasses, the neatly-pleated mounds of cowslips and the mounting tide of cow parsley. Last year I decided to replant, more generously and with several tulips instead of one, starting with an early short-stemmed kaufmanniana group cultivar called 'Scarlet Baby' and following with the blazing *T*. 'Dyanito'.

Funny: mid-March, warm weather and nothing happening. I looked more closely. Kaufmanniana tulips tend to put their tube-shaped flowers up first, or with the growing leaves. Then I saw it: the emerging flower chomped off at ground level. All around leaves nibbled as they came up. And looking more closely still, all the bluebell leaves sampled in the same way.

Deer are choosy. It is the resident muntjac doing it. I am prepared to tolerate the knee-level browsing of any shrub that presents a target. My photinias have had plenty of attention. Now I come to think of it, they are related to roses, however remotely. Presumably Mr Muntjac knows this.

He is an elusive beast; a resident, I'm pretty sure, often glimpsed, no bigger than a Labrador, but instantly lost sight of. Depredations of shrubs I can just about tolerate. But now he has a taste for tulips there goes my wild-flower fantasy.

WITH GOOD ENTENTE

Rarely has a garden restoration had such a fair wind as the one wafting Serre de la Madone back into business. La Madone was the Riviera garden of Lawrence Johnston, creator of Hidcote and garden rooms. It has slumbered for half a century, apparently, in a part of the world where you would think obscurity was a rare commodity, at Menton on the Côte d'Azur. Inevitably a developer spotted the prime site, 7 hectares in sight of the Mediterranean. Remarkably, the French government stepped in to prevent its fragmentation and loss. Local gardeners sprang into action, the town and region found funds, one of France's top garden architects was called in, and La Madone is on the way to complete restoration.

Menton is the last town in France before the Italian border. Just beyond it lies La Mortola, the magnificent seaside botanic garden created by the Hanbury family. The rescue and restoration of La Mortola was the subject of a great deal of nagging in this column in the 1980s. In comparison La Madone seems to have had fortune on its side – enough to make other gardens green.

Do I detect a spot of cross-border rivalry: France and Italy squaring up to each other, trowels at the ready? As visitors (particularly RHS members, who have free access to La Madone) we can only rejoice in our good fortune.

❦ July ❦

ON REFLECTION

Sometimes the reflections on a pond form such a perfect picture that you see nothing else. The upside-down image seems in sharper focus than the reality poised over it. Sometimes a shaft of light pierces to the bottom, seizes on the leaves, twigs and stones lying there and paints them as a pin-sharp still life. Sometimes the surface of the water catches your eye: you see only the ripples, or floating blossom or leaves, and for a moment the reflections and the submarine world are equally invisible. Is it your eye that is changing or your mind? And is there indeed a difference?

I was debating this with a photographer friend, sitting beside our little Red Sea (we gave the name to a woodland pool when the concrete bottom cracked). Beside the seat is a stone conduit that dribbles just enough water to send concentric ripples across the pond like a gramophone record. Opposite, and boldly reflected, four white-trunked birches stand on an isthmus curved like the ripples, both curves being embraced by the curving shore beyond – a design much easier to take in than to describe.

I sit here often, choosing between the three alternative pictures (sometimes a few fish offer me a fourth focal point). 'Let's see', says the photographer, 'whether my camera can do the same as our eyes.' At this point his camera (a Swedish make) jammed. I was not so concerned, though, with the physiological question relating to (presumably) the eye muscles as to the shift in mental perception. Perhaps, I thought, this is the whole secret of garden design. Induce the onlooker to focus where you intend and the rest follows.

It is not easy. I see lusty growth, you see chaos. I see promising buds, you see the weeds. We all learn soon enough that colours draw the eye and that a sundial substitutes for a design of sorts. Some graduate to more imaginative distractions. Whether obvious or simple, though, the whole art of gardening lies in narrowing the choice so that we are all looking at the right thing.

VALE, GST

I recently lined up my copies of as many of Graham Stuart Thomas's books as I possess and added one more, *The Garden Through the Year*, which I had just been sent to review when he died in April at the age of 94 – leaving, as I now hear, his marvellous botanico-horticultural paintings and drawings to the Lindley Library. In this house his books are so often consulted that they live on the hall table; *TGTY* looks set to become battered too.

As a distillation of long experience it is a marvel, but also as a model of appreciation. GST derived such pleasure from everyday things, as well as extraordinary ones, that he could not help passing it on to others in his books, in articles and even on postcards. You don't often get what amounts to a review of a Christmas card, but when I sent him a watercolour of the chapel of King's College, Cambridge (where his grandfather was Senior Porter) his answering card was characteristic. 'It is almost incredible that this wonder of the world' (I edit slightly) 'can have been put up during the Wars of the Roses, stone from three quarries in Northants erected to such a height merely with ropes and pulleys and scaffold poles (no doubt from Scandinavia).' No doubt *Pinus sylvestris*, a tree you loved and photographed and planted so often, you model to all gardeners.

❦ August ❦

NUPTIALS

A wedding in the garden is not precisely a horticultural event, but it certainly concentrates the horticultural mind. Our daughter Kitty was married in the church that shares our garden wall on the warmest May Day for umpteen years. The rest of the proceedings happened in the walled garden, on the lawn, round the ponds, down at the temple and for all I know in the shrubbery. If we could have ordered the weather hour by hour like items on a breakfast menu we could not have asked for more. The photographs are bathed in the golden light of a perfect English spring. That is how it will be remembered, even if the garden was not the first thing in our minds at the time.

Flowers were, though. Flowers in the church, flowers in the tent, flowers in bouquets and buttonholes and in a gothic arch of roses and lilies over the south church door, which needed constant spraying, and a last-minute awning, to keep it lively in the increasingly torrid sun. The garden's contribution to the floristry was almost all green: barrowloads of everything from ivy to elaeagnus, branches of Portugal laurel and eucalyptus, sprigs of box and the early shoots of vines. A florist's eye in the garden is not the same as a gardener's – the shape of one leaf, the sheen of another, odd colours and forms, the fall of a spray have different roles. It is the same vocabulary with a different grammar.

Special preparations? The lawns were our first concern – not the case every year by any means. We (or rather Aileen, whose name I rarely mention, but who keeps the show on the road) gave them a deep spiking and raking to take off barrowloads of moss, fed them with a sprinkle of concentrated dried cow manure called Cowbridge (lawns love it), then raked them some more. In March and April, with no rain at all, they looked bare and brown. When the rain came, though, it was like switching on a green light.

I had splashed out with tulips in October, planting dozens of 'China Pink' on one side of the garden and yellow 'West Point' on the other. We think of tulips as guaranteed performers. Not these: barely half flowered. Thank goodness for winter pansies; they make their most generous show of gleaming satin in a warm spring. The spring woodland flowers were over, the roses only just starting. Is this what gardeners mean by 'the June gap'? Ours came early this year. Not that anyone except me (and Aileen) really cared.

SINGING THE BLUES

The dormice among us have always understood the necessity of delphiniums (blue) and geraniums (red). The best medical advice may be chrysanthemums (yellow and white), but we simply put our paws to our eyes. And I'm afraid it's the same with delphiniums (red).

The first thrilling sight of a sapphire spire happens in mid-June. The buds of the king of delphiniums, 'Blue Nile', have been hinting blue for a week. But when the first flowers open, their brilliance changes everything around them. The strings and woodwind fall quiet when the trumpet sounds.

True blue is a rare colour in the garden. Nor is it easy to define: there are many pretenders. I collected all the approximately blue flowers in the garden on delphinium day (I found 20) and matched them with each other, with *The RHS Colour Chart* as arbiter. Of the 200 pages of this formidable document (mine is the 1966 edition) 12 are headed unequivocally Blue; another ten Violet Blue. Of my 20 flowers only four matched any of the colour-chart Blues. *Delphinium* 'Blue Nile', which has a white eye, is colour 100A, designated French Blue. Black-eyed 'Molly Buchanan' is Union Jack Blue. Love-in-a-mist and forget-me-not also matched the French Blue sample – though with such a tiny flower as forget-me-not it is hard to be sure.

Everything else I collected as more-or-less blue turned out to be in the Violet Blue group, including *Geranium* 'Johnson's Blue'.

❧ September ❧

YOU REALLY SHOULD

It is one of the purest forms of gardening pleasure when a plant you have been watching and waiting for flowers for the first time. There are plants that demand very little patience. *Senecio vulgaris*, for example. Blink, and your groundsel has flowered, seeded and flowered again. The longer the anticipation the greater the pleasure: supposing, that is, you are pleased with what you see. I can only imagine the thrill of watching the *Magnolia campbellii* you planted as a youth in your Cornish garden opening its grey buds to rosy-pink far above your head for the first time before your middle-aged eyes.

What brings me rushing in from the garden to tell you is nothing so spectacular: a smallish flower on a tree considered, I fancy, horticulturally highbrow. Who grows eucryphias? Ah, but you should.

I was pursuing black bryony when I saw the first flowers. A wonderful weed, this bryony, as rapid as any bean and twice as luscious, sneaking up from the shrubbery floor in two shakes and draping its shiny leaves and gleaming green marbles from the highest point it can reach. In this case the 8-foot top of *Eucryphia* x *intermedia* 'Rostrevor'. And there, to my surprise, were the first eucryphia flowers, in masses that at first look like a white hypericum – and wouldn't that be a good idea? – round, virginal (but full of pinky stamens), poised on its slender upright branches among dark, twisted, pale-backed leaves.

Eucryphia is one of those families with branches in South America and Australasia. This 'Rostrevor' is a cross between *E. glutinosa* from Chile (too tender for us, alas) and Tasmanian *E. lucida*. Moist neutral-to-acid soil is all it wants. Its better-known cousin *E.* x *nymansensis* 'Nymansay' is bigger, darker, less choosy about soil and flowers in September. Why should you grow it? Dainty upright evergreen trees that flower, and prolifically, in August don't, so to speak, grow on trees.

COMMON OR GARDEN

Wild Flowers of Britain and Ireland has been my bedside book for weeks. It is the latest in a succession of wonderfully simple and direct Domino Guides by a redoubtable team: Marjorie Blamey, painter, and Richard Fitter, botanist – whose son Alastair maps the range of each plant. Is it ageist of me to add that Blamey is 85 and Fitter 90, and that they are now hard at work on their next book? That is when the painter is not sailing her little boat on the River Tamar.

Wild flowers and garden flowers are polarised in most gardeners' minds. We are trained by horticultural convention, and certainly by nurseries, to regard plants as being either proper for gardens or pretty much weeds.

But what an absurd idea this is. The beauty this book describes and demonstrates may have less raw horsepower than an azalea at full throttle, but it is no less the essence of what gardening is for: the enjoyment of nature's designs. The more you study the ancestral links between the wild and garden forms of plants, the more you appreciate both.

It may not be obvious (in fact it isn't obvious at all) that columbines, and indeed delphiniums, are distant relations of buttercups, but it doesn't seem so strange, when you think about it, that anemones have the same blood. Or marsh marigolds. Or hellebores. And becoming acquainted with the variety of buttercups themselves, from a skulking (but rather handsome) creeper to stately corn buttercups, standing thigh-high, is infinitely more satisfying than measuring out the weedkiller. Look at it this way: would you rather your plants could be identified only by brand names, or in Latin, or bore names that Shakespeare loved to play with?

❦ October ❦

THESE HOT NIGHTS

With the windows open day and night on the shady side of the house, and the curtains drawn on the sunny side (we are learning Mediterranean habits), we hear a good deal from our woodpigeons. Their song is monotonous, but far from raucous. I can (indeed have to) listen to it for hours on end: a low fluting of either five notes or three, either 'I *told* you, you fool', or 'who are you?' Unless the triple-note singer is a stock dove. Expert advice needed here.

We no longer have a single conifer unscathed by them. They flap noisily to the top of every cypress, spruce, cedar and pine and land on the leader, then express indignation when the frail shoot gives way. Spruces are wonderful at recovering; somehow a sideshoot takes the initiative and heads upwards –

only for another clumsy bird to land on it. Pines are less good. Cypresses (including Leyland) often start up again for a while, but I sometimes wonder if the famous tabletops of cedars of Lebanon are not the work of pigeons, starting in Solomon's time.

These hot nights myriad moths flicker and flash in the beams of the light from the house. The bats seem to avoid the light, and go swooping and lunging in the shadows around. Profitably, I hope. An opportunistic spider is trailing his silk, catching light like a vapour-trail. Does anyone see glow-worms these days? I haven't seen one in England for ten years or more. There used to be hundreds when we lived on the North Downs. Indeed when I saw their improbably bright little lamps in France in July I was so surprised I nearly dropped my drink.

ALL IN THE FAMILY

The name of Gertrude Jekyll always comes up when yuccas are under discussion. Perhaps it was her less-than-perfect eyesight that put them so high in her estimation. Is there any plant with so visible an outline? To her they possessed 'the highest degree of nobility of plant form that may be seen in an English garden.'

The yucca event, of course, is the moment when, with speed approaching haste, they elongate their thick flower-spikes and push out their plumes of ivory bells. They flower the way bulbs do, in a sudden surge of fleshy growth, skin-smooth. They are, indeed, cousins of lilies with permanent shrubby bases in dense rosettes of sword-like leaves. We grow two: *Yucca gloriosa*, the most statuesque, its rigid rosettes rising on short stems, and *Y. flaccida*, whose leaves bend in the middle and which, unlike *Y. gloriosa*, flowers in high summer every year. Both smell exotically sweet in the evening, with a hint, I fancy, of liquorice.

Yucca flaccida was in mid-flower this year with half a dozen 6-foot panicles when I suddenly noticed *Galtonia candicans*, the so-called summer hyacinth, doing a passable imitation: whiter, smaller and unbranched, but with a distinct family resemblance. And then *Kniphofia caulescens*, a grey-leaved coral-red (and cool rather than hot) poker, its stance as yuccoid as can be and equally liliaceous. What fun if we could cross them. Think of the glowing spires.

CRYSTAL BALLS

Whether the weather is getting better, or just hotter, is your decision. But that forecasting is improving there can be no argument. Not on the radio, which still makes a sad goulash of it, but on the Internet. The notion of five-and ten-day forecasts worth reading would have been laughable only a few years ago. Now there are websites that offer them routinely, in crisp estimates of temperature and cloud cover, if not precipitation. I have scanned them for a year or so, for East Anglia and parts of France and Italy, and I am impressed. Is the weather more predictable, or is the predicting more skilful?

What has changed, the Met Office tells me, is the amount of detail forecasters can collect and handle. Little of it, surprisingly, comes from out at sea or from above the atmosphere. Satellites can only give a general view of weather systems coming to us over the Atlantic; they can't see, for example, whether there is rain falling from a cloud or not. And there are apparently few ships sending observations. Most of the data are gathered on the ground over north-west Europe and plotted on a grid: a reading for every 12 kilometres. (It used to be 60.) The big difference is in the computers that can calculate and compare an almost infinite number of models from a constant stream of data to discern trends while they are mere glints in heaven's eye.

But then great slabs of weather like this summer's heatwave are much easier to call, as well as more popular, than our routine sunshine and showers.

❧ November ❧

POINT-SCORING

I am ashamed to admit it, but this was my first visit to Stowe. It is rather like confessing that I have just made the acquaintance of St Paul's Cathedral or the Tower of London. In the pantheon of British gardens that is where Stowe stands: the locus classicus in every sense of the word. If there is an excuse (I am not making it) Stowe has been through a long low period, its monuments badly in need of expensive care. That was before the strenuous devotion of The National Trust took effect. Now restoration is going full gallop. More than ever Stowe *vaut le voyage*.

I was all ready for the grand orchestral chords of long-matured vistas, temples settled into ancestral trees, the crispness of chiselled stone and the sweetness of pastoral lawns. And it is all there. Despite the Australian colour of the grass this summer, Poussin was on his throne. Three-score or so pavilions, temples, obelisks, grottoes and statues populate the landscape around one of the stateliest of homes, girdled by the original ha-ha. No joke, this: a stone-walled ditch girdling 250 acres is more like a fortification.

What surprised, shocked and finally delighted me, seeing it for the first time, is how busy it is; how packed with incident. The architectural entertainments are a mere number-two-iron-shot apart; in some cases almost a long putt. Ladies in Gainsborough gowns would not have been great striders, of course. One imagines they were wafted about in post-chaises, or even phaetons, the gentlemen trotting gently within a handkerchief's toss. But before the trees grew thick surely it looked a little overcrowded?

Harder to imagine is that the motive for all this construction was political point-scoring. Even the avenues demonstrated party allegiance: limes were the trees of the Whigs (because a Stuart king had taken refuge in an oak it was the Tory tree). You can't quite imagine Iain Duncan Smith raising an obelisk to the perdition of Tony Blair, or even President Chirac to the confusion of President Bush. Did it do any good, one wonders? Shall I build a temple of Britannia to proclaim my feelings about Brussels 'directives'?

SECOND TIME ROUND

How lucky we were to get through such a summer without a hosepipe ban. Moving the sprinkler became a regular game for weeks on end. We have learnt more than we ever knew about which plants flag first, which lose their lustre for keeps and which can be revived. One thing I will not forget next year: the sight of late-August delphiniums as fresh as the ones I wrote about in June. The secret? A complete chop back to base as soon as the first flowers are over, food, lots of water – and a total relaunch. I looked in the books for more about which perennials are capable of this. Eminent standard works are curiously quiet on the subject. So I have been experimenting. But even without a complete flowering reprise I would rather cut back to fresh-springing clumps of second-growth leaves than look at some of the scorched remains in the border. It is a restoring task, barrowing the top hamper of early summer away in hope of another. Who knows?

Everyone seems agreed, though, that our heatwave brought annuals up to continental standards of brilliance this year. It is Alsace and the Black Forest that always stick in my mind for their window-box power. Perhaps they are more conscientious about deadheading and watering there. In most years they certainly get more sun. But this year has been wonderful. Pubs have made a particular contribution to the gaiety of the nation; they shine out in every village and high street, incandescent with hanging baskets and tubs and windows and wellheads and mangers running the annual gamut from *Ageratum* to *Zinnia*.

In France they give towns and villages stars for the efforts they make to look jolly in summer. A three-star *Ville Fleurie* can be quite an eyeful. Not all their efforts are well-judged. The British effort tends to be more along the lines of Tidiest Village. Perhaps this sensational summer will spur us on next year. In fact I am surprised we haven't yet had a Euro directive about it.

❧ December ❧

EXCELSIUS

Heaven knows I try to prevent this diary becoming too meteocentric. But in gardening weather is often the main driver of events, and this year we have been driven all over the shop. In France (we were there for the grape harvest, three weeks ahead of schedule) the weather played such tricks I thought I was hallucinating. The great drought (still going strong here in Essex) was broken in late August by glorious downpours. The result? A miraculous replay of spring.

What about horse chestnuts in full flower in September? Can you picture hedgerows full of the hawthorn's red berries and its white flowers at the same time? And blackthorn with bloomy blue sloes and constellations of blossom?

The trees that lost their leaves in the great scorch of July and August were so refreshed that they put on complete new suits. Instead of a heavy late-summer green, fields and woods were smiling in springtime freshness. The only trees that failed to recover, turning a terminal brown, were thujas and Douglas firs from the Pacific Northwest. I doubt whether anyone will be planting them again here.

In the garden annuals were arborescent; especially white cosmos, at 6 foot dwarfing the box parterre. Cosmos cannot become a cliché – it has too much class. At eye-level its petals are as snowy, as pleated and primped as a parlourmaid's blouse. Roses came round for a third time with, I swear, more perfume than ever – and in different colours too: the encore from 'Nevada' was in full blushing pink.

We have a little terrace where roses 'Gloire de Dijon' and 'Alister Stella Gray' share two oak beams overhead with grape vines in a tangle of grapes and roses. Heavy translucent bunches (grape 'Perle de Czaba' seems smoothed from marble) intermingle with the silky frivolity of petals, in air so warm and scented that a breath was instant intoxication. On these short dark days it is something to remember.

2004

❧ January ❧

RARE AMALGAMS

Do spiders make a last autumn effort to fill their larders? Are they like the squirrels, so ineffectually half-burying conkers in the lawn? Or are we just more aware of their webs on mornings when they are strung with diamonds of dew?

There has never been a better year to watch the world preparing for winter. After a spring that lasted from February to May, and a summer that finally had us crying for mercy, autumn was more like a snail than a spider. For a wonderful moment I thought that time, which has been speeding up ever since I can remember, had touched the brake.

So seamless have been the seasons that change itself seems to have slowed to something manageable. Or at least observable, like the slow simmering of the sap that produced colours never seen in leaves before. What rare amalgams in their veins turned the oaks to copper, the beeches to the colour of a fox's brush, the limes to gold?

The usual stars of the season, the maples and *Malus*, the larches and poplars, the rowans and *Rhus*, the dogwood and berberis and spindles performed on cue and kept going for weeks, despite the drought. But strange suffusions of pink and purple crept through leaves that most years barely make it to yellow. Even the thistles turned a wan approximation of gold.

There is a cost, in trees and shrubs pushed to their limit. Here the first victims are *Sorbus*: two of the best for their berries, *S. hupehenis* and a little stooping *S. vilmorinii* I loved, planted (its label says) in 1957, tiny-leaved, generous with pink berries. Its last crop is still on the dead branches.

PACKING THEM IN

Some 20 or even 24 houses an acre, the density the government (or at least the Office of the Deputy Prime Minister) is suggesting for future new developments, does not leave much room for gardening. Allow for the parking, the washing, the foundation shrubs as issued and the paddling pool, and any horticultural ideas have to be on the small side. Are we going to see a resurgence of alpine enthusiasm?

It makes me realise how spoilt we are to have a walled garden of almost one third of an acre. John Prescott would agree (that we are spoilt): on the 20-houses-an-acre model it would accommodate six houses and gardens or, on the 24-houses model, eight. I have just pegged out the space, and it looks pretty cramped.

How does it compare with the gardens we have today? Working on what admittedly look pretty crude central statistics, there are apparently 15 million gardens in the country, covering 2 million acres. So the average garden size is an eighth of an acre, or 5,806 square feet (the figures come in imperial, and it's already complicated enough, so let's leave them that way). For comparison a full allotment plot is 30 square rods (to be really imperial), or 3,229 square feet. That makes our walled garden nearly five allotments, or two-and-a-half average gardens.

The Prescott plan calls for eight gardens in this space. And of course houses. Feasible only, it seems to me, if we grow alpines, go minimalist, Japanese-style, stick to Gro-bags, or (the most likely outcome) take up virtual gardening.

MNEMOSYNE

Every garden has an element of biography in it. If only to declare that the owner is a person who has no time for gardening. You can tell the romantic from the obsessive by a glance at their grass. But has any couple ever recorded their life story together as the Strongs have at The Laskett?

Sir Roy's book (*The Laskett*, Bantam Press) about their Herefordshire garden came out in October at a tragic time for him: his wife, Julia Trevelyan Oman, died in the same month. The book is an intimate account of the friendships, the thought-processes, the craftsmen, the seeds and cuttings and hard hands-on graft that moulded their joint creation.

Strong is not a bashful man: he tells it all. The Laskett is a theatrical memorial to personal triumphs; a sort of vegetable (and stone and water) masque; scenes from two immensely fulfilled lives, intensely intertwined. It commemorates exhibitions, books, opera productions, awards. But also the sources of ideas, even the sources of the necessary cash: all the memories that go unrecorded in other gardens.

We were shown round not long ago (see September 2001) by the cherubic Julia and the deceptively lugubrious Roy, holding the stage in turn over their enthusiasms with what seemed utter mastery of every subject. 'Flowers', said he, 'are a sign that a gardener has run out of ideas.' That was something that never happened at The Laskett: flowers became ideas when they were needed, and ideas, flowers.

We are fortunate, all of us, that such creative spirits exist, that they garden, and that they let us share so intimately what gardening can be in their hands.

✤ February ✤

SI MONUMENTUM ...

What else were they thinking about in London in 1804? Top of the agenda, of course, was the founding of the new Horticultural Society. Or so it may seem to us now. In fact that quiet event on 7 March upstairs at Mr Hatchard's bookshop in Piccadilly went entirely unremarked. All the talk was of imminent invasion. London was scared half out of its wits.

If you want a physical memorial to the events of that year, you will find a whopper at Boulogne: a 54-metre (177-foot) marble column beautifully (and rather surprisingly) restored for the Bicentenary. Whenever I pass it on the autoroute heading to or from the Channel Tunnel I salute it as the Society's surrogate monument. It also commemorates Napoleon's Grande Armée: 180,000 men equipped with 2,293 boats for the assault on England – a threat that evaporated only in October the following year at Trafalgar.

These details, and much else, I learn from Patrick O'Brian's life of Sir Joseph Banks, the natural biographical subject for an author fascinated by sailors to the Far Side of the World. Banks was the authority that the founders looked to as their patron. His vast figure, weighing 17 stone and stiff with gout, spelt scientific authority. He was de facto Director of the Royal Gardens at Kew. As President of the Royal Society for nearly 40 years he knew every man of science in England (and many in France).

Up to this time the Royal Society was considered the all-purpose scientists' think-tank, horticulture the business of practical gardeners and nurserymen. Philip Miller's *Gardener's Dictionary* was the Old Testament. But no author, and no garden of the time, could keep up with the flood of new plants from new lands being explored. It was the comparatively young John Wedgwood's idea (he was 38) to pool the best information on gardening in a society for its improvement. Two hundred years later his justification is complete – and old Boney is a distant memory.

SWANS THIS TIME?

I remember Christopher Lloyd, visiting us at an early stage of making our garden, remarking in a meaningful way that new enthusiasts frequently mistake their geese for swans. I hope he had one or two plants in mind rather than the whole garden. But just as new acquaintance can make us undercritical (the first time I saw Japanese knotweed I asked for a piece), so familiarity sends the critical faculty into a coma.

We planted our main borders 25 years ago, on a plan that relies on Irish junipers for its dynamic – if that's the word I want. A single file of them down the centre of each of two long parallel beds gave the plan a strong sense of purpose, anchored by box hedges and box pyramids at the corners. Around them we planted with definite ideas about colours; perhaps less definite ideas about form. The framework was clear enough to forgive some muddled thinking.

Now the junipers are going. A form of *Phytophthora* (not the one threatening oaks, a thought that freezes the blood) hastens the end of what are seemingly short-lived little trees anyway. More than half have now gone: the regular alley is no more. And my muddled thinking lies exposed.

Replanting columnar trees is not an option. I have lost faith in the junipers, Irish yews would be too big, and walking on the bed around them for the annual clip does the soil no good at all. Instead I am thinking of tall grasses to dominate the centre. *Stipa gigantea* is my favourite: high fans of corn-coloured stems and whiskered seed from June to December. Not in a straight line, but bursting from the beds at irregular intervals among the roses, campanulas and phlox, euphorbias and salvias, geraniums and pink late-summer anemones. If they turn out to be geese I have only myself to blame.

WINTER MODE

Winter garden originally meant the Bournemouth variety: a big glasshouse to shelter evergreens and their admirers. Now it means a corner for overcoat plants (who called them that?), de rigueur these days in big public gardens, and increasingly well done as designers look beyond the heather and dogwood basics of the genre.

Anglesey Abbey near Cambridge is developing one of the most ambitious I have seen: a long snaking walk using bark colours en masse as the background to winter flowers, a planting discipline as new in its way as the continental prairie mode of summer gardening.

Winter gardens are not places to dawdle. The days are short, the air cold, the sun low. But it is this low sun catching the colours that makes such powerful pictures – in colours that don't exist in summer. Nor do you need a winter garden to appreciate them. Look at the birch twigs purple-hazy on the commons, and the larch twigs orange in the woods.

❧ March ❧

HORTUS IN URBE

It is worth going down to Docklands to see how two highly conspicuous, very different, grand-scale examples of future gardening are getting on: the Thames Barrier Park and the Jubilee Gardens at Canary Wharf. Thames Barrier Park is the more ambitious, a 20-acre rectangle of redeemed industrial land (it was a tar-oil works) lying north of the nine eerie cowls of the barrier that stride across the tideway. The park is a plateau, formally outlined by massive modules of hedge, yew and Portugal laurel and beech, interspersed with straight beds of groundcover monocultures, as free of whimsy or intimacy as the parterres of Versailles.

Down its centre, to the river, runs the garden, hidden in a broad trench like a dry dock. The planting all follows this line, divided into strips by yew hedges rising and falling like the backs of sea serpents. The strips are long narrow beds of rosemary, of acanthus, of grasses, perovskia, lady's mantle, lavender, Japanese anemones, spurge, sage, caryopteris – each a monoculture. It is hard to wander and impossible to get lost in such powerful geometry. This visitor felt he was being given no choice: the good citizen toes the line.

The Canary Wharf garden disposes of a fraction of the space. It conveys workers to their offices in a gleaming cityscape more like Chicago than London. Playful, though, is the word for the long meandering cascade, built up chest-high in rough stone, that traces the main path. Tall metasequoias, hundreds of them, suggest forests between this moment of liberty and steely reality. Masses of grasses and dogwoods add to the feeling that this is more forest than flower bed. Cheerful sculptures inhabit scraps of sloping lawn that might have been borrowed from St James's Park. After five minutes in this charming place I was bursting to know who was responsible for the design. The answer: Jacques and Peter Wirtz. London should salute them.

❧ April ❧

CRÛG FARM PLANTS

I suspect every gardener has a prime source: somewhere that remains a reference for life. Mine was Keith Steadman's nursery at Wickwar in Gloucestershire in the 1970s, an inspired jungle of a garden responsible for several of the building blocks of my own. I almost felt I was back there when we visited Crûg Farm Plants in Gwynedd the other day. It has many similar features, starting with a country house embosomed in plants out of control, and a walled garden whose walls have disappeared behind the plants they were supposed to shelter. But Crûg Farm has a special buzz. Half the plants are only half-familiar, and a good number not familiar at all. It is the first garden stop for a steady and sometimes spectacular stream of new imports from Asia by Bleddyn and Sue Wynn-Jones.

Crûg Farm is up a country track just outside Caernarfon, in a corner of North Wales where the draught from the Menai Strait can be a bother. The other way, though, the view up the Llanberis Pass to Snowdon, is almost enough to take your mind off the snowdrops. The Wynn-Joneses somehow tear themselves away for three months each autumn to explore the parts of China, Japan, Korea (and last year Taiwan) where Caernarfon-compatible plants of any kind might be found seeding, and the seed collected. Last year the score was close to 300. Far from hoarding these rarities, they sow, propagate and distribute them as rapidly as possible, and on what seems an industrial scale. There must be an acre or more of tunnels and frames, with fields requisitioned from the sheep for growing on. The hugger-mugger of the walled garden, a magic kingdom of choice plants, links straight to web-page organisation (www.crug-farm.co.uk).

What is it that speaks to my inner gardener? Not just rarity, but compatibility: a crowded space where all the shrubs and climbers, the daphnes and hydrangeas and viburnums, the geraniums and anemones and hellebores, thalictrums and trilliums and saxifrages seem happy to have met. It sounds like Eden, but it is just good gardening. There is no mail-order: you have to go. It was the same in Genesis.

HIDCOTE SUR MER

The trouble with an old garden is that proportion tends to be lost. No one can bear to cut down the original trees – especially if they are the biggest of their kind, or indeed the only ones in captivity. This is the quandary of the great collectors' gardens of the Côte d'Azur. Paths, terraces, vistas, pools and views of the Mediterranean become so encumbered with strapping great subtropical evergreens that the founder would not know his own place.

I love these romantic jungles, but they are not easy for a serious conservationist to sort out. Serre de la Madone is the Menton opposite-number of Hidcote, Lawrence Johnston's other creation. He used to pop down there in the Lancia, we are told, while Jeeves drove the Bentley and the ten dogs. October to April was the season. Johnston painted pictures with plants that can only be imagined now, and that with difficulty, although their offspring may well be flourishing in niches they have found for themselves.

Encouraging these, and the dogged survivors of 50 years' neglect, is the starting point for a restoration that is taxing the top minds in French gardening. Serre de la Madone's owners, the Conservatoire du Littoral, will clearly not accept a banal solution: they have delegated design to a committee of the local gardeners who would have been Johnston's friends. One of them, William Waterfield, took us round the work in progress, then back to lunch in the garden of much the same age which he inherited at the other end of Menton. As we ate his home-grown avocados (three cultivars) and marvelled at his tree tomatoes, the problems did not seem so pressing.

✤ May ✤

KING OF THE BUSH

Question: which city marked its foundation by the felling of a tree? Answer: Perth, Western Australia. So I learnt from a plaque in its centre on a visit in March. The early history of the Australian colonies is enough to give a sensitive conservationist the vapours. It was measured in vegetation destroyed. Any tree too big to cut down was simply ring-barked and left to die. But the early history of most civilisations is the same: our ancestors hacked our own countryside out of the primeval forest. And, as I was reminded in the Botanic Gardens of Adelaide, the process continues to this day, only at an accelerating rate.

The spectacular rainforest conservatory in Adelaide, a building like the back of a glass-and-steel dinosaur, is dedicated to conservation of the tropical forest, where one hectare is being destroyed every minute, and two irreplaceable species are extinguished forever every day. In the next 30 years, they reckon, it will be ten a day. But to the loggers, remember, it is just as much progress as it was to our ancestors clearing their assarts and establishing their hamlets. The difference is that they now have bulldozers.

Fascinating as Australia's gardens are, nonchalantly growing so many of our most-coveted plants, to the Tresco limit and beyond, it is the bush, that dismissive word, that steals my heart. Bush seems to mean anywhere where aboriginal plants still predominate, where the gum tree is still king. And king is the word for massive park-like trees with a 50-metre spread, pale bark peeling like an imprudent sunbather.

It is commonly accepted that in England our frosty climate and the chalk soils of our sunniest region spell permanent exclusion for eucalypts. These strange smooth trees, besides, are not to everyone's taste. Those funny round blue leaves are useful, perhaps, in a vase, but they look mighty odd in an English country setting.

Or do they? Have you noticed how many have grown past the juvenile stage in our suburbs in the past few years to become serious dark-domed evergreens? There is none here yet that rivals major planes, but it seems possible that, with no serious cold to stop them, they will.

What should the conservationist think? That all plant-life is good and diversity is a blessing, or that they are out of place, that it is the past we must preserve? Like the plantsman and designer debate, this one is not over yet.

❦ June ❦

BRISTOL FASHION

Are you an edger? It is one of those questions that split gardeners down the middle – or rather, I suspect, in a ratio of about three to one. The three like edges; want, nay need, edges. For this camp, edges are the very definition of a garden: an enclosure where nature knows her place, where you can see where the gardener has been. The edging shears are handy by the door. Any spare minute and out they come. Tidy is pretty.

Shipshape, say the minoritarians, is not garden-shape. A garden should look like a happy accident, and straight edges are not one of nature's outcomes. Tidiness and order are not at all the same thing.

I am in France, sitting by a French window in both senses, watching a little water-jet bouncing up into the sunshine from an old grey stone basin, the garden's central roundel, reconciling all sorts of awkward angles of converging paths. Four box-edged beds are set 'slantandicular', as our old Kentish gardener used to say, their corners convexed to skirt the fountain. The box is shaggy. The house door and the barn door opposite face each other askance, the barn roof appears to be taking a deep breath, the gravel is edged with warped oak board. There is no line remotely straight or trim in the whole scene. And yet it is a picture of order.

Order, as opposed to tidiness, is an inner quality. You might even say a spiritual one. It comes with unity, appropriateness and proportion – concepts from a classical education that sound almost quaint to modern ears. It is not edges that make a garden, but a sense of purpose translated into style. If that style is shipshape, so be it.

ANXIOUS VOID

The four least-musical syllables a gardener can hear fell on my ears last week: honey fungus. The amelanchier had been looking peaky for the past year – but then amelanchiers are not burly trees at any time. Last year it had maybe a half-ration of its little white stars, opening with the leaves a unique shade of tender mole-brown. It was trained on a 6-foot stem, grafted on roots of I'm not sure what sorbus, its trunk leg-thick, its slender branches shading what we call our secret garden. The secret is out now: the tree gone, its roots dug up and its space an anxious void. Should the hellebores that grew under it go on the bonfire too? For the moment they are back where they were, while we ponder.

Healthy vigorous plants, the instructions say, have nothing to fear from honey fungus. I look nervously at the *Nothofagus solanderi* with its minuscule evergreen leaves, one of my very favourite trees, and the ginkgo and the tree peony and the viburnum. The ginkgo must be safe, surely, with its millions of years of survival. But how long can plants stay healthy and vigorous with the fiendish black bootlaces of honey fungus sneaking through the soil around them?

I have two new pieces of information as compensation for the loss of our amelanchier. The telltale bootlaces are elastic – unlike the roots of any plant. So just pull and you have the confirmation you dread. And all products devised to kill honey fungus have been banned.

ROOM TO BREATHE

Revision-time in the garden here this spring has entailed the wholesale cleaning out of the alley in the woodland designated the Long Walk – 90 yards long, as I discovered when I finally asked myself the obvious question.

This straight path from the water garden into the trees ending at a granite obelisk, in a sombre cabinet of yew, was inaugurated 40 years ago or so. So venerable are some of the shrubs that I tend to treat them as permanent features and neglect their toilet. Crowded stems, dead wood, matted ivy … we had it all. Things are a little better now; young shoots have room to breathe.

The perennials that have proved their long-term value in these less-than-ideal conditions, with even the ivy respecting them, include the dull-orange day lily that flowers all summer long, *Hemerocallis fulva* 'Green Kwanso', the mat-forming *Geranium macrorrhizum* and *Phlomis russeliana*, the Jerusalem sage that surprises everybody by seizing on the earth and holding it against all-comers with its assertive heart-shaped green (as opposed to grey) leaves. Then it puts up tiered spikes of mustard-yellow flowers that provoke everyone to ask its name – long into winter, too, when their brown husks still catch the eye. And spurges are wonderful troopers: dark-evergreen *Euphorbia amygdaloides* var. *robbiae* popping up everywhere from running roots, *E. palustris* only where you put it, but brilliant acid yellow-green in spring and flame-orange in October. The primary-colours school of horticulture would call these stalwarts dowdy. I live with them and love them.

❧ July ❧

POST-POWER GLORY

To Northants, to the Heseltines, to see garden-making on an Edwardian scale. It is 30 years since Michael Heseltine began collecting trees in what is now his magnificent arboretum. If he is still short of the complete set it is not for want of trying – especially in the years since the Tories lost power, when his planning and planting redoubled.

We were there at magnolia time, when waxy chalices of a hundred shades of rose and white and ivory crossed your path at every step, mingled with prunus and malus and sorbus choking with blossom. The new yellow magnolias, too: *M.* 'Elizabeth' is planted near the only yellow-flowering cherry, *Prunus* 'Ukon', and the yellow *Weigela middendorffiana*. New plantings, new beds, new labels, new sculpture, new ponds and streams spoke of creative energy everywhere. A new 'rill', modest name for a cascade as long as that of Highbury, foams with 36 water-jets. And the walled garden is 2 acres of exotic virtuosity, of arbours and kiosks and trellis, mirror-ponds and an aviary around a monumental fountain, in which four arching jets converge, by the modern master of moving water, William Pye.

It is 100 years since the Edwardian Golden Afternoon, when Charles Latham, the Jerry Harpur or Andrew Lawson of the age, seized the serenity of its great gardens on black-and-white plates of crystalline quality for *Country Life*. He would feel at home at Lord Heseltine's.

FERTILE GROUND

There is a perfect moment for planting in early May, when the earth is as full of life as the bundles of roots you are holding in your hands, and leaf-green seems to stain the very air. Long soaking in the rain and a week of good draining weather has made the ground so soft and open that you scarcely need a trowel to make a hole, and when I scoop with my hands in the fragrant soil to fondle it round the fragile roots I feel my fingers would take root too if I left them there any longer. Weeds come up as easily as plants go in; there is an almost sexual relationship between earth and plant. The ecstasy is short-lived, but that is the nature of ecstasy.

❧ August ❧

ROSE-CALORIES

What a summer it is for roses. The ones I can see from where I write are all in shades of pink: *Rosa* x *odorata* 'Mutabilis' like some wide-winged watercolour butterfly trying to come in through the window, then 'Albertine', the pale pink known for some reason as 'coppery', then the harsher pink of 'Zéphirine Drouhin' (these all in enfilade down the low brick wall of the front yard), then 'Albertine' again, then 'Bloomfield Abundance' with its airy trusses of tiny flowers. Facing them, out of the other window, in the shade under an alley of Lombardy poplars, are the deep purply-pink of 'Parade', the nymph-pink of 'Kew Rambler', 'Pink Perpétué' (a hard colour, this one), 'Albertine' once more, and the flesh tones of 'Climbing Paul Lédé'. They are all sumptuous this year: old, new, climbers, ramblers and bushes. The scent reaches right across the garden, now more like apples, now more like tea, now on the baby-powder side or mixed with the sharper breath of citrus from a philadelphus.

Does perfume cost a plant energy? There must be rose-calories out there, hoarded from last summer's sun. Petals and pollen and the flesh of fruit are all investments of energy: what about the sweet effusion that washes across the lawn? And why the variety? Does a hint of apple appeal to one bee; will another buzz up excitedly to memories of China in this languid 'Lady Hillingdon', tea-scented old hybrid that she is?

FLORENCE VS SIENA

In Italy roses must always be like this. For Tuscany, May is the month. It is four years since we were there in spring – and that was in April, when rosemary and irises under grey olives paint the garden purple and blue. May was pink and white and red and yellow, box hedges flushing pale apple-green, lavender misty with long shoots yet to flower, mounds of valerian (or is it *Centranthus*?) modulating between pink and red, white and mauve, strong shadows of summer making the cypresses blacker than ever.

The great villa gardens make the most of this pregnant moment. We visited two where, in Geoffrey Jellicoe's words, 'the concept of a domestic landscape is among the most thoughtful the western world has ever known.' He said this of the Villa Gamberaia, often cited as the ultimate Florentine country garden. It is equally true of Cetinale, its match from the hills near Siena. In both, architectural intimacies are played against wide panoramas in perfect harmony.

Gamberaia has the edge in panoramas. It overlooks the valley of the Arno from the north, surrounded by olive groves, with the domes and towers of Florence below to the east and ranks of Apennine foothills to the west. It is hard to know, and perhaps doesn't really matter, how much of the plan goes back to the 16th century when the villa was built, how much to the 18th, how much to the Russian princess who restored the gardens 100 years ago, and how much to recent owners. In such a small space (it is only one hectare, with a long lawn, the bowling green, dividing it down the middle) there is not that much room for manoeuvre. Parterres and ponds, deep ilex groves, the grotto and *limonaia* seem predestined to their places – and the roses to theirs. Strange perhaps that *Rosa* 'Albertine', with its single season of flowering, should be a favourite here, too.

Cetinale has the edge in its plantsmanship: unmistakably by an English hand. The villa, haughty, glamorous and eccentric like its cardinal creator, stands in the fairway of an immense plunging perspective, a mile at least.

Yet under its walls lie arbours and little outdoor salons close-packed with detail – and roses. The modern terminology for successful design is balancing volumes and voids. The juxtaposition of busyness and the long sweep is what these villas carry off to perfection. Especially in May.

✤ September ✤

BOOK-BUGS

How do insects learn botany? It has been another sad season of elm attacks by *Scolytus scolytus* and his little cousin *Scolytus multistriatus*, with their fungus-infected feet, leaving young trees burnt or bare in the hedge. I am hardened to that, 30 years after their brutal arrival destroyed all but one of our elms in, or close to, the immemorial class.

But this year, to my horror, they have been at the botany books and discovered that the graceful zelkovas, cousins to the elm in the niceties of botany but in appearance quite different, are fair game too.

We have three: two of the comparatively common *Zelkova carpinifolia* from the Caucasus and one of the rarer and even more elegant *Z. serrata* from Japan. Our *Z. carpinifolia* turned limp and jaundice-yellow almost overnight in early July. *Z. serrata* is seemingly following, with brown sprays in the canopy and, worse, brown stains appearing on the bark of the lower trunk. One of the last of the East Anglian breed once known as *Ulmus nitens*, the shining elm, for its gleaming dark leaves (most elm leaves are rough and dull), is under branch-by-branch attack, to which we respond laboriously with a saw. How soon will the scholarly scolytus cotton on to *Celtis australis*, the so-called hackberry, another elm relation and one of the best Mediterranean street trees? Ours looks fine now, but how do I tell it not to breathe?

AU REVOIR

For the past 13 years our gardening has been divided between Essex and the Auvergne. It has been a fascinating cultural experience, both horti and otherwise. Lesson one, the real eye-opener, was the difference between a maritime and a continental climate. By central French standards it has not been cold in England since 1981. And, last year apart, we haven't had what you'd call a summer either.

There is scarcely a day in the South of England, and not too many in the North, when it is not pleasant, or at least possible, to go out and do some gardening. Is Britain's equable climate, I wonder, the reason we seem to have invented most outdoor games?

Lessons two, three and four are the different priorities the French attach to everything from lawns to *la chasse*. Everything in France is regulated; there are *normes* for every article of behaviour. And, yes, the free spirit takes these as guidelines only. Their formidable army of civil servants can be implacable, but they can also (and often do) look the other way. Not at all like ours.

Now we are leaving. In a sense the project is over. We have made a garden (and house), planted a vineyard and many, many trees, made excellent friends and learned a whole new set of rules. But there is not enough time to love two homes, and perhaps not enough love either. What makes it easier, or much less difficult, is that we sold Les Boutons to a young friend. We can go back and pat what we planted.

We shall be there this autumn to pick the grapes. I know that when the mist fills the valley and the sun lights the distant hills, when the lakes below gleam in the moonlight and you can hear the stars rustling overhead, or when the grey wagtail pops out from the barn and dips herself in the water tank, I shall not want to leave.

❧ October ❧

FUNGUS FESTIVAL

Four-and-a-half inches of rain is almost a quarter of our annual total. When it arrives in one week in August the effect on the garden is profound. Spring growth is breathless, exciting and confusing; there is never time to appreciate all the thrust and heave, the unfurlings and covering and colouring of the plant world waking up. But August growth is threatening: familiar shapes are blurred, unlooked-for extensions are heavy over the paths; a bulldozer seems more relevant than a pair of secateurs.

And no wonder, when in effect the whole surface of the garden has been ankle-deep in water. Roots had just started proliferating thirstily when glut arrived. Overnight the late-summer scents of dust and spice, of phlox and curry-plant, fig and rue, gave way to cool earthy smells. The first downpour brought a positive installation of fungi: horse-mushrooms, tiny fairies' bonnets and creamy puffballs inflating like balloons. They must have the most hair-trigger reactions of all. Within days, passion flowers and wisteria and jasmine claimed space that was not theirs. Yew hedges turned pale and furry with foot-long shoots. Roses came back to life in subtly different colours: 'Maigold' is orange in spring; this round it is peach. Even Iceberg has a blush.

By the end of each summer the old fuchsia bush under the parlour window has climbed into view. This year it has reached the top of the casement and joined forces with the grapevine hanging from above. I can't bear to cut it. Peering down the drive through its pale leaves and tiny pale-pink pagodas (it is the albino *Fuchsia magellanica* var. *molinae*) is a submarine experience. Or will be unless the rain stops soon.

PATIENT POSING

The variety of our island is scarcely an original theme, yet each summer, when I explore a part new to me, I feel as much on foreign soil as when I cross the Channel. Morecambe Bay last month reminded me of Brittany, the land of hydrangeas and montbretia where the sun glitters on a grey sea. Our hotel garden in Grange-over-Sands ('the Torquay of the North' – but smaller, quieter and prettier) was a relic of Edwardian garden taste: fiercely polychrome bedding in that seaside style that defies taste – just as seaside villas cock a snook at architectural propriety. If Donald 'Postcard' McGill designed gardens it would be in this key.

A wedding in a church high on the fells was the motive for our visit (and the bridesmaids' scarlet satin, in brilliant sunshine against a background of rock and heather, an indelible impression). But to visit Cumbria and not to visit Levens Hall would have been a wasted opportunity.

It is too easy to file away a mental picture of such an iconic garden – the very temple of topiary, with its venerable sculpted yews – and not to nourish it with the reality. I was transfixed. It is not just the age of these marvellous monuments (some are more than 300 years), nor their number (there must be scores) that overcame me, but their beauty.

They stand with the loony logic of a Walt Disney landscape (Snow White, perhaps, or Bambi) among pools of pure colour, primrose and purple, cloistered by grey walls. Light falls in shafts among their strange loaves and mushrooms and hats and arches on luminous bedding (I remember snapdragons and verbena) disciplined by low walls of box.

There are a dozen geometrical compartments at Levens, laid out by a French master of the time of Le Nôtre. They contain some supremely well-planted borders, trim orchards, exotic vegetables, smooth lawns and a wide round pond encircled with limes, a recent addition that the master would have acknowledged as excellently apt. There is high plantsmanship, great craftsmanship and subtle taste; many shrewd plant associations I noted for future emulation.

A few years ago it was voted Garden of the Year, not for its antiquity, but for its quality. You can almost hear the old yews gossiping, complaining about the young, no doubt, and basking in the fame that has come to them after three centuries of patient posing.

⚜ November ⚜

THE PHILOSOPHER ANSWERS

It is important to look at your old garden photos from time to time to see whether you are going forwards or backwards. 'Did that rose really flower like that?' I asked myself the other day, looking at a ten-year-old picture of a 'Gloire de Dijon' nearly eating the house. This year I was content to see one third as many flowers on it, having forgotten its best performances.

The message? I may be getting on a bit, as the ghastly bromide has it, but there is no reason why I should let my garden become middle-aged.

It is not just a question of renewing old clumps of perennials with the sides-to-middle routine, or dispatching the tired stems of shrubs to encourage energetic young ones. It is also the whole question of proportion. Did you intend that bush to be so wide or that tree so tall? And if not, is the sense of disproportion niggling you, or can you persuade yourself that you never cared for the lost view of Snowdon or the Albert Memorial anyway?

The annual ebb and flow of foliage confuses the matter. All gardens are fuller in autumn than in spring. But at some point those annual accretions become middle-aged spread, and then resolve and energy to restore order are what's needed. With trees, a generous budget, too.

There are compensations. Maturity brings patina: textures and gestures and patterns of light and shade that new plants, however exciting, cannot provide. My mossy apple tree, its bole a grey flaking pillar, its branches pruned year after year until they writhe and clench gnarled fists at the moon, is a piece of sculpture it has taken 50 years to create.

The philosopher's answer is that all nature is in perpetual flux, and that you have forgotten your original intentions anyway. Keep pruning and manuring and your sense of worthiness will see you through.

FIGGY SHADE

It can hardly have been this year's weather that has given our fig tree such a productive nudge. I gather that figs around the country are doing the same thing. It must be memories of 2003. In most years we have to rummage among its marvellous leaves (Eve was a good deal more modest than today's thong-wearers) to find the occasional hard little fig. Just now I can reach into its deep-green recesses almost anywhere, it seems, and encounter a slightly yielding little body, cool to the touch, easy to detach and irresistible to bite.

Nothing makes a shadier arbour than a fig tree, or a more fragrant one, if the strange dusty/musky smell is to your taste. The artistically informal garden of the Chelsea Arts Club has a model I am tempted to imitate. Their fig tree is planted against a wall. Eight feet or so in front of the wall is a pergola, or at least a frame, over which the now weighty branches of the fig have been draped, and lean heavily like elbows on a bar, casting members who choose this corner into a deeply figgy shade.

THE SAGE-RISING SEASON

Our friends at the bimonthly magazine *Hortus* have called on the Society's scholarly Librarian, Brent Elliott, to reread Proust (something I shall not be able to do until I finish my first assault) to see what he had to say on gardening and the culture of flowers in that period of French taste best known to us through the paintings of the Impressionists and the more florid of Paris monuments.

The surprises are not in the gardens. So far as Proust gives us any clear picture of what are essentially settings for social comedy they seem predictably banal; not so different from French villa gardens of today, where horticulture plays second fiddle to comfortable seating arrangements.

Plants, in contrast, whether in gardens or the countryside, provided Proust with strong symbols of emotions. Hawthorn and lilac play a large part in any sensitive adolescence: the scents and colours of the sap-rising season, of daylight after dinner and the yearnings that go with it. Proust's yearnings were awakened with the flowering currant, thrusting its flowers through his bedroom window.

It was the age of the water lily, a flower of potent associations, developed into its modern splendour by a nurseryman from the Lot, Latour-Marliac, in the 1870s and by the time Monet had planted and painted Giverny, at the turn of the 20th century. Most potent, though, were the orchids. Darwin's investigation into orchids' wily ways of attracting pollinating insects had recently been translated into French. It provided Proust with irresistible metaphors; indeed cattleya (she wears them in her décolletage) takes on a new and intimate meaning to Monsieur Swann and his paramour.

❦ December ❦

LANDSCAPE WITH WILLOWS

My best thinking walk is two miles of purest Essex, the county 'with valleys but no hills', as one perceptive native put it. When someone else described our county as being flat and boring it could have been the same person who corrected them. 'No, not flat. Undulating and boring.'

My walk, from the garden gate, follows one of these modest valleys. The theme is willows. Cricket-bat willows are the cash crop here, lining every little stream; 15 years from planting a rootless 'sett' to cutting down 50-bats'-worth of prime willow. They are feathery trees, grey flecked with silver as the wind moves their slender leaves and flecked again with yellow as autumn comes on.

The valley bottom is pasture; rare round here, lush green with a pheasant covert of heavy oak and lighter ash to one side. The gentle valley sides are ploughland, just drilled with winter wheat, immaculate rich brown needlepoint with a sequin here and there where the sun catches a slice of shining clay. Our local painters, Constable and Gainsborough, knew the advantage of flat (or flattish) country: an enormous spread of sky for the slow parade of clouds.

October sun flatters gardens, as it flatters the landscape. I always think May and October are the best months for garden-visiting. Or indeed for enjoying your own. There is less work to do in October. But of course the days of May are twice as long as their October counterparts. Better value for money, it has to be said.

THE WELCOME POT

There is a spot just outside our front door (and possibly not only ours) that is a bit of a blank. The house wall makes a corner, half-filled with the pyracantha that hides the bathroom downpipe. What little soil there is, what with drains and roots, is shallow and dry. Next feature: a grapevine, handsome in summer. Then another drainpipe. A good red-brick background, shelter, a moment of suspense as you ring the doorbell: a great opportunity for a memorable plant, but no soil to plant it in.

It took me 33 years for the penny to drop. We needed a vase, something about knee or thigh-height, solid and good-looking in itself and able to swallow a 12- or 14-inch pot for a plant, or planting, to come up to your waist, chest, or even your eyes. We could change the planting as often as we wanted, and easily, by keeping alternatives down by the greenhouse. And why not in buckets with handles (and drainage holes) to simplify the swap-overs?

I soon found the websites of the moulders of reconstituted stone – and fibreglass, too, with a wonderful pattern book. We chose an octagonal gothic vase with the appearance of Portland stone. Its first occupant, a white hydrangea, has been greeting visitors for many weeks now. A box bush comes next, for winter, while I plot more interesting things for next spring and summer. Your suggestions, as ever, would be gratefully received.

2005

THE QUEEN OF MELBOURNE

I have grown to love Melbourne's Botanic Garden during my spasmodic visits over many years. It is full-throttle Victoriana in both senses of the word, part of a great sweep of parkland that invades Melbourne from the south-east on gentle green hills above the Yarra river, but forming a landscape picture of its own with its vast trees, its lake and shady gullies, crowned with the white-towered flag-flying Government House. In detail, in its infrastructure, its plan and paths and ornaments, it remains as it was designed in the 1870s, grand and confident, built it seems to last forever. The garden must be one of the best surviving examples anywhere of a style that combined the grand scale of landscape with the intensely horticultural manner known at the time as 'gardenesque'. It is not a pretty word, but doesn't it sound spot on for much that is going on in gardening today?

It is a tantalising place for overseas visitors, as the natives call us when they are being polite. The plants we grow seem larger than life there and the ones we can't quite manage give me unworthy thoughts about global warming ..... One area in particular I have always wanted to emulate: the Rainforest, where sprinklers among the trees maintain enough humidity for tree ferns to grow luxuriant arching fronds.

The patron of the gardens (and much else; indeed the unofficial Queen of Melbourne) is Dame Elisabeth Murdoch, whose son Rupert has made a name for himself in publishing. The high-point of our visit last spring was an invitation to the house where she has lived since her marriage more than 70 years ago, half an hour south of the city. Dame Elisabeth is a passionate gardener. The first sign of her style is the avenue of lemon gums curving up to the house. *Eucalyptus citriodora* is like a cross between a birch tree and a rugger post, sinuous and startling white, giving off a distinctly citric version of the gum-tree smell – not, I fear, one of the gum trees that has yet proved hardy in England.

The garden itself is England transplanted, but seemingly into richer soil. Each familiar plant (and some unfamiliar) looks extra lusty. It was hydrangea time when we were there: blue and white mops reaching far above our heads. Dame Elisabeth took us on her buggy to see her new plantings, doubling, at a guess, the size of the garden. She needed no prompting on her plants: their names, origins, virtues, problems – and why she loves them.

ON TRIAL

Can we accommodate gum trees in our English gardens? When I wrote about them in May last year a correspondent replied with a powerful point. A neighbour of his, advised by a garden centre, had planted one in the front garden of a cottage already bursting with roses and phlox and the hollyhocks of old England. The tree had reached 20 feet in no time, an anomaly you might think in such a picture. But here comes the point. The cottage is in a conservation area where any work on trees needs planning consent – except, that is, planting them. Once installed they become sacrosanct. Even trees so out of context as to look bizarre and trees out of all proportion to their surroundings.

February

POTTERING ON

The potter garden is a term I heard the other day to describe a plantlover's patch. Doesn't it conjure up a small, much-loved space in which every inch is examined every day? It is the elderly who potter. I rather fancy there is a minimum legal pottering age. Happily I am over it.

If a potter garden has a plan it is an elliptical path (bare patch might be more accurate) worn by the daily circuit. It has little tangential bare patches leading off to favourite plants. One to the greenhouse (small, wooden) and one for the seat. In Japan they have a fancier model: gravel through moss for the path, a lantern, a basin with bamboo dipper, a maple, a bamboo, three hostas and a doorstep plant (*Nandina domestica*, symbol of hospitality).

I don't believe other nations go in for it: their customs demand either productivity or polish. Our potter gardens are products of an Anglo-Saxon passion for individual, personally supervised plants.

They should not be too flourishing. Bursting seedtrays certainly. Cuttings with promising signs of life. But also an invalid or two to nurse and a couple of plants against the wall that have no business in these latitudes – something to tuck up with a rug on cold nights. I should give that *Xia mysteriosa* a hot-water bottle, too, dear. You never know.

My potter garden has defined itself as part of a larger scene – the part I always end up going round last, in the gloaming, reluctant to go in. A visitor might detect it from the relative absence of weeds. It is strong on scented plants, and it is where I grow my only azaleas (soil adjustment needed). The most expensive, five-pounds-a-pop bulbs tend to go in here and those hellebores that require individual inspection, lifting their downcast white flowers to count the purple stains.

NASTY PRICKLY THINGS

Did I read it somewhere, or did I actually overhear somebody say that they couldn't stand mahonias, and lumped them together with their botanical cousins, berberis, as plants to be shunned? Rooted out, indeed, if already present.

Not many plants evoke such visceral reactions. I regularly hear something similar about forsythia. I can understand that: it is loud in spring and gloomy all the rest of the year. But mahonias? I love them all. If it was you I overheard, let me try to convince you.

What else makes mid-November, when things are at their most dire, the moment for its stage entrance? Fatsia does, it is true, with its pallid blow-ups of ivy flowers. They have a ghostly quality among the huge shining leaves that is dramatic, if not exactly heartening. Otherwise garden cheer in the drizzling twilight of the year consists of falling leaves (our ginkgo's are brilliant yellow now, and later than ever) and hardy clusters of berries. I don't underestimate their merry redness, but they are not newcomers to the scene. They are reminders, not harbingers.

Then, with a flourish, *Mahonia* x *media* 'Charity' and its co-workers make their bow. Promising panicles of little yellow buds, 20 or so in a bunch like bananas, expand with a vigour that mocks the limpness of other plants. If mahonia can do this, you wonder, why not all those other shrubs moping out there? In no time the bunches are starbursts of bright little bells emerging from the armoured foliage – though not quite so warlike as that samurai of the tribe, *Mahonia lomariifolia*, whose fallen flowers still make a pale carpet round its feet.

And what was that sweet breath of lily of the valley that caught me at the corner of the woodshed? The first flowers, not so much bursting as gracefully offering themselves, of *Mahonia japonica*. They are the quiet yellow of purity, above sea-green leaves whose spines mean no harm – and they will perfume this pathway until the evenings begin to lighten and daffodils open.

And that is only the ones that perform in midwinter. *Mahonia* x *wagneri* 'Moseri' is best in spring and summer for its pink and yellow shoots, *M.* x *wagneri* 'Undulata' for its deep-green reflecting leaves, *M. gracilipes* for bluish foliage and purply white flowers, *M. fremontii* for tiny powder-blue leaves, *M. nervosa* for dense robust suckering ground cover. Berberis, come to that, is not really so bad, either.

✺ March ✺

SPOILT FOR CHOICE

The conservatory is the source of a good half of my deep-winter garden pleasure. The sense of growth going on, of flowing sap, of buds opening and plants releasing the sweet signals of their smells is a perpetual thrill. But we are just home from a place where the conservatory needs no glass: a hillside overlooking the Mediterranean just east of Nice whose local name is La Petite Afrique – Little Africa.

Floriculture is an industry here. Terraces built for olives and vines are turned over to early carnations and ranunculus for an international market. Ordinary gardeners are spoilt for choice. What do you plant when you can grow almost anything? There are those who play safe, already in love with the native flora (pine, olive, fig, rosemary, broom, mastic) and established exotics (oranges, lemons, pencil-slim cypresses, palm trees, daisies from the Cape, bougainvilleas): the conventional Riviera scene. There are some who relish succulents, not me: cactus is hardly comfortable company. And there are a few who expand into plants that look exotically extraordinary even in this Land of Cockaigne.

If I am asked my advice I hesitate. (I have been, and I'm hesitating now.) There is a sort of good manners in gardening within the local tradition. Too much from the southern hemisphere, even eucalyptus, can look as much of a statement as wearing a suit on the beach. Is it any different at home, though, where the front garden of a determined horticulturist can be like a fruit salad on a forecourt?

A conservatory presents no such problems. If it flowers in the darkest days there is a place for it here. The lemon tree is at it again, perfuming the air in competition with the white *Buddleja asiatica*. Camellias have started dropping petals. The purple flower-spikes of the scrambling *Hardenbergia* are appearing among jasmine buds under the roof. Some are old friends, some new encounters, but everything is a bonus. In Little Africa you have to choose.

❧ April ❧

COLOUR CODE

I t will look ghastly, but I plan a little educational demonstration. It involves tying a coloured ribbon to every plant in the garden. The ribbons will indicate where each plant comes from. Chinese and Japanese plants will get yellow ribbons, American ones red, European ones blue, plants from the southern hemisphere green. No, we can do better than that. I have just consulted my old *RHS Colour Chart*, the one that still used names. China can be Saffron and Japan Tangerine; the eastern States can be Scarlet and the western Ruby. Australia can be Olive, New Zealand Grass and South Africa Bottle. You get the idea. You just need a good ribbon shop.

It will make a bizarre picture, but it does have a point: to remind us of the far-flung, and often astonishing, origins of the plants we take for granted and thrust together without so much as an introduction. Do you think we instinctively, or conventionally, tend to group plants by origin? South Africans on the windowsill, for example. Would it be better, horticulturally or aesthetically, if we did? I think ribbons are the answer.

❧ June ❧

DOG'S BREAKFAST

D o you write lists of plants and tear them up? Do you stand for hours in bookshops leafing though the garden picture books? Do you wander abstractedly round the garden centre reading the labels? Then you must be about to replant your favourite corner. It is a tense time, deciding which of ten desirable plants you can fit in. Play safe or experiment? Think long-term with something choice or whack in an instant explosion of colour? Try six different things or stick to one?

It is worse when your best bed is up for grabs. Best in the sense of sunniest and most sheltered, that is. Abolishing our evergreen magnolia left a 4- x 12-foot bed, facing south-west, the most sheltered we have here. Up the chimney (it did battle with the magnolia) goes a banksia rose whose little double primrose-coloured flowers invade the upstairs windows in May. Below is this anxious-making void.

When does it matter most? (I am trying to do this rationally.) Its shelter could bring on something early in spring, but spring is chilly for sitting out there and watching the sunset. Midsummer is when there are most people around in the garden to see it. Late summer, though, is when we tend to have most time to sit and bask in the warmth of the wall and the paving. August is gardening downtime, when I will read over cups of tea until I suddenly realise it is time for a drink. What should I plant to take full advantage of the site, to look good and smell sweet for the early part of the year and to look great and smell wonderful in August and September?

I could plant a climber to run up the rose, for a start. The ancient pink and blue bricks are too pretty to hide with a clinger like ivy. A twiner like honeysuckle is impossible to untwine when you're pruning. That leaves us plants that go up with tendrils – or indeed without. Could I fit in a *Sollya* for blue flowers, an *Akebia* for fruit (but I'd need a boy and girl) and a *Clematis flammula* for its scent?

It is too dry for hydrangeas, my first choice among late-summer shrubs. Escallonias, perhaps? *Escallonia bifida* is glossy and generous with its flowers (they are white) and attendant butterflies. Buddlejas: *B. crispa* with soft lilac panicles and *B. fallowiana* with strong lavender spikes are two ideas – but deadheading them to keep them flowering would be a duty. *Ageratina ligustrina* (syn. *Eupatorium ligustrinum*) is a shrubby version of Joe-pye weed that has such a strong purple presence in boggy beds. It becomes a cloud of fluffy flowers in August or so.

I could tuck in one or two low cistusy things: x *Halimiocistus* perhaps, for bright midsummer chromatics. *Ceratostigma willmottianum* would give us plumbago blue and autumn red. A little myrtle, perhaps: *Myrtus communis* subsp. *tarentina* with miniature leaves is highly desirable. What about an *Azara* on the wall? Its delicate little leaves and yellow flowers would echo the rose. Salvias, of course: this is the place to grow the ones that are chancy in cooler places.

Phygelius aequalis keeps its little foxglovey flowers going a long time, pink or cream to choice. Is it stylish enough? A really silver *Artemisia* would be cheerful and a *Perovskia* would be graceful. And lavender, of course. And thyme.

Oh, the bulbs. This can be Amaryllis Corner, with great silky red trumpets, and another nerine zone, too. I quite forgot agapanthus. Perhaps the really tall dark-blue ones would be happy. And Mrs Trad has always wanted *Romneya* round the house. So far they have been reluctant, but we had a neighbour who put them in a wall bed and a few years later found them coming up through the floor of his cellar.

You will have other suggestions. The best would be to act on my first sentence. A list like this is a recipe for a dog's breakfast. A vision is what I need, not a shopping list.

❧ July ❧

FOR LIVING IN

Nothing (short of the imminent gallows) concentrates the mind so much as gardening in a small space. It is a salutary experience for a country gardener used to thinking in terms of trees, and indeed avenues. It is my son's London garden I am concerned with, a west-facing stone-paved space 4 yards by 5, bounded by an 8-foot wall. Space in a city is for living in: on a balmy evening I expect there will be a dozen people filling it. Plants have to climb the walls to avoid being trodden underfoot. How to plan it to avoid the feeling of a box with applied vegetation is the question.

The back wall has a raised bed 18 inches wide; the principal planting place, the launch-level for climbers and brink from which soft plants can cascade – and of course just the height to tempt visitors' bottoms. One side-wall is covered with the only established plant. It could hardly be a better inheritance: climbing *Hydrangea anomala* subsp. *petiolaris*, old and trunky enough to have the look of a tree in two dimensions.

Could we, we wondered, reduce the finality of the blank end wall? Why not pretend there is more beyond? A door in the wall, or rather on it, immediately suggests further space. And why not a window, too – shuttered to avoid the blind look of untransparent glass? A climbing rose and clematis can wander across them, as though it is a while since they were used. From the windows of the house, if not from close-to, the illusion works: the wall becomes a beginning, rather than an end.

In the middle of the house wall, between the windows, we have planted an Italian cypress, which in time will reach the roof, but backed by the wall can easily be clipped as a deep-green column. Sometimes filling a room makes it feel bigger; indoors we often manoeuvre round more furniture than seems sensible. By the time the mop-top olive tree, the vine, the bamboo clump, the hydrangeas and the box bushes in pots are up and flourishing it will be as furnished as a parlour. As welcoming too, I hope.

❧ August ❧

A CELESTIAL GLOBE

The Supreme Creator thinks of everything: even the menu. Some think especially the menu. Just as the asparagus supply starts to dwindle, and its flavour becomes almost routine, the artichokes fatten their thistly globes for a different feast. The spring-green taste of asparagus gives way to something milder and riper, more rich and nutty.

We inherited a cultivar that must have been in the garden here for at least 50 years. The globes are almost spherical, an even green with the faintest trace of purple at the base of each leaf and a distinct and characteristic notch in the top. Perhaps a reader knows their name. They are ripe when they reach the size of your fist, and still so tender (at least after a cool bright spring like this year's) that in June you can eat most of each leaf and the whole heart: the fibrous choke is only in embryo. We favour a sauce made with a soft-boiled egg yolk mixed into a mild vinaigrette and the white chopped on top.

Every three or four years in autumn we take the pretty little offshoots of each plant, a few jagged leaves the colour of aluminium, plant them in a new bed, give them to friends, and reap a rich reward.

PEACEFUL ENJOYMENT

I fear there is no landscape equivalent to the right to peaceful enjoyment. You are permitted to feel aggrieved (even if you have little redress) when someone insists on playing loud music in the open air. When they plant bright-yellow conifers in a green landscape you just have to look the other way.

It is a tricky subject, and I may well provoke the sort of letters I received when I wrote about garden-visitors' clothes. Scarlet anoraks, I said, did little for other visitors' appreciation of a colour scheme not including scarlet.

I bring it up again now because we have just been in North Wales, in a valley where forestry trees jostle with ancient woodland in all-green harmony which brings on the cliché of a tapestry faster than I can stop it. Tapestry or symphony, it is soothing, intricate and, during the growing season, when bright young beech, warm oak, soft hemlock and almost lurid shoots of Douglas fir are like the dabs of an Impressionist's brush, quietly beautiful. Thick-walled cottages of dark slatey stone emerge from the vegetation like rocks in a shallow sea. They look less integrated, though, when their owners go down to the garden centre and buy a clutch of deviant cypresses and the rhododendron currently in flower: the red one. The effect is like flotsam (or possibly jetsam) – at any rate the sea polluted with foreign objects: a yellow oilskin, perhaps, and a red lifebuoy. Your instinct is to scoop them up and dispose of them, to restore the picture. Not so easy, though, if they have been chosen, paid for and planted.

Loud colours are not called that by chance. And they seem loudest when they are isolated: a single rhododendron stirs you to pluck it out, while a whole hillside of them is almost soothing – except to foresters. To them the common rhododendron is the worst of weeds. Purple *R. ponticum* is one of the tourist sights of North Wales, especially as a carpet over the barren slate around Blaenau Ffestiniog.

One can see the householder's point of view – from his window yellow foliage may give him a faint suggestion of the not-always-shining sun. And plants contrasting with the surroundings proclaim territory: this is my patch, they say, and I'll plant what I like. I am not suggesting that these pleasures are illicit (any more than a red anorak), only that they affect others more than you might think.

ROSE RAGE

Perhaps it's just a man thing, like punching the air, to run subconscious competitions for the biggest or tallest specimen of different sorts of plants. My summer one is climbing roses: how high can they climb? Climbers, for this purpose, includes ramblers – indeed the difference often eludes me. In fact it includes any rose that attaches itself to something taller than itself and adds extension shoots rather than new ones from the base. We have, for example, a *Rosa* 'Scharlachglut' that evidently prefers the view from halfway up an incense cedar to the relative gloom at the bottom. Our neighbour Ken Akers planted one of our favourites, the apricot-creamy noisette *R.* 'Alister Stella Gray', to cover a little garden arch. Ten years later the arch has disappeared and a nearby grey-blue fir tree erupts with apricot-creamy blooms at house-roof level. Most of the big-scale climbers – appropriately enough with Himalayan ancestry – are once-only performers. Our own star is *R*. 'Wickwar', cascading in great spouts of white over its own glaucous foliage from 50 feet up a long-suffering Christmas tree. The double value in this case comes with its thousands of brown hips among the light-grey leaves. But any repeat-flowering rose you can coax up a tree can be even more desirable.

❧ September ❧

HERON FOOD

I had high hopes of a heavily-pregnant goldfish, the colour and nearly the size of a post-office van, that looped and dived and nibbled in the crowd with the carp, the orfe and the hundreds of tiny red-finned rudd under the wall of the moat (as we Essex folk call a fishpond) beside which I have slung the hammock.

The hammock, symbol and summation of summer, droops between a hawthorn and a crab apple ('John Downie', producer of endless red and yellow fruit) within earshot and nose-range of our little cascade. 'Thrilling, sweet and rotten,' was what Rupert Brooke called the smell of the Cam at Grantchester. Gently mouldy, I would say, between forest floor and farmyard, intermittent on the faintest breeze. I love it. Why do the fish congregate here to feed, and what do they eat? I've never made it out, but the goldfish was a regular luncher, and a great joy, until the heron got her.

I found her dead on the bank, rotten and not so sweet, speared but uneaten by the heron, who found her too much to carry, I suppose. The same heron carried off all seven of a neighbour's 30-year-old fantails in a single night, despite the tripwires deployed to prevent him.

The moat is too deep for the heron to wade in. He cuts an elegant figure in the duck pond on the green, motionless in the morning. I didn't think herons ever fished on the wing, but if not how did he reach the goldfish? Little barking cheeps from the moorhens and a sudden flurry as two dozen rudd break the surface. Orlando the marmalade carp glides serenely by, his tail-fin like a periscope. A summer Sunday, 75 old-fashioned degrees, tea in a few minutes, the best moment in the whole garden year.

PROJECTS

'I've got an interesting project for you,' was my father's formula for trying to get me to help in the garden. 'Project' is a powerful word. It implies a new development, a step forward, an activity leaving its permanent mark. Father's projects, in our garden on the Kentish North Downs, usually involved a red bowsaw and one or other of the sweet-smelling thujas that someone had planted liberally around our part of the chalky hillside. Manky specimens they were in those dry conditions, but the smell, somewhere between apple and pineapple, of their heavy fronds as we cut them is a vivid memory.

A 'project' is sexier than a 'job'. It is a job to mow the lawn, weed the carrots or sweep the path; a project to build a new summer house or install a watering system. The difference defines attitudes to gardening. To some, it is a makeover or nothing. To spend a day in the garden and leave it as you found it, only cleaner and tidier, has no appeal for projectors. Is it another of these gender distinctions? Put me down in the feminine camp, to live in quiet communion with my plants. To sweep paths, not to lay them. 'How come you are always planting new beds, then?' says Mrs Trad. 'You can't see a tree without planting a rose to climb it.' Ah, but that's just so as to have more plants to quietly commune with.

PLANT OF THE MONTH

It has been growing here for 40 years or more, yet every summer it fills its corner, and all the lower parts of a senior wisteria, with its unique peppermint-fresh muddle of white and green, of sepals pretending to be petals and then having second thoughts and trying to be leaves. Everyone asks its name. *Clematis* 'Alba Luxurians' is lengthy for a modest little flower. Not excessive, though, for a plant of such wayward charm and cast-iron performance. 'Late, small flowered' is how the textbook description starts for all what the botanists now call Viticella Group and similar clematis. Nobody should be put off. 'Late' means precisely when clematis-power is called for, in midsummer (and lasting till autumn). 'Small' is in relation to earlier, showier, shorter-lived performers. The size of flower, of course, is less important than the numbers, and looking along the wall now, where *C.* 'Venosa Violacea' stains a big escallonia purple, *C.* x *triternata* 'Rubromarginata' has clambered in a froth of pink through a philadelphus into the overhanging branches of a cherry, and *C.* 'Rubra' sprawls maroon velvet over everything in reach, I'll take my clematis late and small every time.

SUMMER'S HUB

I call it the Buddleja Moment. Summer seems to pivot round the moment when buddlejas (don't they look funny with the pedantic 'j'?) start ladling their honey into the air. The wild ones seeded in walls often go first. In this garden phlox, crocosmia, many day lilies, agapanthus, Japanese anemones … all the late-summer plants – and even the first autumn berries – seem to sniff the honey and take their cue.

❧ October ❧

WHITE: FRESH OR DULL?

What is your attitude to white flowers? To some gardeners they are the purest form of floral beauty, a sort of flowery ideal: all freshness, form and texture. Others tolerate them as safe and easy, useful and bright with no danger of clashing hues. To others they are a cop-out: boring, unimaginative, evidence that the gardener has no aesthetic spine.

I am of the first school, with guilty traces of the second. The first especially in the evening, when the wattage of white appears to increase. In August, too, when the risk is dowdiness, and the leaves of trees and shrubs have lost what was fresh and original about their first appearance. I have waited years for a *Hoheria*, that underrated little Kiwi tree, to flower. It looked peaky and wan as though the lime from the wall was unbalancing its diet. This spring we gave it some Epsom salts: now its froth of white stars challenges the eucryphia across the path; eucryphia dark and formal, *Hoheria* all tousled light. Brighter still is my favourite scrambler, from midsummer to the frosts: *Solanum laxum* 'Album'. White is not a single colour: there are warm whites and blushing ones, cold ones and brilliant ones. The little stars of the solanum have a crystal brilliance that makes each one tell.

In August, white-variegated leaves are most eloquent, too. *Cornus mas* 'Variegata' makes one of the brightest bushes, with more cream than green in its leaves (which presumably accounts for its slow increase in stature: an underdose of chlorophyll). Its little cherries are just showing the first traces of red. After years of patience the white-variegated aralia has made a luminous parasol over a broad patch of border, half-shading a group of yellow and orange lilies. The lilies are in pots; it is a bad idea to dig under an aralia: the result is thick thorny suckers, without even the redeeming feature of variegation.

BAMBOUSLED

I had promised myself a visit to the Bambouseraie for years, but it is in a part of France I rarely visit: the foothills of the Cévennes. Behind its faintly comical name I thought I would find a botanical collection and a nursery where the abstrusities of the woody grasses would at last be made clear. It takes a special kind of mind to grasp the differences in culm and node and sheath blade and auricle in a group of plants with many hundreds of species – all bamboo. I find I get too carried away by their behaviour. How fast they grow (up to a yard a day), how tall (up to 30 yards), how wide they spread (up to acres, breaking pavements as they go) and their beauty.

The Bambouseraie is a garden that demonstrates all these things, a park where the theme is the usefulness of bamboo, a great day out for the family, one of Europe's most original and beautiful plant collections and, apparently, the world's biggest bamboo nursery. This year it celebrates its 150th anniversary: 1855 was the year when an importer of oriental spices, Eugène Mazel, bought the land in the valley of the Gardon and brought in plants of the tall timber bamboos from the Far East. As a contemporary wrote: 'Bamboo is an essential of life in China and Japan. Houses, boats, furniture, musical instruments, weapons, bedding … everything is made of bamboo. Even the paper on which the artist paints his favourite subject: bamboo.'

Timber bamboo had never been grown in Europe before. Mazel spent his fortune on it. He canalised the river to irrigate his 34 hectares of deep alluvial soil. He watched his tree grasses grow to tree heights and colonise with their thick rhizomes every centimetre he allowed them. He planted avenues of the newly-introduced sequoias, and specimens such as a ginkgo you would guess is 400 years old. Then he went bust. But his successor, Gaston Nègre, was as smitten as he was: three generations later Gaston's descendants are still in charge.

As evidence of the universal utility of bamboo they have built a precise copy of a village in Laos, in which every detail, from structure to sieve and spoon, is made of home-grown material. In celebration of the spectacular verticality of bamboo they invite artists to follow their fancies in the seabed light of its forest of stems. And tellingly, in the nursery at the gate where every visitor feels compelled to buy a bamboo of his own, they sell rolls of black polypropylene as thick as a gramophone record. Nothing else, they warn you, will stop their rampaging rhizomes. *Phyllostachys* at full tilt can take over the entire neighbourhood.

✤ November ✤

A RUNNING JUMP

Wisley in early September: hot sunshine on the great herbaceous borders in full cry. No wonder the crowds pour in – this is iconic horticulture, a national treasure like the Guards at the Palace. And, some would say, just as tenuously related to modern life. Such gardening seems not so much aspirational, these days, as theatrical: a great performance. Performing is what great gardens used to do, before they became anxious about sustainability and biodiversity. When you can carry off the hat-trick, which is what Wisley does, it is worth more than a detour.

Wisley was, in fact, my detour that day: my main object was Painshill. I had been putting off a return visit, as one does, reviving the memories of my first, before restoration began, when it held the mysteries of a romantic ruin and the allure of the forbidden. It was a rainy weekend. We were staying with Chris and Jeanette Brickell when he was Director of Wisley. 'I've always wanted to explore it,' he said. It is only 3 miles from Wisley. It could have been 100. This was the 'lost garden' before Heligan: padlocked, barbed-wired, a jungle of sycamore, on lease, apparently, to a fishing club. Chris led me to a cedar of gigantic proportions, its roots in a ruined stone bathhouse, to a giant waterwheel, built to fill the weed-filled lake from the River Mole. 'Somewhere up there', he said, pointing through the sycamores, 'is a gothic gazebo and a Turkish tent. And over that bridge is a grotto.'

It took a running jump over the missing planks to reach the island. Part of the grotto had collapsed; its felspar walls gleamed in the rain. Trees had sprung up everywhere. It was the wood that hid the Sleeping Beauty.

More than 20 years later the beauty is revealed. What seemed irreversible decline has been reversed. Charles Hamilton, who lavished his fortune on this Surrey hillside in the 1760s, must be hugging himself as he sees his project, his plantations and his prospects, in their glory.

VOTED FIRST

Verbena bonariensis must surely be the plant of the year, if not of the new millennium. It is the tall spindly one, shoulder-high, carrying tight little bunches of bright-purple flowers and little else. It started as an accent plant, a touch of spice in the border, graduated into a feature and threatens to become, it seems, the main crop.

Penelope Hobhouse used it to great effect in her 'country garden' at Wisley, massing it as you might lavender, chopped down to give it many stems and far more flowers, round her central fountain basin. Others take advantage of its enthusiastic self-sowing to plant points of purple at random. The National Trust seems particularly smitten: by August the rose garden at Mottisfont Abbey might have been renamed Verbena Vale, or after the plant's origins, just 'Buenos Aires'.

COULD TRY HARDER

I was surfing the property pages of *Country Life* at the dentist's the other day when it dawned on me just how far from wonderful most big English country gardens are. It is an instant cure for any smugness about English gardening. Do we, as we like to think, have the world's best? Page after page of some of the world's most expensive real estate says 'Oh dear: what must the rest be like, then?'

I dare say they give their owners pleasure, these incoherent acres dotted with ill-considered trees, these spindly roses and worn-out borders, these clashing colours, impractical levels, trite ornaments and shameless swimming-pools. Members of the RHS, of course, are guilty of none of these things. I'm afraid there are not nearly enough of us.

AUTUMN QUIZ

'Few plants give such an air of settled distinction to a garden.' Three guesses at what Graham Stuart Thomas was writing about. Yes, cyclamen. Every autumn when the ivy-leaved *Cyclamen hederifolium* produces its throngs of bright-pink flowers from the dry brown ground, I wonder that anything can be so understated yet so brilliant. What a strange package, a brown lump rooting absurdly from its upper surface. What are these coils, as intricate as a nest of adders? Which are its roots and which its branches? Why did a primula turn its petals back like a spaniel's ears in a high wind?

It is as fertile as it is tenacious, this peculiar little creature. Tiny leaves are announcing new ones while the old are still flowering. The flowers gone, the marbled, sculpted leaves will jostle like the flowers to smother any competition, and hold their ground all through winter and spring.

In one corner of the garden here, in the light shade under larches, the whole colony is white: not my planning, just another mystery to add to the list.

❧ December ❧

TREES UP CLOSE

Home from the American West Coast, the heat of California and the autumnal cool of the San Juan archipelago. The San Juans live in the rain shadow of Vancouver Island and the Olympic peninsula (where the Hoh Rainforest collects 14 feet of rain a year). You can pick your preferred precipitation among these 50 or so rocky wooded islands, from 35 inches on one to as little as 11 on another. In October they feel and smell like Japan, fir needles damp underfoot, warm in the sun, cool in the shade. Their simple flora, like ours decimated by the Ice Age, gives something of the feel of a Japanese garden, too, where planting is limited to a handful of species. Douglas fir and western red cedar are the matrix, with red-barked madrones, the king of the arbutus tribe, firing up the sober palette. Madrone carries arbutus strawberries in bunches like grapes. Bigleaf maples drop yellow leaves the size of napkins on ground covered with low mahonias, *Gaultheria shallon* and 'ocean spray': botanically *Holodiscus discolor*, a prime example of a plant whose old, now incorrect, name gave you the idea perfectly. It used to be *Spiraea quercifolia* – a spiraea (its creamy flower panicles droop) with leaves lobed like an English oak's. It thrives in Essex.

America, the west especially, marries houses and trees in a way that is made impossible in Britain by building regs and insurance qualms. Trees swerve across roofs and poke out of porches, putting their shade precisely where it is wanted, soaring to the sky or stooping to the ground. In the Napa Valley they are often massive 'live' oaks, in Washington, firs or madrones. Don't they fall and crush your house? Not if they are close enough. Don't their roots split the foundations? Not if they are built with proper allowance for future growth. I quizzed a builder. 'I've never had a problem,' he said. The 60-foot Lombardy poplar 5 yards from my window at home has never troubled this house either.

Not everyone wants to live in a tree, but are we programmed to reject the idea? If it works in America, why not here?

WHY HURRY?

If there were a beauty contest between the months of the year, May and October would be the finalists. They can be tempestuous, true, but the prevailing weather is temperate, the sun is not too high in the sky, and the garden is moving between the extremes of being bare and fully clad.

May is all excitement and activity, October the opposite. Go-for-it gardeners become restive as plants go nowhere, holding their flowers through uneventful days. I have friends who say 'Let's have a good frost and get it over. I want to put the garden to bed.' Not me: I love the yellow leaf lodged in the fading spire of flowers, the roses on half-power, the wan attempts at a second or third display. It divides us, as so many things do, into the proactive tidiers, who see how things should be, crisp and clear, and the dreamy (you might say idle) observers, who find the seedhead as worthwhile as the flower. No, I'm in no hurry to cut down, pack away, dig over and divide. I can go on making quiet adjustments until nature does something decisive.

MATCHING

'Occult symmetry': what a wonderful expression. Occult is such a suggestive word: 'hidden', simply, at one end of its range, but positively supernatural at the other.

Jane Brown (whose books started with Lutyens and Jekyll and so far have reached Lanning Roper) used it in a lecture to the Essex Gardens Trust on 20th-century garden history. We can all do symmetry: planting the same thing on both sides of the path. But hidden symmetry, symmetry lurking ready to pounce, mystical, magical, symmetry unseen; the idea gave me goose pimples.

Jane's slide showed a path between a hedge and a canal. Another showed a strongly sculpted plant, fatsia perhaps, matched by one with tiny leaves like box, denser, therefore apparently weightier. Not so much symmetry, to my eyes, as balance, but balance by putting on the scales two items with quite different mass-to-weight ratios; candyfloss to a pebble. Do we have some instinctive measure that can even the odds and give equivalence to two such disparate things?

2006

❧ January ❧

SALIX PETROVICH

Moscow is scarcely the world's top horticultural destination at any time of year. In October, with early sleet in the air, I feared my visit might be barren. There are squares, avenues, vast parks, trees without number. The Kremlin is as green as St James's and Moscow University sits in a forest. Where could I find gardeners, though, and the soothing activities of cultivation? The answer was in the little botanical garden that goes back to the great modernising Tsar, Peter the Great – and through him, indirectly, to our own John Evelyn. It celebrated its tercentenary last year. Tsar Peter rented (and wrecked) Evelyn's house at Deptford during his English tour to study shipbuilding. To claim Evelyn as the godfather of Moscow's little garden is far-fetched, but they do say Peter planted the towering larch at the centre, and the oldest plant in the garden, a battered old pollard willow, is pregnant with memories of ancient, unreformed Russia. Unreformed romantic and plant-tourist that I am, I begged a cutting. Perhaps in 300 years someone will read this, identify a crumbling old willow growing here at Saling, take a cutting and keep the story going.

❧ February ❧

WE ARE ALL GARDENERS

I missed the RHS debate on whether we are still a nation of gardeners (the conclusion was 'only just'), but I did note the remark by one of the speakers that a garden does not need plants. True, up to a point (although it will soon acquire some unless it has a supply of weedkiller). Kyoto's most famous garden, after all, is only rock and gravel (and a touch of moss).

It's not the garden, I would argue, that needs plants: it's the gardener. And in this we are all, to some extent, gardeners. Is there a spider plant in your office? Do you eat your sandwiches under a tree? Do you walk home across the grass?

You don't need to bud your own roses or keep an allotment to be a gardener: merely to understand that we have an innate relationship with plants, and the more we cultivate it the more fulfilling it becomes. Especially in the space reserved for the purpose we call a garden.

BLAST FROM THE NORTH

I was in the water garden when Boreas arrived. All the winds used to have names: the gentle western Zephyr, the icy easterly Eurus and the boisterous Typhoeus from any direction, just as the Mistral has its name today. Boreas, the blast from the north, was the very embodiment of a wintry spirit as he forced his way in among the trees.

It was a calm afternoon. There was sunshine in the yellow leaves and the fountain jet was perpendicular when I saw the north grow menacingly dark. The bare branches of poplars were bright-etched against a roll of serious grey. In five minutes it had covered the sun, a scatter of raindrops fell, then the air started to move and the fountain to waver. One minute was hesitation, the next brutal impact. Leaves raced across the grass, a cold roar filled the air and the tallest trees, pines, larches and swamp cypress, swept together in a bow that seemed impossibly low. Straight trunks 60 feet high flexed like withies as the front bullied them aside. A sailor caught unreefed in this, I thought, would be in the drink. It was like a bully slamming open the door of a saloon. For five minutes the trees tossed in a frenzy, then he was gone.

A weather front shows as a sudden fall of the barometer. Higher pressure is suddenly displaced by lower. I am simple-minded: it seemed to me that all the pressure was coming with Boreas from the north. When I asked the Met Office they quoted Buys Ballot's Law. In the northern hemisphere, it says, if you stand with your back to the wind the low pressure is always on your left. Is that clear?

❧ March ❧

THE NEAREST JUNGLE

We make it a habit, while the world is in its post-Christmas trance, to take advantage of empty roads and hotels to get some fresh air. Once I put the point of a pair of compasses on where we live and described a circle reaching the nearest serious hills.

By serious I mean, rather arbitrarily, over 2,000 feet in old measure, 600 metres in new. In our latitudes, it's where you begin to feel exposed, out of the rut. (I wonder who started the canard about mountains starting at 1,000 feet? Molehills, perhaps.) To the east it's a long way to anything that high: Cambridge folklore says to the Urals. To the south the nearest qualifier is deep into France, the Morvan, woody and gothic but not exactly fresh air. That starts in the highlands of the Auvergne. To the north, the High Peak makes a start, continued on a bigger scale by Great Whernside, the old West Riding, good bleak country for striding. To the west there is Dartmoor, just qualifying, then the Brecon Beacons, then the Cantabrian mountains, bald, cloud-mottled and neglected, culminating in the wastes of Snowdonia, 250 miles from home, and another world. The Welsh mountains not only inhabit the clouds, they come down to the sea.

Hills mean valleys. Broad geological dishes, and sudden torrential slashes where earth gives way to crashing water. Plants find shelter in these chasms, grow in ideal conditions of humidity and still air, and fight their ecological battle to the death – of most things except the tall trees.

The Afon Gwynant pours from the north face of Cader Idris in a narrow gully to the River Mawddach. Beech, ash and oak, and sometimes sycamore, throw into plantless shade the white water and the black rocks, the winding paths and the plunging slopes. Only ferns, and straggling hollies, and listless ivy, survive the dark of summer. But in January the sun sneaks in, low-angled and deep-shadowed, making diamonds of water-drops, painting the beech trunks silver and the ash orange. It is the nearest we have to jungle, this climax vegetation in scraps of ancient forest. It is where we start the year, between moor and fireside, slipping and scrambling among the ancient trees.

✣ April ✣

ALPINE FASHION

There is a certain look in people's eyes at the RHS early spring show. They pile through turnstiles at the Lawrence Hall panting for flowers, as though the months since autumn had been interminable. The jewels start right at the door: three stands of them, the predictable sweet-shop assortment of cyclamen and alpine iris, aconites and snowdrops, miniatures seemingly magnified by being promoted from where they belong at your feet to tabletop height. The crowd presses, in big coats, carrying shopping, murmuring Latin like nuns at prayer.

Just in case anyone is stuck in the rut of convention, there are little notices among the flowers to bring you up to date. This is, after all, the season of London Fashion Week. 'The fashion is for bolder colours', says one little card deep in snowdrops, '… even orange', it goes on. And 'black is never out of fashion', says one next to that dreadful spiky *Ophiopogon* that seems to have been dipped in soot; scarcely, I should have thought, the little black dress of gardening.

Deeper into the hall for dreamers with their minds on more distant seasons. Scuffles, or nearly, over a stick in a pot labelled *Tilia mongolica* or *Viburnum cylindricum*. There is a different kind of instant satisfaction in capturing a rare shrub or tree: the thrill of the chase, not the glow of contemplation. For that there are the paintings. Cascades of minutely detailed cherry blossom from a Japanese artist who spends three months on one work. A red and white camellia with the startling realism of the Dutch masters from a German painter. Fir cones drawn with nightmarish precision by a lady from Dorset. Panel upon panel of those gentle studies that denote devotion as much as they delineate botany.

The February show was about survival: jolly little conifer buns, dogwoods with loud barks, and the hellebore that walks by night. The show in March is like coming up for air. The next is serious anticipation: new ideas for a new season.

MULTICULTURALISM

I sometimes think trees and shrubs are the easy part of gardening. You know where you are with them. You can see them in winter: there's no searching around with fork and fingertips, trying to locate, and then identify, a cluster of dormant buds. Anything in straight lines is easy. Lawns are hard; you never know what problem is lurking. Water? A ticklish medium of unknown chemistry. But perennials in borders, especially borders that pitch them in with roses and bulbs, cause a crisis every year.

It is predictable. We should have precisely located and labelled everything when we were cutting it down to tidy it up. The moment comes and goes, though, with only a half-hearted attempt. There is no scheduled fix-the-border date in our garden. If a plant is mush in November I clear it away; if handsome it stays. And by January hidden assets are appearing in awkward places.

First to show is arum, always somewhere unexpected, usually in a clump of something I intended to split or move. Is it the marble-leaved *A. italicum* 'Marmoratum', this perky little scroll of green, or just a plain old cuckoo pint? It is so bright in the bare ground that I can't bear to touch it. Next are bulbs. I think I know where the crown imperials are, and the tulips, but can I have put that iris there? Aconites, snowdrops, alliums, scillas pop up randomly, it seems, in what is supposed to be a bare field for herbaceous operations.

I pick my way gingerly to prune a rose, asking myself whether the soft crunch under my foot was lysimachia or phlox. The label that says delphinium is feet away from the telltale patch of gravel put there last year to teach the slugs a lesson. Cress is coming up in the crown of, I think, *Campanula lactiflora* and, oh my Lord, that's celandine.

It's all William Robinson's fault. Bedding by numbers was much less stressful. If we must pretend we just happen to live in a random community of plants with different calendars, tastes and habits from the four corners of the globe, we can't expect them all to fall in line with our fashionable foibles.

❧ May ❧

PANICULATION

We had to cut down only one tree to have a whole new garden zone to plant: a beauty, sloping gently down to the pond we call the Red Sea, sheltered from the north and west by a cypress and a juniper and a fair-sized *Sorbus*, one of my favourites, *S. scalaris*, with leaves like combs.

Gardens easily and quickly become habitual. We each carry a little ecology map of our plots in our heads. Aspect, soil, wind … memories of lessons learned tidily computerised. A cistus there? Absurd: too shady. Hostas there? They'd frazzle. But I can reprogamme the computer for this bit. The tree was a sweet chestnut. Its shade was absolute. After 30 years I realised I had only planted it to see if it minded our clay. It didn't, but nor would I miss it in comparison with what I would plant in its newly unshaded, ideally sheltered, place.

Hydrangeas were my first thought – rashly (second thought) in view of what now feels like long-term drought. I was inspired by near-trees of *Hydrangea paniculata* in the arboretum at Thorpe Perrow in North Yorkshire, an enchanted place of thickets and unexpected glades. In late summer *H. paniculata* 'Grandiflora' and 'Kyushu' dangle and thrust their respective panicles in mounds cottage-high of yellowing, purpling, greying leaves – an outcome improbable in Essex, I admit. Perhaps if I stratify the soil deeply with leaf mould and ladle on water from the pond ….Anyway, I'll have a bash.

Then one or two Japanese maples, I thought, and while they are getting up speed, a little elder; the parsley-leaved one in particular. I've already planted the challenging maple, *Acer pensylvanicum* 'Erythrocladum', pictured on *The Garden* cover in January. You'll remember its nail-varnish gloss. So bark for winter, flowers for summer, plenty of autumn colour; what about spring? I shall wake it up with scillas, keep the blue going with camassias, then deploy the cream froth and feathery leaves of goat's beard, *Aruncus dioicus*, in paniculate anticipation of the main event.

DIPLOMATIC BAG

Could the ambassador's sweet tooth be the writing on the wall for *Sciurus carolinensis*? Nothing else seems to halt the advance of the tree rat. Grey squirrels have been driving out our native red, *Sciurus vulgaris*, ever since they were introduced from North America in Victorian days. They now outnumber our own, apparently, 66 to 1, have colonised almost all of England and Wales and are doing the same in Scotland. It is not only red squirrels they devastate: they prey on birds' nests, steal their food and strip the bark from broadleaf trees. They carry a pox that acts like myxomatosis on red squirrels that catch it, while being immune themselves. Even if everyone agreed the task of controlling them would be almost impossible, but we are far from that. While our urban population still finds them cuddly all efforts to eliminate them will be frustrated.

And the ambassador? So far the grey squirrel has been a British problem. There aren't any in France or Germany. Brussels has paid no attention. But 50 years ago they were introduced into northern Italy; they have become established in Piedmont, and have found the hazelnut orchards that supply

Ferrero Rocher – and on a humbler level, Nutella. The Alpine valleys are full of beech and sycamore, their favourite trees to destroy. So far they have been treated as a local issue, with no pressure on regional authorities to do anything about them. But now France is worried: no country in Europe has more broadleaf woods. Letters are going from Paris to Rome. Could there be an international solution? The European Squirrel Initiative is the body, based in Suffolk, lobbying for action before it is too late. Better to load your gun than hold your breath.

ON HOLD

I have rarely appreciated the conservatory so much as in this finger-drumming spring. Outside there has been a go-slow for weeks on end. Tree buds may be fattening, but the early bulbs are wan, the grass barely green. Any day now the soil will reach the magic temperature: 6 degrees, they tell me, and away we go. There will be too much to take in as the whole flora shifts into bottom gear.

It is the curse of modern times, I fear, the short attention span that demands constant change. I certainly would be no good with a garden that was intentionally static; a scatter of sulky rocks in gravel or an embroidered parterre that looked up at me every day of the year with all the vital energy of a sofa cover. For the same reason equatorial gardening would leave me, so to speak, cold. Is it winter or summer? The same old palms, all those noisy birds, dark at six …. No, there has to be a sense of progress. Even a temporary hitch (this March, for instance) makes us impatient.

❦ June ❧

QUEUE GARDENS

To the Royal Botanic Gardens (so fashionable these days that I have seen them spelt Queue) on a bright day with a north wind to see the new alpine house. Everybody says what a beauty it is; a design worthy to follow the glass masterpieces of the Temperate and Palm Houses. I find it in the brown stone canyons behind the Princess of Wales Conservatory, a place where plants, I always think, must feel like soldiers in a barracks: orderly, well-housed, properly fed and watered, but with no prospect beyond the institution.

The new house soars up like a shining sail or the ridged back of a sleek and streamlined reptile, smaller than I expected, but finer: a jewel of glass and steel proportioned to the tiny treasures it displays. A dozen worshippers filed past miniature narcissi, an ivory erythronium and a Chilean blue crocus, *Tecophilaea cyanocrocus*, a colour to make gentians feel dowdy. They must feel most luxuriously housed.

On the way back I joined the photographers around the magnolias. My pocket digital looked silly beside their Hasselblads and tripods and black trunks of equipment. I'm happy with my picture, though: a silver Boeing among the succulent pink petals of *Magnolia sprengeri* var. *diva*.

NUPTIAL BLISS

Think of all the things you do in the garden: weed, prune, hoe, mow, plan, ponder, rake and even relax. Is there one activity, one deed, that stands out as climactic, the Big Moment? Planting, surely. Committing roots to the ground can be done in a trice. Its consequences, though, are the success or failure of the whole enterprise.

It is a moment I love. Taking out the barrow, loading up compost, bonemeal, spade and trowel is stage one. Then the intended in its pot: yes, this is a marriage of plant and place – and I am responsible for its happiness. I look around before I dig. Have I taken everything into account? Will the hedge shade it, or the run-off drown it? Is the soil too sticky here? Am I leaving enough room for its eventual size?

This afternoon I married half a dozen plants that may, if all goes well, still be in the same beds in 50 years. I dug deep, loosened the soil and mixed in compost to make it match, in texture at least, the compost around the roots. I teased out fibrous white threads that were circling the pot. I knelt to gauge the depth, bent with both hands gently to place plant in earth. I scooped soil with bare hands, fingered it among the roots and drew up a counterpane of soil. It felt like holy water in the can as I gave them my blessing.

PSYCHOTOPIA

Most gardeners, I suspect, react to the word Philosophy in the way Goering did to Culture. They reach for the safety-catch of whatever tool they are carrying. Perhaps they admit to a little of the homespun kind, as in 'A peck of dust in March ...' or 'The best time to prune is when you remember'. But rigorous thought – examining, comparing and rejecting abstract ideas – they are happy to leave to, for want of a better word, philosophers. I have just been reading one who is also a garden critic. It made me think.

Tim Richardson is concerned with the sense of place all agree is essential to a good garden. Alexander Pope's advice was 'consult the genius of the place'. What, asks Richardson, is this 'genius'? He has a new name for it: Psychotopia.

Psychotopia is the centrepiece of a recent collection of essays, *Vista*, which has faint echoes of that manifesto of half a century ago, *Declaration*, in which Doris Lessing, John Osborne, Colin Wilson, Ken Tynan and John Wain set out their stalls. John Osborne wrote, 'There has never been so little to say to one another, and so little desire to say it.' *Vista* (Frances Lincoln, 2005) says something similar about our gardening. Style is lacking because content is lacking. We just rehash the same old ideas ad nauseam. It is an argument that crops up from time to time in these pages.

So what is Psychotopia? A combination of spirit and place. I shall not try to reproduce what takes Richardson 30 closely argued pages to expound. You must read him. One obvious example is the atmosphere or mood that visitors to a garden encounter: cheerful or gloomy, calm or troubled. Is it inherent? It often seems to be.

What else may be inherent, then? Certainly the ecology. A Surrey garden on heathland, a Wealden garden on clay, a Cotswold garden on limestone and a Scots one on granite start with different natural flora and should always, surely, keep at least that much sense of where they are. Add history (if any), artistry (ditto) and all the baggage of what you may have heard or read about it, add in memories of it in other seasons, add in your own inclinations and mood, and the garden you visit is much more than the sum of its parts.

❧ July ❧

NOW SERENE

Spring is over like a flash in New York – and indeed in most of the America that I know. There is no shilly-shallying between warm and cold spells: it goes from cold to hot. Bud burst is bud explosion. How lucky I was, then, to see Central Park at the very height of its spring glory, a week in April of cool air and warm sunshine, when the cherries were just going over and the crabs coming out, the snowbells and shadblows frothy white (plants don't seem to have Latin names in the States) and the flowering dogwoods doing what they do only in the continental climate of their home.

Central Park is the finest city park on earth, on a scale and in a style that perfectly matches the swagger of Manhattan. Its lakes are vast, its rides monumental, its rocky bluffs like fortresses – but its detail is improbably perfect too. A generation ago it was almost abandoned, filthy and dangerous. Then came a truly remarkable woman, Betsy Barlow Rogers, the first ever Park Administrator, who convinced the city it was trashing one of its greatest assets. How she transformed the huge space – more than 800 acres – from sordid to serene is an inspiring story.

Walking to the Boathouse with her (Venetian gondolas on the water are her latest inspiration) reminded me of a wide-eyed walk at Alnwick Castle with the Duchess of Northumberland. A determined woman, I thought (was this reprehensibly sexist?) can achieve anything. These two have left enormous legacies already, thrilled millions with only the benign weapons of horticulture.

SUPPER DISH

We have been eating Swiss chard since April, from last year's plants, while this year's get going – and always with a sense of occasion. It is a leaf we would grow for its looks even if it were poisonous: so bold and smart with its brilliant white central stem and great spade of bottle-green, glossy on one side and matt on the other.

What is Swiss about it I'm not sure. We met it, as *blette*, in French markets. But the recipe that makes it dressy at table, too, is to cut up and cook the white stems to serve in a cheesy béchamel sauce, surrounded by the greenery, cut up and cooked separately. It is more delicate in flavour and less tannic than spinach. With a fried egg or two on top it makes a feast of a summer supper.

❧ August ❧

JUVENILE PLEASURES

Senior gardeners, I have often noticed, seem to look straight through variegated plants, as though it was not quite cricket to attract the customers with anything so flashy. I must be a junior gardener: I find them fascinating. The different effects of chlorophyll and the lack of it in leaves are not only eye-catching, they can add extraordinary grace to a plant that would hardly score without them. Sometimes they add to a list of virtues that was pretty strong already. The dogwoods are a case in point. Is there a more low-maintenance shrub for long-term cheerfulness than the variegated forms of *Cornus alba*, the red-barked 'Siberian' dogwood?

There are three dogwoods competing at the moment in their own private beauty competition: *Cornus mas*, *C. alternifolia* and *C. controversa*. The cream-variegated form of the first, the so-called cornelian cherry (does anyone actually call it that?), is an airy bush, growing here in the relatively light shade of a koelreuteria. Like most variegated plants it luxuriates in some shade, and reaches out longer shoots than it would in the sun, spraying its creamy leaves to lovely effect.

Cornus alternifolia 'Argentea' is its immediate rival, the same sort of size but white-variegated and fine-twigged, the branches forming horizontal layers that can be exaggerated by judicious pruning almost into wedding-cake format, recalling, but with less emphasis, the variegated selection of the 'giant' dogwood, *C. controversa*.

It is a hard plant to place, this last, and one of the boldest statements in the woody world. What do you do with a tree that thrusts plateaux of whipped cream in all directions? I saw the perfect answer recently at Powys Castle: give it a stony courtyard of its own to posture in. It is too look-at-me for most garden settings.

I give the crown to *Cornus mas* for two attributes the others don't have. One is a haze of yellow flowers in early spring, the other a crop of scarlet fruit.

❧ September ❧

SUSSEX SUR MER

Paradise is a garden – or so we're told. Presumably every gardener imagines, or anticipates, or hopes for, a slightly different heaven. The one most talked about is the Islamic model. A Wisley one must surely be popular, with departments for all tastes. There will be a public for sylvan glades, and I'm sure for a plantsman's glory hole of rarities. And will it be someone else's garden or our own: can we actually do any gardening?

Up to now I had never put my mind to it. But at the end of an afternoon at Le Bois des Moutiers I was ready to settle for where I was. All the ingredients were there, from Alhambra courts to immense cedars, from borders in calculated harmonies of colour to leafy hollows echoing to the sound of a rill. I would be happy, I thought, to wander here forever, with or without secateurs and spade.

Le Bois des Moutiers is a Sussex garden on holiday by the French seaside, at Varengeville-sur-Mer near Dieppe, on the west-facing coast of Normandy. It has been cherished by three generations of the Mallet family, since the first commissioned Edwin Lutyens to build the house. Lutyens, in his 20s, was on a roll. He never did anything more playfully modern. He designed the formalities, the courtyards and steps and pergola and garden houses, full of his whimsical ingenuity. The Mallets have played the Gertrude Jekyll part, playing chromatic scales in deep borders, modulating between purple and silver with a descant of pink and white, or white and gold in frames of green box.

True heaven for me, though, is in the wooded valley between the house and the sea, a picture composed with a Claude or a Poussin in mind, where high trees frame magic glades and light slants through screens of leaves. In summer it draws you deep into a world of massed hydrangeas, pools of white or blue, of irises and astilbes lining mossy paths, of monstrous gunneras and soaring bamboo, down and down, until in the distance, framed in trees, as blue as a hydrangea, lies the Channel.

OUSE WATER IS IT?

It amounts to cruel and unusual punishment, both for gardeners and their plants, to ban the free flow of water essential for life. Back from an early-morning trudge with a can to a distant plant (my fault, I know: I should have put it nearer) I can almost see the struggles of young roots underground. Established plants have come to terms with their neighbours' roots. They may flag under the sun, but they have reserves. Until all the soil is saturated, though, new ones are locked into the compost you planted them with. Other roots are claiming all the unturned earth – and theirs, too, when you water it.

In Britain we don't often see our gardens when it is 90 degrees in the shade. It is fascinating, if painful, to see how different leaves and flowers react: some taking it bravely, some flopping as they lose their turgidity, and some burning to a sad irredeemable crisp. New plants are always the first to go.

I feel almost guilty saying it, but we have no hosepipe ban around here in Essex. By what seems an extraordinary contract with the Almighty, Anglian Water does what others say they can't: redistribute supplies via our little rivers. This is the driest part of England. How come the tiny River Pant was surging happily under Great Bardfield bridge yesterday? I hope no one in Cambridgeshire objects, but it carries water pumped from the Great Ouse to our Essex reservoirs. Where does the Ouse find so much water? From deep in the chalk that lies under most of East Anglia. An adaptable river, the Ouse: in the 17th century, or so I read, it flowed in the opposite direction.

Then why can't we do something similar with the surplus rainfall of the north and west? It falls, after all, on high ground, which means that gravity should help it along. (Gravity, Mrs Trad once pointed out, should bring it down from the north too. She regards the Nile, and other rivers that flow northwards, as unnatural, or possibly bogus.)

Too massive an undertaking, say the authorities. The pipes and pumps involved would bankrupt us. A better solution, perhaps, would be to go and live where the water is.

❧ October ❧

EDINBURGH FESTIVAL

There was no great drought-busting downpour; no darkness at noon and the gutters spluttering. Just a patter on the open window in the night and the curtain swaying. I had thought the garden almost past hope at the beginning of August. We had cut down the dustiest and most hangdog plants to escape their reproachful looks.

What a gear change. Even the first few millimetres of rain started green shoots. From idling along in overdrive, nature double-declutched into bottom. We have still had only 300 mm, or 12 inches, in 2006, but with a new flush of roses, phlox reviving, salvias starting, galtonias and creamy kniphofias breaking cover, perovskia in its element, the emergence of anemones and the promise of Michaelmas daisies, things are looking up.

We have tended to plan the garden in the past on the basis that the summer, at least the end of it, could take care of itself. All the emphasis is on May, June and July, when we are open for the National Gardens Scheme. August is holiday time, we are often away, annuals are in full cry and later flowers emerging. There can be a sense of fullness. Not this year: the three-week heatwave of July exhausted all the garden's reserves. August, besides, is a good month not to go on holiday. Sweetcorn, tomatoes, carrots, salads, spinach, courgettes, beetroots, beans are all good reasons to stay. Need the border look like a hotel room at checkout time?

Edinburgh, I thought, should have the answer: the August festival is the climax of its year and 'the Botanics', as everyone calls them, a model for the world. Even here, though, the great herbaceous border had entered the dowdy phase. Its splendid support system of canes, nets and woven hazel branches was still keeping most things upright, but aunty colours had taken over:

purples, mauves, yellows and greys. An impressive sight, but not a festive one.

One side border, though, seemed planted precisely to answer my problem; brilliantly cheerful without quite the hectic palette of the late Lloyd style at Great Dixter. No cannas or gladioli and not many dahlias. It used the hard red-on-red of *Lobelia cardinalis* 'Queen Victoria' and *Dahlia* 'Bishop of Llandaff', but wove it into a pattern of complementary colours. There were penstemons: *P.* 'Windsor Red' and pink 'Peace', scarlet *Phlox* 'The King' and purple 'Harewood', and mounds of the purple-on-grey of *Salvia leucantha*. At either end were thickets of *Helianthus* 'Lemon Queen'. I shall follow its example at revision time – coming soon.

COMPOUND INTEREST

Is anyone asking how long it takes to grow box hedges? They well might, seeing the price of any sort of potted box in some garden centres. Five years, I now know, will give you a respectable well-knit hedge halfway up your calves, and seven a really weighty ancestral-looking one.

Back from a visit to our sometime garden in France, now being nurtured by enthusiastic friends, it came as a shock to see how much happens in a year behind your back. Not only has the box parterre taken on something like dignity, but our fruit trees have formed an orchard, and lopping a few lower branches from the 12-year-old walnut has made a shady space for a long table. The competition between our favourite rose, the orange-yellow *R.* 'Ghislaine de Féligonde', and a muscat vine needs the umpire's final decision, and the persimmon tree has finally looked itself up in the manual and produced a crop of fruit.

Time is of the essence to gardeners. It is to everyone. But the price put on impatience is usually excessive – and it leaves out of account the quiet satisfaction of compound interest, let alone the delight of seeing a long-term project coming to fruition.

❧ November ❧

SAD SPACES GONE

However well you know where they are, some things always come as a surprise – and are all the better for it. Crocuses in autumn always startle me. Whatever suddenly happened in that dusty ground to trigger such tenderness, to break out such exquisite satin skin and such radiant colour?

They don't even wait for rain. Temperature or day-length or some mysterious combination of the two tells them the moment has come; the dry corm with its silent tick explodes into a beauty looking for a mate.

The whole garden had this effect on me this autumn. You could not imagine, in the desolation of the dog days, how September would fill the borders again. In this country we are not used to the summer shut-down that Mediterranean gardeners know as routine.

Where have the sad spaces gone now? Michaelmas daisies, anemones, penstemons, fuchsias and salvias have smothered them in a great duvet of pink, white and purple. Not all of it is benign: there are things seeding, multiplying, roots darting about that I will regret later. But at the moment it is better than spring.

COUNTY SHOW

There were some supremely golden moments last summer, and November is not a bad time to recall them. The day that comes back most clearly, easily and often was in late July, before the heat had turned gardens brown, when we were given licence to roam in a score of Suffolk's most splendid gardens.

The object was to raise money to restore the Theatre Royal at Bury St Edmunds, one of the country's few remaining Georgian playhouses. The day started with lectures in churches scattered round the county, a neat device to prevent everyone from following the same itinerary. I drew George Carter on 'The Garden as Theatre': precisely apposite.

I am not sure which contributed more to a memorable day, the jewels of gardens we were allowed to visit or their setting, the English landscape at its golden best. True I plotted a course that avoided main roads, towns or almost any uncomely sights. The farms and fields and woods, the churches and gardens glimpsed behind hedges rolled on mile after unsullied mile. There is no rural England left? Don't you believe it. It made me wonder what gardening can add to perfection – until I saw some of the gardens.

What gardening adds is a point of view. Literally, in many cases: a church tower framed in a dramatic way or trees reflected in a lake. What George Carter meant by 'theatre' is something extra: additional self-consciousness, as it were, with an element of look-at-me.

Was there anything radical on show? There was no East Ruston. Glorious horticultural maturity is the label I would apply to what we saw in Suffolk that day.

❧ December ❧

TWO MODELS

Did you grow restive in October, too? Day after day the thermometer clung to temperatures we are lucky to see in some summers. Nature was in a trance. It was hard not to feel that something unwelcome was impending. I had to get out and see what was happening in other gardens.

I chose (why not?) two that in their different ways are the most momentous of all in our gardening history: Rousham and Hidcote. They are 20 miles apart in space, 200 years in time, and plain opposites in spirit: Rousham the serenely classical, Hidcote the intensely personal. Or are they? In the golden calm of an October morning each was an enigma.

Rousham implicates the entire landscape in its vision of an Arcadian world. I tried to picture William Kent roaming on the hill above the Cherwell with his client, the millionaire General Dormer. Did Kent bring a master plan, or did Dormer have a wish-list: a cascade, a grotto, an eye-catcher, statues of Apollo and Pan, Venus of course, covered seats for rainy days? He must have stipulated a plunge pool, they are not part of the standard repertoire – and Kent probably hit on the wonderful notion of feeding it with a serpentine rill. Was there a learned argument about their siting, quotations from Horace over port by candlelight; was this really philosophy in stone and turf and water?

Or could it be, I wondered, that the whole thing was a country-house lark? Did they stride around in leggings, tricorn hats and coats with side skirts, wine on their breath, laughing and blowing horns, perhaps pushing someone in the river? It is the inscription that casts the doubt: in the heart of the mystery, below the statue of Venus, it commemorates 'Ringwood, an otter-hound of extraordinary sagacity.'

Rousham and Hidcote have nothing in common. Hidcote is intellectual. It starts with a quiet stone courtyard, a modest house hemmed in with trees, and thinks its way outwards in a series of episodes, each self-contained, hiding the landscape beyond, then claiming it in calculated glimpses, as heaven might look down on earth – or earth, indeed, up at heaven.

Isn't this more Italian in spirit than English? It reminds me of Gamberaia, the Florentine villa on its promontory above Settignano. Hidden gardens huddle by the house, parterres and the long bowling green extend the views – but always to a hedged-in limit. The world beyond is brought to you, when it is, as premeditated revelations.

Hidcote of course is the one we imitate – and not only in its perfection.

It has all the ingredients modern gardens need: private spaces, colour schemes, contrasts of scale, water under strict control, a wide range of plants ecologically arranged, whimsy in topiary, limited horizons. It is domesticity elevated to art. In the serenity of October, with flowers nodding, and yellow and russet creeping through the leaves, it felt the safest place on earth.

HAVING WRIT, MOVES ON

It was inflation that brought me to *The Garden*; the eye-watering inflation of the 1970s. 1975 was a particularly trying year for treasurers, however prudent and sanguine – and Lord Blakenham of the RHS was both. The Society, he told us, was facing a deficit of more than £50,000. Subscriptions would have to go up, and sacrifices be made. One that was discussed was to publish what was then called *The Journal* quarterly instead of monthly.

Lord B asked me, as a man who had worked in magazines, for my opinion. 'You must keep it monthly,' I said, 'or you'll lose your members.' (Members were called 'Fellows' in those days.) 'Add colour. Make it a magazine for everyone. Hire the best writers, print more and better pictures, and call it *The Garden*.' 'When can you start?' he said. I had found myself a job, associates and friends that have lasted 32 years.

We made the changes in June, aiming, as I said in my first editorial, 'to be the link between serious gardeners everywhere.' We borrowed the title from William Robinson's magazine, where, in what seemed a happy omen, precisely 100 years before he had first met Gertrude Jekyll. For that matter *The Journal* was in the middle of its 100th year. It all felt neatly auspicious. Why did I choose Tradescant as my nom de plume? It was a resonant name from garden history that was lying unused.

With this column Tradescant says goodbye to *The Garden*. It is time for a new voice. The RHS continues to evolve – faster, in fact, than ever before. It has almost six times as many members, different priorities and different tastes. Have I run out of things to say? How could anyone, with gardening in all its richness as a subject?

PS I duly popped up next month in Gardens Illustrated ....

2007

ACCEPTABILITY BROWN

How would Capability Brown have got on with English Heritage, I wonder? Or with Planning Guidelines or Building Regs? He would have had a fit, and we would be looking at a different landscape. No greensward sweeping down to winding water, no hanging clumps of oak or beech. Overgrown topiary would be towering everywhere, and avenues fanning out all over the country. Still, the weeding industry would provide thousands of jobs ....

How did we let ourselves be dictated to like this? It is one thing to acknowledge a public interest in what we do with our houses and gardens, but quite another to accept dictatorship by bureaucrat. We all have our stories. Mine is how we invited all the relevant planners for coffee and a tour of the house. In its 500 years everyone has had a go, adding wings or subtracting them, building new staircases and corridors and chimneys. The listed buildings officer dropped himself in it. 'What I love about these old houses', he said, 'is that each generation leaves its mark.' 'Funny you should say that. This', said I, producing plans, 'is the conservatory we are going to add.'

Don't try to chop a tree down without a permit, though. Not even a self-sown sycamore. Not even an elder. Plant whatever you like; no one questions the innocent little tree you bring home in a pot. Just remember when it reaches 50 feet high to ask permission to cut it down.

FASHION EXTRA

Will *Salvia uliginosa* be the next *Verbena bonariensis*? I hope so. *V. b* is the lanky but resolutely upright plant with tiny purple flowers that has filled fashionable gardens in the past three or four years. Seedlings take until late summer to flower, but gardeners, even gardeners with thousands of visitors and doubtless strict planting plans, can't resist letting it spread. Wisley, the Savill Garden, the rose garden at Mottisfont – it's everywhere.

And this salvia? Another lanky self-sower, with an even later season but with flowers of a unique sky-blue. They are tiny too, in little panicles at the end of many branches, but wave high above the border, here among pink Japanese anemones, white cosmos, pale pink roses (and of course *V. b*), in just the sort of nursery colour combination that made Christopher Lloyd so indignant.

Uliginosa means from boggy ground. Compared with some heat-seeking salvias, maybe, but droughty summers here have only encouraged it. It comes up everywhere, especially in the brick path. Just like *V. b*, but brighter, later, prettier and so far more special.

❧ February ❧

VIVISECTION

New gardening picture books are all very well, and all very glamorous, but they don't absorb the mind. At least this is what I find, snug under my lamp in front of the fire. Turning the pages of delectable borders and enviable vistas is fine – but don't you become listless? I scribble notes: 'Vinca to cover stump' or 'Valerian for dry wall', but I lose the thread of the text among the pictures and get angry about captions that say 'Previous two pages ...'.

Old books are another matter. Books from the days when colour was a luxury and black and white had a different way of telling a story. There is a quality in old-fashioned thought that shames our facile age, too. I have just been reading E A Bowles's *My Garden in Spring*, the thoughts of a passionate Edwardian plantsman. It is his curiosity that brings him alive today. He took nothing for granted. Perhaps you know someone – perhaps you are someone – who discovers how plants work by cutting them open to look. Bowles on *Iris unguicularis* (winter you might think, rather than spring) is awe-inspiring. He is on intimate terms with half a dozen cultivars, harvests them in sheaves for his study every week for months, and explains just how they work (and why they used to be called *I. stylosa*: his razor blade reveals that the plant has a style extending the whole length of the stem).

Other old writers have other qualities. Gertrude Jekyll conveys precision with poetry. Lucas Phillips is a blunt military man who keeps his flower beds in order, Michael Howarth-Booth a nurseryman who could sell a shrub with the best. William Robinson went in for open, angry criticism of a sort that would never be published today. Christopher Lloyd came closest. And then there is the gentle sage Graham Stuart Thomas. I will never tire of him.

SNUG UNDER GLASS

Our conservatory is no hothouse, but such a relatively warm autumn, with endless sunny days, kept it on the boil for week after week until a score of things were flowering at once. We rarely get a chance like this to play with colours in winter. One group of pots worked specially well: the golden yellow flower of *Allamanda cathartica*, like a big jasmine without the scent, the lemon yellow spike of *Salvia madrensis* and the cool lime-yellow bells of *Correa backhouseana*. The pinky-red *C. pulchella* is a Christmas cliché, its cousin a much cooler plant in every sense. A tall camellia, the early-flowering *C. sasanqua* 'Narumigata', with white flowers 10 cm wide, framed the picture. Scent is not normally a feature of camellias. But sniffing 'Narumigata' makes me think it's just as well.

❧ March ❧

IMPOSSIBLE TO REEF

Yesterday it blew harder than it has since 1990 – judging, at least, by the toll it took. It is the proprietors of avenues I feel for when it roars this loud. No one but I will notice, when we've cleared up the mess, what trees are missing from my seemingly random planting, but a gap in an avenue is like a missing tooth.

What a mess there is, all the same. Seven trees down – never the ones that looked particularly fragile or exposed. Our tallest tree, a Canadian poplar, *Populus* x *canadensis* 33 metres high, landed largely in our neighbour Ken's garden and partly on the road. Miraculously there was no one around and only one pine was crushed. Long-suffering Ken says he won't miss it. The ones I shall miss most are a big bird cherry, *Prunus padus*, by the church gate and another poplar, a shapely and fragrant black cottonwood *Populus trichocarpa* I planted as a cutting 30 years ago, which is leaning dangerously with its roots above ground. One of the bluest of Scots pines,

Hillier's *Pinus sylvestris* 'Argentea', simply snapped (and not even at the graft) in a sustained gust that gave no relief for a full five minutes.

The bird cherry tore its roots out, revealing that honey fungus had been rotting them. There was no sign of it in the healthy crown. Other trees split at high forks, points of weakness I had not even noticed before. Most trees were simply cleaned of their dead twigs, a litter-storm that covers lawns, shrubs and beds. It would have been worse – as it was in 1987 – if deciduous trees had been in leaf; sails impossible to reef. We have a chipper roaring away, spreading minced tree as a deep mulch in all directions. Soon only I will see the gaps and, of course, set about filling them. The catalogues are open at my side.

THE MEMORY GENE

I'd never thought of a garden simply in terms of the number of different plants it can hold, but if you are a plant-addict with a frustratingly small garden it makes sense. Logically, I suppose, they should all be tiny alpines. The true cottage gardener, though, thinks differently. Each plant must have a reason to be there. Being pretty or good to eat is important, but more important still is sentiment: who gave you the seed or where you took the cutting.

It is not only cottage gardens that have this dimension, of course. I dare say Louis XIV had flashbacks (guilty ones, I hope) of the gardens at Vaux-le-Vicomte he had plundered for Versailles. In botanical gardens it was all down on the dog-eared accessions cards in the old files before they were transferred on to the computer. It isn't the same: no more traces of compost or clipped-on postcards of the Yichang Gorge. The memories, though, the history and the accumulated know-how are part of the gene-bank of every garden as much as the genes of the plants themselves. You can say of any place that its reality is as much in perception as in bricks and mortar. But of gardens this is doubly true: they only exist to be perceived.

A garden of any size, in fact, is as rich as the mind of its creator. Someone who is always curious, always acquisitive, will have a garden of many layers of meaning; something that a designer, however fashionable, can never offer.

❧ April ❧

SHRIEKS OF SPRING

I don't want to spoil the spring for you, and it may be your idea of the jolliest colour scheme on earth, but when the pinks (and mauves and magentas) of spring appear among the predominant early yellows, the grinding of my teeth can frighten the horses.

I know. Nothing can be done. The Creator put the forsythia and flowering currant on the same planet (though not on the same continent) and his other creation, man, planted them together. Daffodils and honesty are pretty powerful, and yellow daffs with *Prunus* 'Kanzan' even more so. Swearing is the polite word for what these colours do to one another. They flash before my mind's eye as I write: bergenias and daffodils, daffs and purple heathers ... daffs have such a long season that swearing is hard to avoid. And then come the azaleas in every colour. What we can avoid, though, is some of the hardest shades of yellow, and some of the more lurid manifestations of magenta. And planting them side by side.

If there is a ground rule of colour it is not to cross the meridian of the colour wheel that runs from green to red. You're safe on the arc between blue and yellow, where together they make various shades of green. The tricky bit is the quadrant opposite, where they shade from purple to orange.

I admit a colour-coordinated spring garden sounds more than precious. Spring, after all, is spring. But you can avoid, ban, veto, dig up and burn the plants whose only tone of voice is a shriek.

PLAGUE AND TRADE

The two greatest threats to our native woods and their flora are deer and the nursery trade. So says Oliver Rackham in his new book *Woodlands*, published by Collins last year in the New Naturalist series and a surprisingly bracing read.

We have never had so many deer in this country, he says, and there is little hope of controlling their spread. Even if we all chose venison instead of beef, it is too dangerous to shoot them in the suburbs where they lurk. Unless we deer-fence our woods, their seedlings, coppice stools, wild flowers and before long their whole structure will be destroyed. The victims even include birds. Nightingales no longer nest in woods where undergrowth is hollowed out by muntjac. Fenced out of woods, of course, the deer will make straight for our gardens.

The nursery trade? It is the pattern of modern commerce we should be worried about. Mass production is the order of the day, wherever it is quickest and cheapest. British nurseries have almost given up propagating their own material, let alone local strains of anything. It matters less, certainly, that your azaleas come from Belgium than that oaks are grown from whatever acorns are most plentiful. It may be 50 years before we discover that Italian oaks are useless in Britain, by which time nothing can be done.

The most immediate threat, however, is the fungus *Phytopthera*. Rackham asked a Dublin conference whether Ireland had not seen enough of it to last 1,000 years. In the 19th century it caused the potato famine and depopulated the country. 'That's tricky,' came the official answer. 'If we exclude foreign plants we'll be done for restraint of trade.' In other words fingers crossed. In the dispute between plague and trade, which side are you on?

HINT FROM A MAPLE

I wonder if you have the same fetish as I do about Japanese maples. Towards the end of winter I find myself drawn into their twiggy interiors to rid them of the wood they seem anxious to shed. As many as a quarter of their slender fishbone twiglets have died, and by March stand out white among the darker living ones. You only have to press them to hear a little snap. Best to gather them up and burn them, because dead maple wood attracts one of the more sinister fungi: coral spot. Once its tiny pink pustules appear, usually on the snag of a torn or broken branch, there is not very much you can do to save the branch, or even the tree.

This habit of shading out their own older shoots is what gives mature maples their graceful floating look. As their branches extend all their fresh growth and all their leaves are bunched near the tips. A Japanese gardener prunes to exaggerate this effect, taking out the weaker branches until only four or five remain, to pose like outspread wings in a tableau. He does the same with pines, to imitate the effects of age and exposure on a rocky shore. It is one thing, though, to take a hint from a maple and another to impose on a pine. I can't see this particular form of topiary, seductive as it is in Japan, ever sweeping the home counties.

❧ May ❧

HOMECOMING

Home from three weeks in New Zealand, glowing and confused. Glowing from the pin-sharp sunlight that turns every landscape into a cinematic panorama; confused by the kaleidoscope of plants, native and (mainly) non-native, that makes Kiwi gardens some of the richest anywhere. I was wary of 'Kiwi' when I went. Was it a loaded word like 'Pom'? Far from it, I found: it is a proud label for everything New Zealand.

'Bush' is the other term that commands respect. It means the native flora, where it still covers the land, whether as high forest or low scrub or an exotic coastal tangle of palms and flax (the phormium of our gardens) in total control of dunes and cliffs mile upon mile. You can't keep out of the constant discussion about native and non-native nature. Predatory mammals introduced from abroad play havoc in a land that had none of its own. Our problem with grey squirrels is nothing compared with the damage done by rats, mice, stoats, deer, rabbits and especially Australian possums to a fauna that includes birds that can't fly.

New Zealand's Department of Conservation is an impressive organisation. Its combat troops fight for its native animals and plants. Its communications arm provides, among much else, interpretative trails through Bush of every kind. Five miles into a walk in rainforest you can still come across labelled trees. Getting your mind round the towering podocarps, the immense cypresses, cousins many times removed of the ones we know, the six species of southern beech, the prolific ferns soaring into trees and wonders such as tree fuchsias and the bizarre lancewood is not easy. Nor is it helped by the mix of Maori and Latin that confronts you. Hebes and olearias and pittosporums are the genera that feel at first most like familiar ground – until the ground gets boggy with unfamiliar species and strange behaviour.

Bush tends, admittedly, to be brown – or rather a mixture of greens and tans and greys that fall somewhere short of conventional garden 'colour'. Perhaps the pollinators of the antipodes are colour-blind. You can make a comforting, well-furnished garden with Kiwi plants alone, but scarcely a cheerful one. 'Our' garden plants, on the other hand, do spectacularly well in the brilliant light and ample rainfall. The national arboretum, Eastwoodhill near Gisborne on the North Island, grows trees from round the world at alarming speed and the roses of Christchurch, on the sheltered east coat of South Island, are enough to give you a complex.

The shift back from late summer in the southern hemisphere to early spring in this one is brutal. I confess it took me a couple of days to see the point of my own garden again. Perhaps the most important factor is transparency. There is a good deal of everygreenery here, more than in most gardens. Plenty of walls and hedges too. But how sketchy and unclothed – unpainted might be a better image – an English garden looks as colour starts to erupt in March. The severity of winter in Britain is at least simple. Coming home it all seemed too complicated. Colour is in spots rather than blocks, shape in lines rather than masses. I know – it is my garden – where the volumes are meant to be and where the voids, but it is my mind, not my eyes, telling me.

By the third day, jetlag receding, I was happy: things had clicked into place. Instead of random detail I was seeing my own intentions. Had I learned anything by going away? To make things simpler and more obvious, perhaps. How else are other people to know what you are trying to say?

❦ June ❦

WINDSOR V PARIS

The curtain went up with the carpenters still banging away on stage and the actors learning their lines. I had scarcely ordered the plants I need, let alone planted them, when spring went into overdrive. Plants I was planning to move and clumps to divide suddenly looked inviolable, on the point of flowering. Besides, the soil was rapidly drying out: a peck of dust in March was a bushel in April. With no rain in prospect it was time to go visiting; to cast off self-reproach and see the spring displayed by gardeners who really know how.

The Savill Garden at Windsor with its splendid new visitor centre is drawing crowds these days. The soaring oak-roofed building is the best piece of modern garden architecture we have. But even better in April, to my mind, and much less visited, are the Valley Gardens, a mile to the south on the ridge of the Great Park that overlooks Virginia Water. If ever there was an idealised landscape, a forest of exotic flowers, it is this. Sir Eric Savill and his successors have groomed 200 acres of ancient hunting forest, carved vistas, nurtured rarities, planted amphitheatres and wound paths until a wander in these woods in spring is pure intoxication. When magnolias melt in petals on azaleas it goes to my head. A sailor with a perfect beam wind might feel like this, or the audience of a sublime aria. Life doesn't get any better.

You could call it the abstract painting of gardening, this entirely English style. There are no functional parts, no symbolism, no representation, no eye-catchers; just the landscape itself, coloured with flowers. Sometimes at the end of a plunging forest-ride you see silver water. Immense oaks and beeches support the sky. Reality is suspended in horticultural heaven.

French garden nirvana is as different as could be: nature not idealised but domesticated. It would be the perfect moment, I thought, to compare what London and Paris do best. For years my favourite French April garden has been La Bagatelle in the Bois de Boulogne: the prettiest possible potager all primped up for spring. The heart of it is a walk under arches of wisteria; each arch a different species or cultivar. *W.* 'Multijuga' dangles pale tassels a yard long, *W. sinensis* sweet-smelling purple ones. There is pink and white, and a graceful form nearer to grey. All are pruned tight for maximum performance.

But the gardener is drunk on bulbs. They even scale the walls of his bothy and sit in pots on the roof. Tulips are marshalled like dancers at a ball, swirling among pansies and wallflowers, disciplined by low box hedges and little skirts of pear trees in flower at knee-height. A positive embankment of sand and manure announces asparagus: the first tips, no knobs, of grey and cream are poking through. Later there will be grand displays, the immaculate rose garden and the border where Michaelmas daisies stretch for 100 yards. For now the union of function and frivolity is quintessential Paris, and pluperfect spring.

❦ July ❦

CHLOROPHYLL SURGE

'Time', said some philosophical wag, 'is nature's way of stopping everything from happening at once.' Until this spring, that was, when something went wrong with the mechanism. A month of near-summer weather, and not a drop of rain in six weeks, had this garden (and certainly this gardener) seriously disoriented. Tulips and roses together upset my sense of propriety, not to mention colour. Fauve is the word for the cerise of *Rosa* 'Zéphirine Drouhin', the red of a tulip called 'Bastogne' and the bright amber-brown of my favourite wallflower. 'Go back in and wait your turn,' I said to the rose. But no.

After six weeks the rain came reluctantly, unable to cure the chapped and ravined clay. Rabbits could still get their paws trapped in the cracks. At one point you felt horses had better watch where they put their hooves.

Don't think I'm complaining. Blossom has never been more bountiful, nor early May a more sensuous moment. When hawthorn fills the hedges round magnolias in voluptuous bloom all is well. I have been going out daily at dusk to marvel at the *Staphylea colchica* I grew from one of the seeds in a purloined 'bladder' years ago. Bladdernut is the purportedly common name of this estimable bush, now 5 metres and weighed down with intricate bunches of white flowers. Poppable green bladders follow. Dusk is its moment (it is for all white flowers) because then, I have discovered, it transmits to the maximum its creamy gardenia smell. I didn't know anything else could do gardenia.

The colour theme now is searing spurge-green. Did I intend euphorbias to take over? You might think so: a chlorophyll surge has that effect. Brightest of all spurges is *Euphorbia palustris* – which also offers orange leaves in autumn. Box hedges join in as they put on new growth, and I seem to have let the brilliant-green alexanders (*Smyrnium perfoliatum*) get out of hand again. Two years ago 300 volunteers were needed to scour Kew of this menace to the bluebells. Perhaps we should put it back on the menu, as it was before we had celery.

❧ August ❧

DEAD OR ALIVE

All bamboos of one species, the story goes, flower at the same time and then promptly die. You may have been a witness. It certainly happened here, 20 years ago, when our three clumps of the common *Fargesia murielae* blossomed. Tiny as each flower is, they transform the plant, dyeing it smoky-purple and freighting each culm with tiny dangling wheat-like seeds that arc it almost to the ground. Within six months all three were dead, and gardeners far and near reported the same – with feeling: digging out the remains of clumps 5 feet across was no joke. Mysteriously, replacements were available. I should of course have asked the nursery how and whence, since obviously not all fargesias had perished. For reproductive purposes the flowering seems a great waste of effort: the millions of seeds we must have had produced only one seedling, which to this day is barely waist-high. My replacement plants, meanwhile, have flourished, grown, and to my horror, this spring flowered again. Twenty years is surely far too short a lifetime for a bamboo.

This time, though, I cut out the flowering shoots just as they reached the low-bowing stage and gave the depleted clumps a feast of food and water.

That was in April. To my delight the few remaining shoots have put out new leaves: recovery seems possible. And just in case, I have planted a clump of the near-related (and perhaps even more beautiful) *Fargesia nitida*.

PS A year later: one clump dead, one still flowering. Fingers crossed.

THEM THERE HILLS

We tell our friends it is not really a garden at all, because when they find out that we tend a plot around a defunct gold mine in Snowdonia they all say 'How can you possibly garden in two places at once?' It's better than counting sheep is my response.

It is only a sketch of a garden, in any case – but to me all the better for it. It lies by a stream in the middle of a wood, deep among thriving oak, ash and birch, with a distant view of that most noble of rather short mountains, Cader Idris. Wales had its gold rush at much the same time as California and Australia, in the middle of the 19th century. The Cae Gwian mine was floated on the London Stock Exchange. Shafts were dug, railways installed and a crushing-mill built, powered by a towering waterwheel. All they fetched out in the end was copper, but the grey stone buildings stood – and 150 years later motivated our garden, round the stream that runs from the mine-mouth, our deep dark grotto.

The old mine office, gabled but roofless, is the sheep-proof part for precious plants. The rest is defined only with low stone walls. One roofless shed is home to a hydrangea that fills it to overflowing with deep-bluey-purple blooms. A gunnera guards the path up to the grotto. Embothriums stand round it like flaming brands. Strawberry trees stand at the corners. There is a graceful myrtle gleaned as a seedling from a Scottish forest, a *maiten* from Patagonia, and ferns ranging from the Royal (one day I hope in these conditions the size of a small tractor) to the exquisite little thing with 2-inch fronds that grows between the dark-grey stones. In such acid soil with 60 inches of rain a year, things become possible that in Essex are out of the question.

PLANTSPERSONS

A plantsman is as hard to define as he (or she) is easy to recognise. His (or her) garden is easy to recognise, too: a place where plants subtly out of the ordinary form a thriving community. It's where the rare, the newly discovered and the elite of the plant world are cherished with passion (and where there is never room to accommodate all the newcomers).

We went to such a garden the other day: White House Farm on the Kentish Downs, the creation of Maurice and Rosemary Foster. It was a journey through layers of discovery: from smiling lawn through classic pergola into a forest of flowers where all horticultural inhibitions have been thrown away. Up every tree clambers a rose, and up each rose a vine. Clematis scrambles through magnolia, actinidia through azalea, and the earth below and between is pulsing with competing growth. The pergola snakes for 100 yards among maples and bamboos, rhododendrons and roses, dripping with every wisteria known to man. Seven more acres of arboretum are planted with trees from wild-collected seed. If plantsmanship like this is exhausting to view, what must it be like to practise? To judge by the Fosters' purposeful serenity, pretty close to heaven.

❧ September ❧

BLITHE SPIRIT

I lean on clematis in summer like a drunk on the bottle. They seem to be doing half the work of keeping a sparkle in the surging masses of green, a handful that time has shown keep producing wonderful colour week after week. Of all the midsummer ones *C.* 'Perle d'Azur' is queen: climbing, spreading, drooping and generally distributing its pale violet-blue flowers, individuals that tilt this way and that, catching different lights. It wanders up my favourite climbing rose, the buff/white/pink *R.* 'Alister Stella Gray', and dances over my favourite white/pink/red hydrangea, *H. serrata* 'Grayswood'.

At the same time *Clematis* x *durandii* takes care of the deep-blue end of the spectrum – with less elegance but equal generosity. *C.* x *durandii* has no means of climbing, but we have made it brushwood wigwams in beds where perennials crowd around. *Alstroemeria ligtu* is the perfect pink to set one off. Buff plumes of *Macleaya cordata* and blue spikes of delphiniums jostle round another.

The only clematis in the garden when we arrived was *C.* 'Alba Luxurians'. The second name is apt, the first less so: flowers can be white or green, and are usually harlequins of the two. It belongs to the later-flowering and smaller-flowered category that gardeners refer to, rightly or wrongly, as viticella. I scarcely mind which of this featherweight tribe I grow: their casual little flowers pour off the vine from June to September. *C.* 'Kermesina' is like velvet wine, 'Minuet' a merry muddle of purple and white, 'Polish Spirit' close to

C. x *durandii*, 'Madame Julia Correvon' more red wine, but with narrow petals widely spaced. All these grow here with blithe good humour.

SUDDEN DEATH

Those prone to nervous anxiety should stay away from the July issue of the quarterly *Journal of Forestry*. It describes a new disease affecting gardens in Cornwall. What is known in America as Sudden Oak Death has been flagged as a threat here for the past five years. The new find is another strain of *Phytophthora* all too well adapted to destroying Cornwall's precious trees and shrubs.

Phytophthora kernoviae takes its name from Kernow, the old name for Cornwall. It loves Cornwall's jungle conditions where big-leaved rhododendrons and magnolias thrive, spreading through mist and water-drops where breezes rarely stir. Eighty Cornish gardens have so far been infected, among them Trengwainton, where The National Trust has set up a monitoring station. *Phytophthora* there has already claimed magnolias, acacia, jasmines, rhododendrons and kalmias. In other gardens camellias, viburnums and drimys have caught it. Worse, there are cases of beech (but not oak) being affected. Given the right conditions *Phytophthora* of two strains -- *kernoviae* and the original Sudden Oak Death strain, *ramorum* – seem able to kill almost anything.

The conditions are specific, and rhododendrons are important hosts. *R. ponticum*, that ineradicable weed (however pretty its flowers) of broadleaved woodlands, harbours *Phytophthora* and passes it on. The precautions to take are to reduce the damp shade element, clearing undergrowth to let light and air in, to get rid of weak old wood and promote strong growth. Bleeding bark cankers are the principal symptoms. None of it makes pretty reading.

With this year's weather I had just been relishing the almost Cornish feel (at least for an Essex garden) of our establishing woodland, the damp mulch and the dense foliage. For how much longer, I wonder?

❧ October ❧

A RIDDLE

If it takes duckweed 30 days to cover a pond, how much of it is covered on day 29? Half, I was told: it doubles overnight. I don't quite believe that, but it is a prodigious grower: one week scattered green spots, the next a lawn on your water. I used to think it pernicious and attacked it with herbicides. Now I consider blanket weed far worse, and try to love the world's smallest plants as they proliferate.

The arguments against them are obvious. They hide the surface, abolish reflections, darken the depths and cling to anything that touches them. The arguments in favour? They feed on nutrients in the water that cause other problems. Removing them is a way of cleaning the whole pond. On a small one it is not such a bad job, skimming off the mass of tiny leaves. You wait for a windy day to push them to one side of the pond, then drag them to the edge with an improvised broom, or fish them out with a paddle-shaped net. Each leaf is a plant trailing a tiny white root. They reproduce by growing little buds that split off and grow on.

Once you focus on the tiny things you can even find beauty in them. Skimming them you encounter a world of bugs, beetles, tiny snails and tadpoles. You can polish your water surface clean and gleaming, or tolerate a few green rafts. When your weeding is finished, everything is pruned, the car washed, potting shed tidied, and you've swept behind the dustbins, amuse yourself by watching them grow.

GHASTLY GOOD TASTE

I'm not guilty of planning it this way, but ghastly good taste has broken out again in our borders this summer. Could I really have chosen such Mabel Lucy Attwell colours? It must be my inner little girl outing herself: there is nothing to disturb a dormouse in their almost inaudible harmonies. Goodness, I like it, though.

It is all pink, white and blue. The pinks are pale phlox, Japanese anemones, roses 'Felicia' and 'Comte de Chambord'. Only slightly more assertive are *Penstemon* 'Andenken an Friedrich Hahn' and *Salvia involucrata* 'Bethellii'.

The blues run from agapanthus and *Salvia patens* (its sapphire almost the only sharp note in the border) to somnolent blue rue, the azure pinpricks of *Salvia uliginosa* and the purple exclamation marks of *Thalictrum dipterocarpum* and *Verbena bonariensis*.

As for the whites, *Phlox paniculata* 'White Admiral' is in stratocumulus mode after all the rain, Iceberg roses are glacial, cleomes are threatening arachnids and cosmos becoming shrubs. There is shape and variety: tall spires of cool *Veronicastrum* and plump creamy ones of *Kniphofia* 'Little Maid', a low tangle of *Aster divaricatus* – white daisies on black stems. Later, fire will break out with sedums and crocosmias, chrysanthemums and turning leaves. Just now it reminds me of Katharine Hepburn's acting which, according to Dorothy Parker, ran the whole gamut of emotions from A to B. For the moment I'm extremely happy with A.

❧ November ❧

HEDGE FUN

Where do you stand on grasses? I mean the ones you don't stand on, the pale fans and waving feathers of the border. If they were a political party they might not yet be forming a government, but they would be shaping up for a coalition. My vote was undecided for a long time, but I'm beginning to be swayed.

It started at Wisley, where the old grass collection, on the way to the restaurant, always seemed out of place. It was grass for grass's sake, a pattern sheet of height and textures and colourways. Then came Piet Oudolf's vast new borders overlooking the new glasshouse. Grasses are the vital element in his bravura herbaceous palette. All the earth and fire colours of summer into autumn are there in broad brushstrokes and knife-smears. Fauve master does wild-flower meadow.

What happens when the two revolutionary parties of our gardening age converge? The Wirtz family in Belgium, renowned for their sculptural approach to evergreens, have been leading the hedge party for decades, infiltrating our consciousness until hedge and garden are almost as synonymous as garden and topiary were to the ancients. Mark my words, the hedge and grass garden is almost upon us.

There is a feint in that direction just down the road here in Essex, at Marks Hall near Coggeshall, in the splendid walled garden attached to the very considerable arboretum. Brita von Schoenaich, the designer, has used grasses as formally as anyone can in a pattern of hedges and deliberate rounded shapes to create an entirely novel effect. It certainly gets my vote.

PS: www.markshall.org.uk

ALL LIT UP

'Has that always been there?' asked a quite regular visitor the other day. It self-evidently had, being a shrub of some 20 summers' growth. I saw exactly what she meant, though. The sun was holding it in an evening halo against a shaded background. It was suddenly the focal point.

Light is always the most important influence, in planting a garden as in looking at it. You don't know when the clouds will part, shooting a ray of light to earth. You do know where the sun will be in the heavens, and can plan accordingly. It's not just a question of the plant's preferring sun or shade, but of your preferring a plant well lit, and which window you will be looking out of when it is.

Our bathroom window faces south-east. When I opened the curtain this morning the vine leaves that assault the window at this time of year were like art deco glass, a Lalique lampshade sparkling green, amber and gold. At teatime they merely block the view of the trees beyond bathed in afternoon sun.

Back-lighting is one of the strongest effects a gardener has at his disposal. Name me a plant that doesn't look its best outlined against streaming sunlight. We were at Beth Chatto's the other day, marvelling at her dry garden (and her wet one too). The grasses (again: it's that time of year) were golden filigree – no jeweller could deck his window like this. But not all the beauties were deliberate. A glimpse of water through willow and bamboo was ethereally beautiful in a way not even Beth could have planned. What she had orchestrated to perfection, though, was the self-lighting touches where pale colours seem spot-lit in preordained gloom. White Japanese anemones in her oak wood, for example. But lit from any angle there is no end to the beauty and usefulness of this paragon plant.

OWZAT?

I have a wine-loving friend who can prove that there is a correlation between the number of runs scored in first-class cricket and the quality of that year's claret. The more runs the better. Firm batsmen's wickets mean ripe grapes.

This year will test his rule. The figures are not quite in yet, but an Indian summer can save a vintage when it is too late to score runs. August may have been awful, but while the garden basked in September sun the grapes were making up for lost time. Now there's a correlation: a wet summer and a fine September mean bowlers' wickets, the garden at its best and a juicy vintage in the Médoc.

❄ December ❄

REFLECTIONS

I have always wanted to play the mirror-trick somewhere in my garden. It is something I associate with town gardens: well used, a mirror can startlingly expand a tiny space. My son tucked a mirror in a picture frame on a wall behind the serpentine stems of a climbing hydrangea, doubling and drawing attention to their hairy snaking on a background, confusingly, of sky. What can reflection bring to bigger spaces? For one thing, it can bring light.

Here at Saling Hall we are making a new vista that calls for an eye-catcher at each end. One end has a spy-hole in a wall opening on to a pond with a tall jet of water. The other has nothing except a wall of dusty ivy perpetually in shade.

I fetched a mirror down from the attic and hung it in the ivy at the end of the axis, facing the spy-hole. It instantly drew attention to the symmetry of the arrangement – but too brightly; and it is hard to walk by without seeing yourself reflected. It provided the answer, though: what I need is not brilliance, but a mere suggestion of light. A window in fact; or rather a dummy window stuck to the wall with glass that reflects light but no clear image. It will suggest that the woodshed wall is something more interesting and motivate wanderers to try my new path. Now what shall I plant along it to reward them?

A YEAR'S DISCOVERIES

It is rather fun (and a good memory-jogger) to make Christmas lists of the discoveries of the past year: people met, music heard, pubs with good beer – and crucially of course, for gardeners, plants encountered for the first time. Then to make a pick of favourites.

My list starts with a mini-euphorbia given to us by Annie Turner, a neighbour, last April. It has been in flower ever since – but not at all the flower you might picture. *E.* Diamond Frost has tiny white bracts (where most euphorbias have green to yellow ones). The plant positively sparkles, mimicking, if anything, a gypsophila. Last year I believe it was the darling of American nurseries, a bedding or conservatory plant unlike any other. There is little commercial interest, though, in something that roots as easily as a spider plant.

Perennial discovery of the year is *Thalictrum* 'Elin'. It was standing proud in July, a pale-purple haze way above head-height, in a border at Gresgarth Hall, Arabella Lennox-Boyd's garden near Lancaster. A plant that sustains itself in mid-air seems miraculous. Thalictrums were already my passion. I have rarely been wetter than I was on that day, but it was impossible to stop exploring a garden with such riches.

Tree discovery of the year is harder, but I give it to a little maple with the odd name of *Acer palmatum* 'Shishio Improved'. It was a beacon across Savill Garden in May, its spring leaves a unique scarlet. What was this autumnal colour doing among the magnolias? Better still, it repeats the show in November.

Nursery of the year is easy. On a dusty August day Spinners, at Boldre in the New Forest, was heady with woodland flowers. Towering euphorbias dropped their white petals on a mauve, pink and purple tapestry of hydrangeas and Japanese anemones. In broad sunlit beds yellow clematis clambered among the yellow fruit of *Viburnum opulus* 'Xanthocarpum', and scarlet lobelias mingled with scarlet schizostylis. It was here I discovered my shrub of the year, a revelation of beauty I had never expected.

Peter Chappell of Spinners is inevitably one of the first nurserymen to offer a variegated eucryphia. *E.* x *nymansensis* 'Nymans Silver' is a sport discovered recently at Nymans Garden in Sussex. Its serrated oval leaves are outlined in creamy white. Even 4-foot-high plants were full of wide, white, innocent, many-stamened flowers.

The preposterous idea of gardening a whole Norfolk broad makes my garden discovery a simple choice. Who could imagine primulas, gunneras and skunk cabbage by the acre, along miles of paths under ancient oaks? Lord Fairhaven is the answer, in the 1950s. His gardens are near South Walsham.

As for my New Year resolution ....

PS And here I took to the ether, appearing as www.tradsdiary.com ....

2008

❦ January ❦

THE SOMEWHAT HAIRY CHERRY

Floods, thank God, at least of the rising sort, are not going to engulf us on a gravelly flat in Essex. We all say it would be nice to have a bit of good crisp weather, even to see a frozen pond, and to get the skates out for the first time in years. Half-thrilled, half-uneasy (even, illogically, with a pang of guilt) we are enjoying an absurdly early spring. January 18th saw the warmest January night (at 13°C) ever recorded in England. Birds are not necessarily good meteorologists, but their singing this morning sent a thrill through me like the first smell of growing grass. The sense that we have got through the darkest part is a powerful pleasure, and how can you not revel in plumped up primroses?

If I were limited to a single small tree in this climate my choice, I've decided, would be the 'autumn-flowering' cherry, *Prunus* x *subhirtella* 'Autumnalis'. Its November flowering, a scatter of pink or white confetti among its slender branches, is hardly a spectacle. Nor does it bravely outface ice and snow. It is an opportunistic flower, a chancer that will flower whenever the weather smiles.

In London, where the temperature rarely dips to freezing these days, it can dress itself time and again in its pale frilly flowers all winter long. Other cherries lugubriously block the view all summer with their heavy leaves. Little *subhirtella* (it means 'somewhat hairy', a sad indication of a botanist's poetry-free soul) has tiny leaves that cast hardly any shade and turn pleasantly yellow and orange in autumn.

I'm not sure whether I prefer the pink- or the white-flowering version. Having the luxury of space I grow both, several of them, scattered through the garden wherever I have stopped on a winter's day and seen a dark background that needed cheering up. Even now I can round a corner and be surprised by a starburst (okay, sub-starburst) of pink or white against gloomy green or grey.

In France, when we lived in the Auvergne, we grew a scaled-up version of what seems to be the same tree, a little more vigorous, with slightly larger and it seemed to me more numerous flowers. I found it in a nursery, its name lost. The only name I have found that seems to apply is *Prunus* x *subhirtella* 'Fukubana'. I must find it and plant it here in England to be sure.

Little *subhirtella* seems to be a long-lived tree by Japanese cherry standards. The real painted geishas of the race, in my experience, grow and flower furiously at first but burn out disappointingly young. *P*. 'Taihaku', the so-called Great White Cherry, lasted only ten years here and none of the wide-spreading 'Shirofugen', with their billows of double pink flowers, has survived longer than 15 years from planting. Our latest loss is a great favourite, 'Jo-nioi', a tall vase-shaped white-flowering tree with single flowers that have the best scent of any I know. Last May people were reading its label and writing down its name. This spring it will have a score of flowers and leaves and die.

❧ February ❧

FRIGHTS OF SPRING

Couldn't the daffodils contain themselves until the snowdrops have had their go? Not this year. The ghostly calm of white in the woods is shattered by trumpet-blasts of yellow. I thought someone had dropped a Kodak box, so out of place was the first daff to open. I picked the head off and hid it. Snowdrops must have the brown and grey of February to themselves. Small chance when hawthorn is already in leaf, bluebells are rich green, even forming buds, and you can see a hint of colour through the furry bud-scales of magnolia.

I imagine there are gardeners up and down the country making lists of premature flowers. With so many anomalies, where do your start? From where I'm sitting, at the kitchen table, with the fat pink buds of *Staphylea holocarpa* 'Rosea' visibly swelling under the workshop gable. Frost at the end of April is its usual problem.

Surely nothing now can restore it to its routine. The question is how damaging will it be, to the whole plant as well as its flowers, if proper cold weather sets in this month or next and interrupts this frantic activity? These buds look as though they are almost in labour: how long can delivery be postponed?

It is absurd, isn't it, to let anxiety cloud skies that are serene from the moment the mists clear to dazzling pink and orange dusk?

✻ March ✻

CYBERIA

I often reflect what it would have been like to live at the beginning of history, when experience, information, the past itself was in short supply. I'm sure it didn't feel like that, and that Adam and Eve considered yesterday's breakfast as a precedent, if not a landmark. Sometimes it feels as though we do the opposite: we live almost at the end, with overwhelming quantities of history around us. Is there more behind than in front? No one knows.

I think this sitting at my computer, having just Googled the name of a plant too new in cultivation to be in a reference book, and found reports on its performance from nine different locations; indeed a lively exchange about its value and needs between plantsmen in four different parts of Europe. It all makes such well-used formulae as 'sun or part shade in a well-drained, moisture-retentive acid to neutral soil' sound very much like history. On the Internet you can not only learn from current experience, you can also participate. Nobody will appreciate it much if all you can add is 'Mine died', but there is room in cyberspace for everyone's contribution.

AT THE CAPE

You plan a winter holiday these days and find when you come home that you've missed a good chunk of spring. I'm not sure who is more confused – the plants or me. Back from two weeks in South Africa I find *Magnolia sprengeri* with one flower out, the big pink cup looking very sorry for itself, and rather absurd in incipient snow, while all its other flower-buds had followed standing orders and waited. Anyone organised enough to have a timed detonation of colour must be cursing.

Down on the Cape there were days when the temperature was not so different from that of home. It's been a wet summer, and a 30-knot easterly brought no cheer. It was the first time I had investigated the bizarre flora caught between mountains and sea known as the Fynbos (and pronounced, near enough, 'fainboss'). Its mixture of proteas, ericas and restios (various kinds of reeds, tall and short, green and brown) flourishes on thin sand and rock. Here and there I recognised a geranium, a heather or a *Buddleja salviifolia*. There are arborescent and everlasting-flowered asters to confuse you, looking rather like people wandering up a hill with flowers in their hair. The nature reserve at Hermanus was an accessible place for a bit of botanising, with good paths, useful labels and a charming garden of Fynbos plants before you set off up the hills and into a ferny gully of assegai trees. A large part of the reserve had recently been burnt – but that's the system. The fire restarts the cycle, clears the ground for seedlings and for alarming bright-pink eruptions of amaryllis and nerines.

Inland, in the beautiful wine country of Stellenbosch and Franschhoek, the hills are covered with what looks a similar mixture of plants – although the species change, I was assured, almost by the yard. In one spot on the Simonsberg a fire five years ago had cleared the ground (including a vineyard) and set in motion a wonderful glinting grove of silver trees, *Leucadendron argenteum*. I'm not sure how rare they are: we didn't see any others outside Kirstenbosch, the botanical garden on Table Mountain. Certainly the proprietor was proud of them. Nothing in the plant world is more exquisitely silver-silky. *Convolvulus cneorum* gives you the idea, but these grow upright to make handsome spiky trees.

This was at Rustenberg, a name well known for wine, for Jersey cows and for being one of the loveliest and most fertile of Cape farms. My last visit there was 25 years ago, but I vividly remembered the English garden, the work of Peter and Pamela Barlow in the 1950s. It has gone full circle, from the formality of an almost Edwardian design, brick-walled and -stepped around a handsome white Cape Dutch manor house, through flowering profusion, English-style, to an almost jungle phase, ready to be cut and cleared and started again by the next generation. Not the oaks, of course; at 60 years old magnificently shading the lawns. The surprise to me was how very English a garden can look here on the latitude of North Africa. (Africa is balanced across the equator: the Cape and Tangier are both close to the 35th parallel.) Given the water, all our plants seem to grow here with vim and flower with abandon. The difference is the light: our pastel colours almost disappear by day, to emerge at dusk. The current Barlows, Simon and Rozanne, have created a new garden next door before starting on the old one at Rustenberg. Judging by the new creation the next cycle in the old garden will be as deeply romantic as the last.

❧ April ❧

PARADISE ISLAND

If spring has been uncertain here, it has been the same all over Europe, the moods of April testing gardeners' nerves and creating memorable effects of sun and rain in the same picture.

Are you ever reluctant to test the reality of a cherished dream? That must be the reason we had left the Italian Lakes for so long unvisited. So long, in fact, that my mental pictures of them were mainly in black and white: memories of parents' photographs of their honeymoons. Could such an innocent dreamland still exist?

It depends when you go. The Lakes are on Milan's doorstep. In summer the coaches, I'm told, are bumper to bumper and the cafés round the boat-landings no fun at all. In early April, with trees just starting to green and little squalls corrugating the water, visitors are as tentative as flower-buds. It is the magnolia moment and the camellia climax, and yet (at least on weekdays) a good proportion of them are born to blush unseen.

We went with a party from the International Dendrology Society. Dendrologists walk with heads high, eyes on the treetops. Some even carry tapes to measure any specially girthy specimen. Parts of the Lakes have the sort of rainfall combined with summer warmth that makes trees luxuriate. The biggest tree of all, though, and one of Europe's most famous, had had a terrible accident. The Kashmir cypress, *Cupressus cashmeriana,* on Isola Madre in Lake Maggiore was brought down by a freak tornado in 2006. It was worth the journey to see the efforts being made to save the life of this marvellous creature. Winching its 70 tons from prone to upright was only the beginning. Step two was to cut off most of its glorious blue tresses while feeding its roots with the rarest delicacies. It towers again over the palace of the Borromeo family on the summit of their garden-island, surrounded by white peacocks – and so many other remarkable plants that a dendrologist is left reeling.

The two islands transformed by the Princes Borromeo into gardens are a mere brisk boat-row apart. Isola Madre is the plantsman's island; Isola Bella the famous architectural fantasy of a galleon riding the waters, a garden of amazing ingenuity, fantasy, craftsmanship and panache. Strict formality was the original plan, as the Head Gardener, Gianfranco Giustina, explained. The extravaganza of its terraces and statues, fountains and cascades was to be coloured by bedding and punctuated by pots but unobscured by climbers and trees. Vain hope. More romantic ideas prevailed in the 19th century. Little trees grew lofty, wisteria mounted the terraces and the cult of rhododendron brought towers of scarlet blooms. The massive Borromeo palazzo still forms the prow, and the poop is still a soaring theatre of baroque statuary; in between and all around horticulture holds sway.

Wisteria is a principal motif of the lakes and their gardens. Pruning it is an art Italians well understand. No pillar or plinth or lintel is too modest to be given its climber; the wisteria, though, with its potential to become forest-sized, is precisely pruned to fit its billet. Years of pruning give it astonishing character; with arabesques of branches under severe control, plump buds releasing curtains of scented purple. Thickets of camellias, parades (even pergolas) of lemons and forests of magnolias in voluptuous flower make such a feast of petals that your eyes turn almost with relief to the level waters of the lake.

A NASTY SWIPE

What message (to use an ugly political term) does it send to our young people to brutalise hedges the way farmers and local authorities do? Uttlesford District Council is reputed to have one of the most privileged living environments in the country. The Dunmow bypass today is like a horrible wound, its trees (they were never a hedge) smashed, splintered and torn, jagged white wood wrist-thick mangled by the tractor, minced branches in tangled heaps. The beauty of spring, the sacredness of nature totally trashed – to save ratepayers' money, as I'm sure the council would say.

Among the 'services' the council provides (with a profligacy that suggests spending other people's money gives it no pain) could it consider training young people with nothing special to do to use a saw and a billhook? Working with nature is learning to love her. The brutalised roadsides seem to express nothing but hate.

❧ May ❧

AUGUSTINE BLUES

We were in Snowdonia for the spring: all six days of it. We went in what felt like the end of winter: branches all but bare, fat flower-buds on the ashes but not the oaks (last year it was the other way round). We came home in early summer; the biggest difference of all being the beeches, which had managed to unfurl, shake out and spread at least their first four leaves per twig. They were still in that state of infinite tenderness when the shoot is a slender, silky green–grey extension weighed down by almost transparent wisps of leaves, but the sky was full of them, green in the majority over blue as you looked up. Bluebells, open only on sheltered primrose banks before, were jostling in deep violet crowds. Birches and larches were a haze of bright yellow–green.

I admit I felt cheated. I need leisure to revel in spring. A long day at the office and I would have missed the best part of it. Happily I was in the woods, trying vainly to capture the metamorphosis on my camera. I lay under a rhododendron under a beech, knowing that the picture could fail dismally to convey the filtering light, the pale purple, paler green and intense sky-blue woven in restless shades; knowing that the only way really to see is to put away your camera, stop even thinking, and live in your eyeballs.

The rhododendron is *R. augustinii*, the nearest (admittedly not very near) to blue. Among the shades of violet and lilac, in dappled sun and shade, they can seem as blue as bluebells. When we acquired our wood, 13 years ago, I planted a dozen *R. augustinii* along streams and by little waterfalls. I pretty much left them to take their chance. A wood is not a garden; the dustpan and brush have no place in forestry. Despite neglect, nine of the 12 have flourished. Last autumn I cleared the invading birch, gorse, bracken and brambles around them. This spring their slender framework and little flowers, as elaborate as orchids, graced the shifting light under beeches and larches like puffs of smoke. I shall plant more. To plant anything else would be gardening.

Of course we went to Bodnant. I had never been there at the cusp of the rhododendron season before, and was *ébloui* (there are English words, I know, but don't you love the French?) by the colours, the scale, the mastery of this extraordinary garden-cum-forest. It made me concentrate on the question of colour. It goes wrong when a bright or strong colour is isolated. A single red flower among pinks is effectively a weed. Red and white are the colours to be most careful with: they need careful grouping with plenty of green. One path in the upper garden is dedicated entirely to red rhodos, with truly regal effect. Down the cascade by the old mill, on the other hand, red fights pink and white, not so much a patchwork as an outbreak of measles.

Even blue, soft as it is, is best played alone.

FELLOW GARDENERS

The RHS is evolving at a dizzying rate these days. It has to, of course, to keep up with a world that spins faster every year. I sometimes wonder, though, if in its headlong expansion it risks losing sight of the quiet pleasures that attract so many gardeners. Carlo Petrini, the founder of the Slow Food movement, reacted to the arrival of the first Golden Arches in Rome with a boom worthy of his friend Pavarotti. 'Food', he thundered, 'should be slow' – and pronounced it ZLOOOOOW. Gardening, too. Slow means tranquil, private, considered, personal, uncompetitive, contemplative ... all the unfashionable adjectives you can think of. Show gardens are one thing: showing off is what they do. Private gardens exist to nourish the soul.

Does the RHS recognise that among its members there are many (how many?) whose love of plants and nurturing them is a lifelong affair, going far beyond fashion? Its earlier members (earlier than the 1980s) used to be called Fellows, until that came to seem an inflated appellation for every recruit.

Wouldn't it be an apt recognition, though, for those who remain loyal to the Society for, let's say, 20 years? Seniority, you may say, proves nothing. Some of us will be ignorant and idle however long we live. Perhaps Fellowship should be earned in some more demanding way. It will always be a very long way from the Victoria Medal of Honour, which is held by only 63 outstandingly distinguished gardeners at any one time. There is such a thing as Honorary Fellowship, awarded to a select few. It seems a pity, though, that the concept of Fellowship of what remains, at least in part, a learned Society should disappear by default.

❧ June ☙

SHARP FOCUS

A week away in early June and you come back to a different garden. It was wet while we were gone, and warm enough for plants to make their main thrust of growth, to bulk up and cover ground. Last night, just home, I walked round in a daze of excitement, surprise, shock and, I confess, dither. So much needs to be enjoyed, so much needs to be done. Instinctive priorities are new plants, just planted. Have they survived my disloyal absence?

A fresh eye for your own garden is never easy to achieve. Homecoming gives you your best chance. Has the fatsia grown too bulky (yes), or the hedge too tall? Does the *Robinia* 'Frisia' shout too loud beside the purple cotinus? This is the moment to decide. But how do you prevent yourself from stooping to pull up an egregious weed ... then another and another? Contemplation and quiet consideration go by the board once you start stooping – which is why they are fragile commodities around here.

I love weeding. After propagating, it accounts for my happiest gardening hours, most absorbed and closest to my plants. There is gross weeding, when I straighten up all sweaty with armfuls of goosegrass and nettles and dock, and fine weeding, which scarcely fills a trug but leaves a bed looking like a jewel-box.

Both make me focus and concentrate. Weeds rampaging intertwined disguise themselves as their betters. Tiny seed leaves, mere hints of a plant, challenge me to identify them and decide whether they are going to add to or subtract from the picture in question.

Herb Robert its everywhere at the moment. Who can possibly dislike this lusty little geranium, so agile in scrambling? Its fragile pink stems, forking and forking again, its tiny pink flowers and its odd smoky smell have a potent charm, whether procumbent, when it is a great improvement on bare soil, or clambering up on the shoulders of a stronger plant. Its giant exotic cousin, *Geranium maderense*, almost identical in construction and behaviour, is after all a showpiece we have been proud to welcome to our ever-warmer gardens.

Tom Stuart-Smith, speaking about his triumphant Chelsea garden last month, said how important it was to finish planting several days ahead of the show, so that plants could settle down and adopt their natural positions – a thought that hadn't occurred to me before. Of course flowers and leaves turn to take best advantage of the light, manoeuvring in relation to one another like people in a crowd. It is easy to see where something has been added or, if you are weeding, subtracted. Even easier to see where the gardener's boot has been. It is one of the joys of this time of year that beds brim with leaves in pristine condition and perfect alignment, flower stalks getting ready to go, as blithe and beamish as schoolchildren.

Intricacy can't be taken in quickly; a fact that Tom's garden eloquently expressed. There were brilliantly decisive touches: a single white peony, for example, against one of his grey rectangles of perfectly polished water. But between there were passages of soft planting to slow down the eye. It is a fact of garden-making that big and simple is quick and easy – not necessarily satisfying for longer and quieter contemplation. The natural embroidery of many kinds of leaves rewards focused concentration – especially, for that matter, when some of them are weeds.

❧ July ❧

FRANCE TRÈS PROFONDE

Utter originality, you would think, is a tall order in the world of gardening. Influences are all around us: we copy, we refine borrowed ideas – everything comes round again.

Not so at Orsan. The Prieuré de Notre Dame pretends to be in the monastic style of six centuries ago. It certainly evokes in shapes and symbols a strict and devotional mood. No priory or abbey, though, ever had a garden like it. It came from the imaginations and the drawing board of two Parisian architects to transform a tranquil valley in the almost abandoned centre of France – and to lodge in my mind as a piece of perfection to emulate and aspire to.

The architects, Patrice Taravella and Sonia Lesot, found and bought the one-time priory in the same year, 1991, that we found our French property 50 kilometres away. It was an offshoot of the great Benedictine Abbey of Fontevraud by the Loire to the north. Its setting would have suited the Cistercians: buried deep in wild country, among woods and stream, like Tintern or Cîteaux or Rievaulx.

There was no church left, and certainly no garden: just a three-sided court of dignified stone buildings open to a shallow pastoral valley, a stream and high woods. The architects' minds, though, immediately parcelled it into a grid of strict formality. 'Every designer', says our friend Tara, 'must start with *une trame*' – a word that means a weaver's pattern, suggests underlying order, and in this case is a set of squares imposed on the country like monastic discipline on unformed novices.

We have almost forgotten what pleasure lies in discipline, regularity and repetition. It is so far from the fashions of our times. What we forget, perhaps, is that a pattern preordained, predictable and precisely applied feels like a straitjacket only until it is accepted. Once it seems normal it has the opposite effect: it solves all problems and leaves the imagination free to wander. The hedge-walled cloisters of Orsan can become a gardener's spiritual home.

Symbolism is important, too. You enter through a garden of simples: healing herbs in beds like a pharmacist's stockroom. Windows in high hornbeam hedges reveal an inner courtyard where only beans and wheat grow, in strict-ruled rows; then others where the one crop is grapes, from vines trained on chestnut trellis copied from a Book of Hours. The hornbeam walks dividing and linking the spaces are cut with rigid precision, then ornamented with roses, also precisely trained in elaborate figures. No shoot but is tied in, often to a chestnut trellis that soars above a hedge or describes some whimsical figure to break the pattern. Whimsy plays the role here that it does in illuminated manuscripts: the gardening monk is allowed his little jokes. One is a potager that turns out to be a maze, another a wicker orchard chair far too big to sit in.

At the crossing point in the centre of these green enclosures stands the fountain. Not a glittering display of the beauty of water, though; just a sober pedestal with four pipes dribbling barely enough to wet the stone. The subliminal message is that water is precious, scarce and to be carefully conserved.

We stayed at Orsan in the priory buildings, in the modern hotel Taravella has installed and where he is chef using his own produce. Walking at night and waking in these decorous surroundings is a kind of cure. There could scarcely be a garden so different from my pragmatic and unruly domain. Yet coming home I felt revitalised by its real, intense, marshalled and directed forces.

INDEX